UNBREAKABLE

UNBREAKABLE

>>> Building the Resilience of the Poor in the
Face of Natural Disasters

Stephane Hallegatte
Adrien Vogt-Schilb
Mook Bangalore
Julie Rozenberg

WORLD BANK GROUP

ISBN (paper): 978-1-4648-1003-9
ISBN (electronic): 978-1-4648-1004-6
DOI: 10.1596/978-1-4648-1003-9

Cover design: Brad Amburn Creative, LLC

Library of Congress Cataloging-in-Publication Data has been requested.

CLIMATE CHANGE AND DEVELOPMENT

The Climate Change and Development Series was created in 2015 to showcase economic and scientific research that explores the interactions between climate change, climate policies, and development. The series aims to promote debate and broaden understanding of current and emerging questions about the climate-development nexus through evidence-based analysis.

The series is sponsored by the World Bank Group's Climate Change Cross-Cutting Solutions Area, which is committed to sharing relevant and rigorously peer-reviewed insights on the opportunities and challenges present in the climate-development nexus with policy makers, the academic community, and a wider global audience.

TITLES IN THIS SERIES:

Unbreakable: Building the Resilience of the Poor in the Face of Natural Disasters (2017) by Stephane Hallegatte, Adrien Vogt-Schilb, Mook Bangalore, and Julie Rozenberg.

Shock Waves: Managing the Impacts of Climate Change on Poverty (2016) by Stephane Hallegatte, Mook Bangalore, Laura Bonzanigo, Marianne Fay, Tamaro Kane, Ulf Narloch, Julie Rozenberg, David Treguer, and Adrien Vogt-Schilb.

Decarbonizing Development: Three Steps to a Zero-Carbon Future (2015) by Marianne Fay, Stephane Hallegatte, Adrien Vogt-Schilb, Julie Rozenberg, Ulf Narloch, and Tom Kerr.

CONTENTS

ACKNOWLEDGMENTS

This report was written by a team led by Stephane Hallegatte and composed of Mook Bangalore, Julie Rozenberg, and Adrien Vogt-Schilb. It benefited from contributions by Laura Bonzanigo, Shun Chonabayashi, Martin Heger, Steffen Lohrey, Christian Lovell, Ulf Narloch, and Emily Jennifer White. The team thanks Scott Vincent Andrews, Aziz Gokdemir, Patricia Katayama, Shaela Rahman, and David Charles Tucker for their help in the preparation of the report, and to Francis Ghesquiere, manager of the Global Facility for Disaster Reduction and Recovery who initiated and supported this project.

Guidance was provided by the report's peer reviewers. Internal peer reviewers included Carter Brandon, Niels B. Holm-Nielsen, Alanna Simpson, Emmanuel Skoufias, and Ruslan Yemtsov. Ilan Noy, Professor of Economics at Victoria University of Wellington, New Zealand, also provided invaluable comments and suggestions.

For important contributions and advice, the team thanks Abby Baca, Henrike Brecht, Daniel Jonathan Clarke, Christophe Crepin, Carlo del Ninno, Marianne Fay, Julien Gagneur, Rashmin Gunasekera, Steve Hammer, Maddalena Honorati, Oscar A. Ishizawa, Abhas K. Jha, Jolanta Kryspin-Watson, Barry Patrick Maher, Olivier Mahul, Samuel Munzele Maimbo, Juan Jose Miranda, Rick Murnane, Israel Osorio-Rodarte, Artessa Saldivar-Sali, Zuzana Stanton-Geddes, and the World Bank's Geospatial Operations Support Team, and especially Keith Garrett. The authors also thank Ted Veldkamp, from VU University in Amsterdam, and the United Nations' International Strategy for Disaster Risk Reduction team, and especially Gabriel A. Bernal, Mabel Cristina Marulanda, Andrew Maskrey, and Sahar Safaie.

Detailed comments on drafts of this report and on the background papers were provided by Paolo Bazzurro, Charlotte Benson, David Bevan, Sebastian Boreux, Jinqiang Chen, Patrice Dumas, Nate Engle, Chico Ferreira, Chris Field, Francis Ghesquiere, Ruth Hill, Kazuko Ishigaki, Brenden Jongman, Tamaro Kane, Kouassi Kouadio, Norman Loayza, Hugh MacLeman, Reinhard Mechler, Martin Melecky, James Newman, James Orr, Richard Poulter, Valentin Przyluski, Rob Reid, Adam Rose, Rae Rosen, Vladimir Stenek, Tse-Ling The, Maarten van Aalst, Claudio Volonte, and Sebastian von Dahlen. Useful comments were also received from participants of the 2015 Disaster Risk Financing and Insurance workshop organized by FERDI, CERDI, and GFDRR in Clermont-Ferrand, France; the GFDRR's 2016 Understanding Risk Conference in Venice, Italy; and the 2016 ENGAGE workshop hosted by the Potsdam Institute for Climate Impact Research in Berlin, Germany.

Editorial services were provided by Sabra Ledent and Paul Holtz. Brad Amburn designed the report. Visibility and launch of the report were supported by Elisabeth Mealey, Scott Vincent Andrews, Lisa Thalheimer, Nicholas James Parker, Gayle Young, Peter Vincent Von Elling, Edgar Buckley, Nicholas Andrew Keyes, Gerardo Spatuzzi, Camila Perez, and Shaela Rahman.

The report was sponsored by the Global Facility for Disaster Reduction and Recovery (GFDRR) and the Climate Change Cross-Cutting Solutions Area of the World Bank, under the leadership of John Roome.

OVERVIEW

**Building the resilience of the poor
in the face of natural disasters.**

"Economic losses from natural disasters totaled $92 billion in 2015, and average annual losses have been estimated at more than $300 billion a year."[1] Policy makers, analysts, and others are used to such statements, which measure the severity of disasters and their socioeconomic impacts using the value of the damages inflicted by disasters on buildings, infrastructure, equipment, and agricultural production.

Although these numbers are useful—they provide information on the trends and costs of disasters—they fail to detail how disasters affect people's well-being. Obviously, $1 in losses does not mean the same thing to a rich person and a poor person, and the severity of a $92 billion loss depends on who experiences it. The same loss affects poor and marginalized people far more because their livelihoods depend on fewer assets, their consumption is closer to subsistence levels, they cannot rely on savings to smooth the impacts, their health and education are at greater risk, and they may need more time to recover and reconstruct. A flood or earthquake can be disastrous for poor people, but have a negligible impact on a country's aggregate wealth or production if it affects people who own almost nothing and have very low incomes. By focusing on aggregate losses, the traditional approach examines how disasters affect people wealthy enough to have wealth to lose and so does not take into account most poor people.

This shortcoming is not just a monitoring issue. When projects to reduce disaster risk are assessed on the basis of the value of damages that can be avoided, analyses favor projects that will protect or support richer areas or people. Imagine two flood protection projects with similar costs. The first would cover a wealthy neighborhood in a capital city. Because of the density of high-value assets, it would avert on average $10 million a year in damages. The second project would target poorer areas in a second-tier city and prevent just $5 million a year in losses. A traditional analysis would unambiguously select the first project. But a $5 million loss may matter more to poor people than a $10 million loss to richer people. If the second project benefits very poor people, it may generate greater benefits for well-being. And because well-being is the ultimate goal of public policy, the second project may be more attractive.

Moreover, not all risk management policies can be assessed using metrics that include only asset and production losses. Policies such as increasing access to financial services and expanding social safety nets make it easier for people to absorb, cope with, and recover from damages caused by natural disasters. Thus such policies can mitigate the impact of natural disasters on well-being even though they have no impact on direct damages from disasters.

This report moves beyond asset and production losses and focuses instead on how natural disasters affect people's well-being. Here, natural disaster risk and losses are measured using a metric that can capture their overall effects on poor and nonpoor people, even if the economic losses of poor people are small in absolute terms. This metric can be used in the analysis of disaster risk management projects so that investments improve the well-being of all people and are not systematically driven toward wealthier areas and individuals. And this report proposes and uses a consistent framework to assess traditional approaches to reducing disaster risk (such as building dikes or reinforcing building regulations) and strengthening resilience (such as adopting adaptive social safety nets) to help design consistent risk management policies.

By examining well-being instead of asset losses, this report provides a deeper (and grimmer) view of natural disasters than does the usual reporting—indeed, this view takes better account of poor people's vulnerability. This analysis also identifies opportunities for action and policy priorities at the country level, with three main messages:

1. Efforts to reduce poverty and disaster risks are complementary. Estimates for 89 countries find that if all natural disasters could be prevented next year, the number of people in extreme poverty—those living on less than $1.90 a day—would fall by 26 million. The impact on poverty is large because poor people are exposed to hazards more often, lose more as a share of their wealth when hit, and receive less support from family and friends, financial systems, and governments. In fact, disasters can push people into poverty, and so disaster risk management can be considered a poverty reduction policy. And since poverty reduction policies make people less vulnerable, they can be considered part of the disaster risk management toolbox.

2. Natural disasters affect well-being more than what traditional estimates suggest. Poor people suffer only a small share of the economic losses caused by disasters, but they suffer disproportionately. Based on estimates of *socioeconomic resilience* in 117 countries, and including in the analysis how poverty and lack of capacity to cope with disasters magnify losses in well-being, the effects of floods, wind storms, earthquakes, and tsunamis on well-being are equivalent to a $520 billion drop in consumption—60 percent more than the widely reported asset losses. The design of disaster risk management should, then, not rely only on asset losses. Targeting poorer people with disaster risk reduction interventions—such as dikes and drainage systems—would generate lower gains in avoided asset losses but larger gains in well-being.

3. Policies that make people more resilient—and so better able to cope with and recover from the consequences of disasters that cannot be avoided—can save $100 billion a year. Action on risk reduction has a large potential, but not all disasters can be avoided. Expanding financial inclusion, disaster risk and health insurance, social protection and adaptive safety nets, contingent finance and reserve funds, and universal access to early warning systems would also reduce well-being losses from natural disasters. If all countries implemented these policies in the proposed "resilience package," the gain in well-being would be equivalent to a $100 billion increase in annual global consumption.

Efforts to reduce poverty and disaster risks are complementary

Natural disasters keep or move people back into poverty and are one reason that eradicating poverty is so difficult. Between 2006 and 2011, 45 percent of poor households in Senegal escaped poverty, but 40 percent of nonpoor households fell into it, leaving the poverty rate almost unchanged. Natural risk contributed to this lack of progress: households affected by a natural disaster were 25 percent more likely to fall in poverty during the period (Dang, Lanjouw, and Swinkels 2014). Among Guatemalan households hit by tropical storm Agatha in 2010, per capita consumption fell 5.5 percent, increasing poverty by 14 percent (Baez et al. 2016). After Ethiopia's 1984–85 famine, it took a decade for most asset-poor households to restore livestock holdings to pre-famine levels (Dercon 2004).

Poor people suffer disproportionately from natural hazards. Natural disasters hit poor people particularly hard for five reasons:

Overexposure. Poor people are overexposed to floods in many countries, such as in Panama and Zimbabwe, where they are greater than 50 percent more likely than the average to be flooded. Such overexposure is also true for drought and high temperatures in most countries. More important, poor people are often exposed to frequent, low-intensity events, such as the recurrent floods that affect many cities with insufficient drainage infrastructure. These events do not attract media interest and are poorly documented, but they can have significant cumulative impacts, especially through their effects on health.

Higher vulnerability. People's vulnerability—that is, how much they lose when they are hit—is also a critical determinant of the impacts of natural disasters. When poor people are affected, the share of their wealth lost is two to three times that of the nonpoor, largely because of the nature and vulnerability of their assets and livelihoods. A global analysis suggests that poor people are nearly twice as likely to live in fragile dwellings.

Less ability to cope and recover. The impact of natural disasters on well-being also depends on how well people cope and recover, which depends on the support they receive. Coverage of poor people by social protection is often low. And after they are hit by a shock, poor people receive less postdisaster support than do nonpoor people. For example, in response to the floods and landslides in Nepal in 2011, only 6 percent of the very poor sought government support, compared with almost 90 percent of the well-off (Gentle et al. 2014).

Permanent impacts on education and health. Disasters force poor households to make choices that have detrimental long-term effects, such as withdrawing a child from school or cutting health care expenses. In such cases, children are often the main victims (Kousky 2016). In Guatemala, Storm Stan increased the probability of child labor by more than 7 percent in areas hit by the storm (Bustelo 2011). In Ethiopia, children under 3 at the height of the 1984 famine were less likely to eventually complete primary school, leading to income losses of 3 percent (Dercon and Porter 2014). And in Peru, the impacts of the 1970 Ancash earthquake on educational attainment can be detected even for the children of mothers affected at birth, demonstrating that the effects of large disasters can extend even to the next generation (Caruso and Miller 2015). Irreversible effects on education and health can reinforce the intergenerational transmission of poverty.

Effects of risk on saving and investment behavior. The losses the poor suffer are not the only way in which disasters and natural risks keep them in poverty. Sometimes, the impact exists even before the disaster hits (ODI and GFDRR 2015). For example, smallholders tend to plant low-return, low-risk crops because they cannot afford to lose one year of production in case of bad weather, so their income is reduced even when the weather is good (Cole et al. 2013). And people are less likely to invest in their house or production equipment if these investments are likely to be washed away by a flood.

Natural disasters increase global poverty

Poverty is thus a factor in the vulnerability to disasters. Similarly, disasters are a driver of poverty. Although it remains impossible to quantify the full effect of natural disasters on the number of impoverished, it is possible to assess the short-term impacts of income losses (see Rozenberg and Hallegatte forthcoming). To do so, a counterfactual scenario was built of what people's income would be in developing countries in the absence of natural disasters. This scenario uses surveys of 1.4 million households, which are representative of 1.2 billion households and 4.4 billion people in 89 countries. The analysis concludes that if all disasters could be prevented next year, 26 million fewer people would be in extreme poverty—that is, living on less than $1.90 a day. Although this estimate is subject to large uncertainties and cannot capture all impacts, including those on health, education, and savings, it still shows how severely natural hazards affect poverty.

Vulnerability to natural hazards and disasters can be reduced through development and poverty reduction efforts that enable people to settle in safer places, make their livelihoods and assets less vulnerable, and provide them with the tools and support needed to cope with shocks. Thus policies that help reduce poverty can be considered part of the disaster risk management toolbox. But the connection between poverty and disaster risk goes both ways: disasters make it harder for poor people to escape poverty. Disaster risk management can thus also be considered a poverty reduction policy.

Natural disasters affect well-being more than most people think

For hazards such as floods, storms, tsunamis, and earthquakes, risk assessment typically focuses on:

» Hazard—the probability of an event occurring
» Exposure—the population and assets located in an affected area.
» Asset vulnerability—the value lost when an asset is affected by a hazard.

These three factors constitute the *risk to assets*—that is, the average monetary value of the damages that disasters inflict on assets (often measured as replacement or repair value). But the risk to assets is an incomplete metric.

This report extends risk assessment to measure the well-being losses caused by natural disasters (figure O.1). To do so, risk assessment was conducted separately for poor and nonpoor people, defined as the bottom 20 percent and the top 80 percent in terms of consumption in each country. The analysis takes into account the various dimensions of inequality of poor and nonpoor people in the face of disasters and the distribution of losses across individuals. Indeed, losses concentrated on fewer or poorer individuals have a larger impact than the same losses affecting richer people or shared across larger populations.

Figure O.1: This report moves beyond asset losses to estimate how natural disasters affect well-being

ASSET LOSSES

1. Hazard   2. Exposure   3. Vulnerability

WELL-BEING LOSSES

1. Hazard   2. Exposure   3. Vulnerability   **4. Socioeconomic resilience**

Specifically, the analysis considers the different abilities of poor and nonpoor people to cope with asset losses by modeling the effects of asset losses on income (accounting for capital productivity and diversification of income sources) and consumption (accounting for savings, remittances and social protection, and postdisaster transfers). Consumption losses are translated into well-being losses, taking into account the different impacts of a $1 loss on poor and nonpoor individuals. Well-being loss at the country level depends on the distribution of impacts within the population, but it is expressed as the equivalent loss in national consumption. Thus a finding that a disaster causes $1 million in well-being losses means that the impact of a disaster on well-being is equivalent to a $1 million decrease in country consumption, perfectly shared across the population.

Socioeconomic resilience measures an economy's ability to minimize the impact of asset losses on well-being. It can be defined as the ratio of *asset losses* to *well-being losses*:

$$\text{socioeconomic resilience} = \frac{\text{asset losses}}{\text{well-being losses}}$$

If socioeconomic resilience is 50 percent, then well-being losses are twice as large as asset losses—that is, $1 in asset losses from a disaster is equivalent to $2 in consumption losses, perfectly shared across the population. Socioeconomic resilience can be considered a driver of the *risk to well-being*, along with the three usual drivers of risk assessment:

$$\text{Risk to well-being} = \frac{\text{expected asset losses}}{\text{socioeconomic resilience}} = \frac{\text{(hazard) * (exposure) * (asset vulnerability)}}{\text{socioeconomic resilience}}$$

The impacts of natural disasters on well-being are larger than asset losses

In all of the 117 countries studied, well-being losses from natural disasters are larger than asset losses (Hallegatte, Bangalore, and Vogt-Schilb, forthcoming). According to the *United Nations Global Assessment Report on Disaster Risk Reduction*—the so-called GAR (UNISDR 2015)—total asset losses from natural disasters in these countries average $327 billion a year.[2]

Because disaster losses are concentrated on a small share of country populations, imperfectly shared, and affect more poor people (who have limited ability to cope with them), this report estimates that well-being losses in these countries are equivalent to consumption losses 60 percent larger than asset losses, or about $520 billion a year. Globally, poor people are disproportionately affected by these losses: people in the bottom 20 percent experience only 11 percent of total asset losses but 47 percent of well-being losses. Thus poor people experience asset losses that are only half of the average but well-being losses that are more than twice as large.

Maps O.1 and O.2 show this report's estimates of socioeconomic resilience and risk to well-being. Risk to well-being decreases with country income (figure O.2b). This decrease is driven mostly by better protection against floods, higher-quality buildings, and widespread early warning systems in wealthier countries, but resilience also matters.

The average global socioeconomic resilience is 62 percent, ranging from 25 percent in Guatemala to 81 percent in Denmark—meaning that $1 in asset losses in Guatemala has the same impact on well-being as a $4 reduction in national consumption. Figure O.2a shows that, overall, resilience grows with GDP per capita.

The fact that rich countries are more resilient than poor countries is not a surprise. But resilience varies widely across countries of similar wealth because it depends on many other factors, including inequality and safety nets. Thus all countries, regardless of their geography or income, can reduce risk by increasing resilience.

Map O.1: Socioeconomic resilience measures the ability of a population to cope with asset losses

Socioeconomic resilience (percent), 117 countries

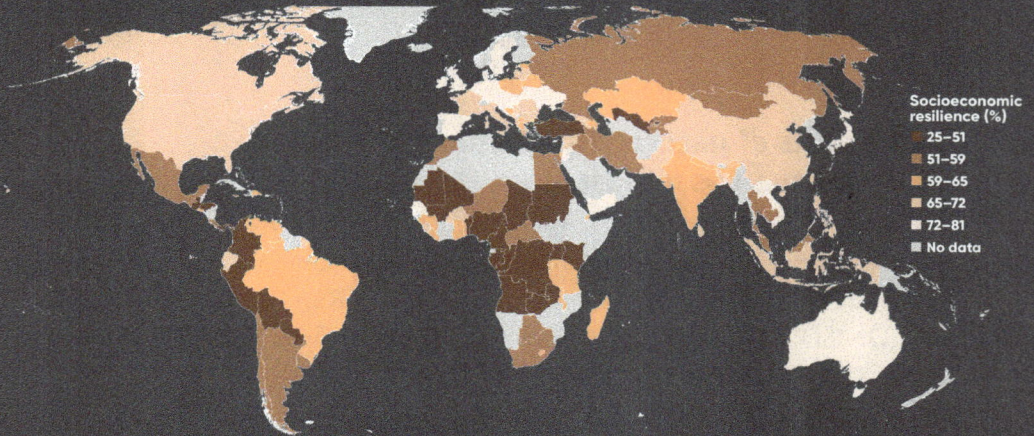

Socioeconomic resilience (%)
- 25–51
- 51–59
- 59–65
- 65–72
- 72–81
- No data

Map O.2: Risk to well-being combines hazard, exposure, asset vulnerability, and socioeconomic resilience

Risk to well-being as percent of GDP per year, 117 countries

Risk to well-being (% of GDP per year)
- 0.00–0.30
- 0.30–0.50
- 0.50–0.80
- 0.80–1.50
- 1.50–6.55
- No data

Sources: World Bank estimates.

Figure O.2: Socioeconomic resilience tends to increase with income, whereas risk to well-being decreases with income

Source: World Bank estimates.

The socioeconomic resilience measure used here captures part of the United Nations' definition of resilience: the ability to resist, absorb, accommodate, and recover from the effects of a hazard in a timely and efficient manner. But it does not cover all the areas discussed in research on resilience (see Barrett and Constas 2014; Engle et al. 2013). For example, this framework does not take into account direct human impacts (such as death, injuries, and psychological impacts), cultural and heritage losses (such as destruction of historical assets), social and political destabilization, and environmental degradation (such as when disasters affect industrial facilities and create local pollution). For a broader view of resilience, it is useful to also consider indicators that use different methodologies and other aspects of resilience (see chapter 4).

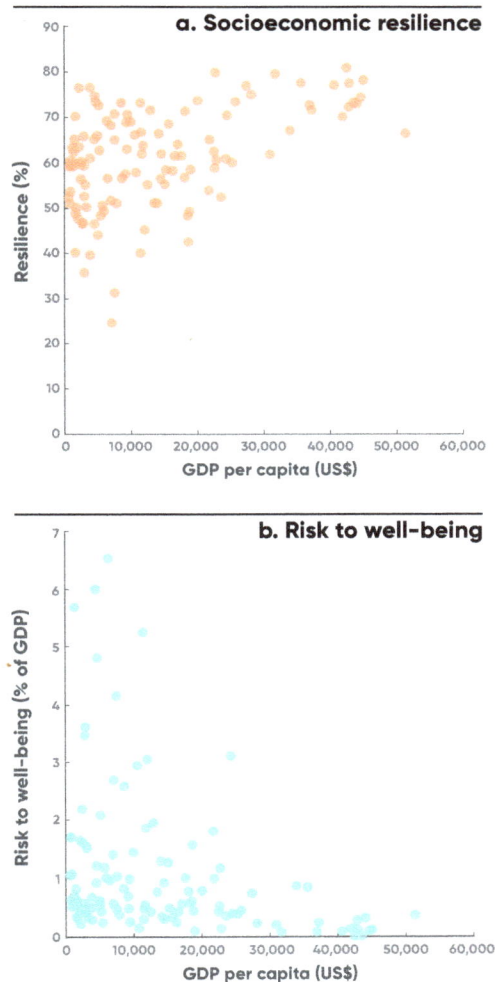

a. Socioeconomic resilience

b. Risk to well-being

What matters is not only how much benefit a project generates, but also who benefits

To assess the potential benefits of projects that protect populations against hazards, consider two similar interventions. The first would reduce by 5 percent the share of the population exposed to natural hazards, but target only the poorest 20 percent of people in each country. If the entire world implemented this intervention, avoided asset losses would be $7 billion a year—but global gains in well-being would be $40 billion because the intervention would benefit poor and highly vulnerable people.

The second intervention would also reduce the share of the population exposed to natural hazards by 5 percent, but target only the top 80 percent. Because richer people have so many more assets than do the poor, avoided asset losses would be much larger—about $19 billion. But gains in well-being would be smaller—$22 billion.

Where would such interventions be the most attractive? In absolute terms, reducing the exposure of poor people to disasters would provide the most benefits in large and high-risk countries (figure O.3a). But in relative terms, reducing the exposure of poor people is more efficient in countries in which they have limited social protection and access to finance (figure O.3b). In such countries, resilience is low, magnifying the benefits of lower exposure. In Mali and Niger, for example, reducing exposure to natural disasters by 5 percent could cut asset losses by more than 10 percent and well-being losses by 25 percent—but only if such efforts target poor people.

Figure O.3: Reducing poor people's exposure to disasters could prevent large losses in well-being and assets

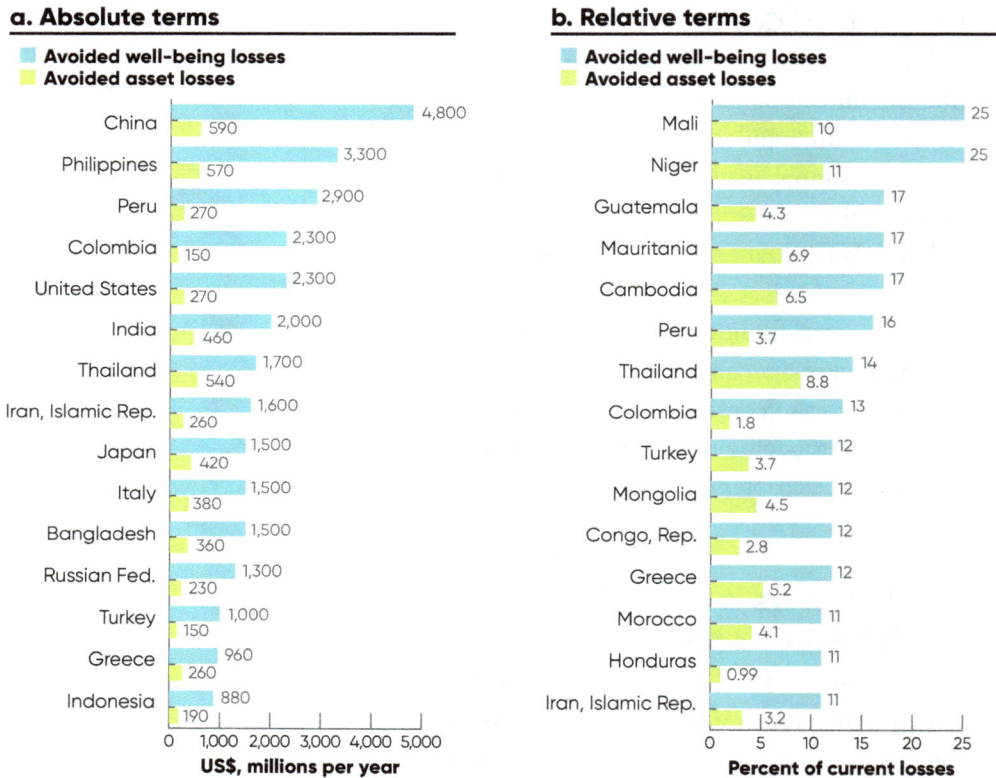

a. Absolute terms

Avoided well-being losses
Avoided asset losses

Country	Avoided well-being losses	Avoided asset losses
China	4,800	590
Philippines	3,300	570
Peru	2,900	270
Colombia	2,300	150
United States	2,300	270
India	2,000	460
Thailand	1,700	540
Iran, Islamic Rep.	1,600	260
Japan	1,500	420
Italy	1,500	380
Bangladesh	1,500	360
Russian Fed.	1,300	230
Turkey	1,000	150
Greece	960	260
Indonesia	880	190

0   1,000 2,000 3,000 4,000 5,000
US$, millions per year

b. Relative terms

Avoided well-being losses
Avoided asset losses

Country	Avoided well-being losses	Avoided asset losses
Mali	25	10
Niger	25	11
Guatemala	17	4.3
Mauritania	17	6.9
Cambodia	17	6.5
Peru	16	3.7
Thailand	14	8.8
Colombia	13	1.8
Turkey	12	3.7
Mongolia	12	4.5
Congo, Rep.	12	2.8
Greece	12	5.2
Morocco	11	4.1
Honduras	11	0.99
Iran, Islamic Rep.	11	3.2

0   5   10   15   20   25
Percent of current losses

Source: World Bank estimates.

Note: The figure shows avoided annual average losses from a 5 percent reduction in exposure, achieved by reducing the exposure of the poorest 20 percent of people, expressed in absolute terms (millions of U.S. dollars per year, adjusted for purchasing power parity) and relative terms (percentage of current average asset and well-being losses).

These results highlight the trade-offs between monetary gains and well-being gains. If a disaster risk reduction budget is allocated based only on avoided asset losses and monetary benefits, most investments will go to rich areas. Instead, investments in disaster risk management need to balance the need for economic efficiency with the imperative to protect the most vulnerable. Measuring benefits in terms of increased well-being instead of avoided asset losses is a way to do so.

The same approach can also be applied at the subnational level to identify regional priorities within countries. For example, it can help prioritize between two similar risk reduction projects in two different provinces in Vietnam. A project that would prevent $1 million a year in asset losses in Binh Dinh province, which has an estimated resilience of 69 percent, would generate well-being benefits valued at $1.4 million a year ($1 million divided by 69 percent). By contrast, a project that would prevent $1 million a year in asset losses in Kien Giang province, which has estimated resilience of 29 percent, would increase well-being by $3.4 million a year ($1 million divided by 29 percent). Thus the project in Kien Giang would do far more to increase well-being.

Increasing resilience is good economics

Despite efforts to reduce people's exposure to natural hazards or make their assets less vulnerable to hazards, natural risk cannot be cut to zero. Disasters will continue to occur, and they may even become more frequent because of climate change, urbanization, and increasing population densities in coastal areas. Thus it is critical to supplement actions on exposure and vulnerability with improvements in people's ability to cope with unavoidable shocks. Such efforts require a flexible, holistic risk management strategy that uses different tools for different types of disasters and populations (figure O.4).

Revenue diversification. Diversifying revenue and receiving remittances or cash transfers from social programs help households at all income levels cope with small shocks (Bandyopadhyay and Skoufias 2012). People suffer less from a local disaster if some of their income comes from outside the area through government transfers or remittances.

Financial inclusion. Financial inclusion helps poor people save in forms less vulnerable to natural hazards than in-kind savings like livestock and housing, which diversifies risk. It also enables the poor to access credit, thereby accelerating and improving recovery and reconstruction. But improving poor people's access to formal financial instruments is a long-term challenge in many developing countries and is insufficient for larger shocks.

Market insurance. Market insurance can protect against larger losses, but efforts to provide universal access to insurance face multiple obstacles, including weak

Figure O.4: Risk management should include a range of tools for different types of disasters and households

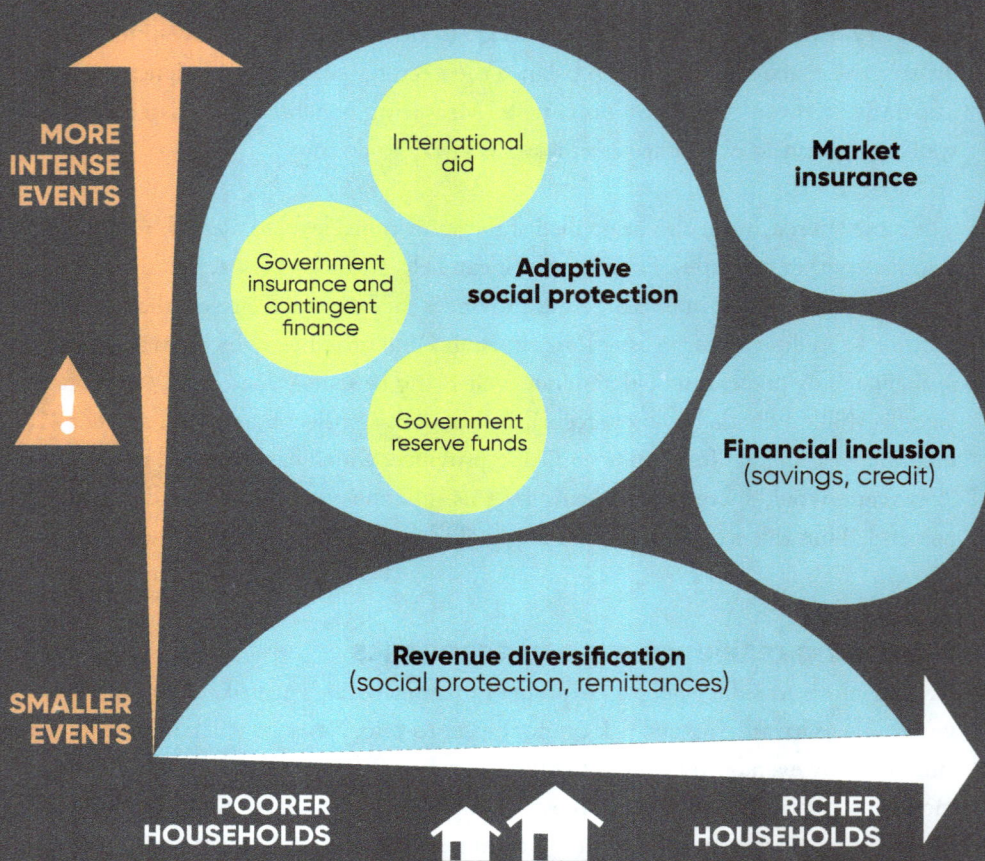

MORE INTENSE EVENTS

SMALLER EVENTS

POORER HOUSEHOLDS

RICHER HOUSEHOLDS

International aid

Government insurance and contingent finance

Government reserve funds

Adaptive social protection

Market insurance

Financial inclusion (savings, credit)

Revenue diversification (social protection, remittances)

Source: Hallegatte et al. 2016.
Note: Instruments in blue target households; instruments in green protect governments' or local authorities' budgets.

institutional and legal capacity, affordability issues, and high transaction costs—especially for poor people.

Adaptive social protection. For poor households—and to cover the largest shocks— easily scalable social safety nets are needed. Although social safety nets always improve resilience, a growing body of evidence reveals that such instruments are even more efficient when their targeting and delivery are flexible enough to transfer resources to disaster victims in a timely fashion. Postdisaster transfers have a benefit-cost ratio above 1.3 in the 117 countries studied. And in 11 countries—Angola, Bolivia, Botswana, Brazil, Central African Republic, Colombia, Honduras, Lesotho, Panama, South Africa, and Zambia—every $1 spent on postdisaster transfers yields well-being benefits of more than $4.

Quick action through existing social protection programs can be especially effective at preventing humanitarian emergencies and cutting intervention costs (del Ninno, Coll-Black, and Fallavier 2016). In 2015 Kenya's Hunger Safety Net Programme delivered support to more than 100,000 additional households in response to drought, and added a special transfer to 200,000 households in anticipation of expected droughts. In Ethiopia, rural farmers affected by drought in 2005 and 2011 and covered by the Productive Safety Net Programme had consumption losses 25 percent lower than those of other rural farmers (White and Porter 2016).

Disaster risk financing. These types of adaptive social protection programs create liabilities for governments, which may require them to draw on various tools such as reserve funds (for smaller disasters), contingency credit lines (such as World Bank's Cat-DDOs), regional risk pools (such as the Caribbean Catastrophe Risk Insurance Facility), or transfers of part of the risk to global reinsurance or global capital markets (such as with FONDEN bonds in Mexico) (Mahul and Ghesquiere 2007). Such tools make it possible for governments to support the affected population, and they improve the transparency and predictability of the postdisaster response (Clarke and Dercon 2016). Meanwhile, combined with institutional preparedness and contingent plans, they can accelerate recovery and reconstruction, reducing overall losses (de Janvry, del Valle, and Sadoulet 2016).

A resilience package. These instruments increase people's ability to cope with asset losses without reducing the asset losses themselves. Implemented together as part of a *resilience package*, they could reduce global well-being losses from natural disasters by $78 billion. Adding universal access to early warning systems would raise well-being benefits to $100 billion.

The analysis described in this report reveals the powerful complementarities between interventions, as well as the importance of designing each intervention as part of a consistent package best developed at the country level (box O.1). For example, policies that facilitate access to financial resources after disasters and interventions that make safety nets more responsive generate much larger benefits combined than the sum of the two performed independently. There is also a strong complementarity between market insurance and adaptive social protection, with insurance providing protection for the middle class while adaptive social protection is most efficient when focused on the poor.

A package of resilience-building policies would generate benefits that go beyond the avoided well-being losses estimated here and contribute to a broader development agenda.

BOX O.1

RESILIENCE PACKAGES SHOULD BE TAILORED TO EACH COUNTRY

Figure BO.1.1: Many actions could reduce well-being and asset losses in Malawi

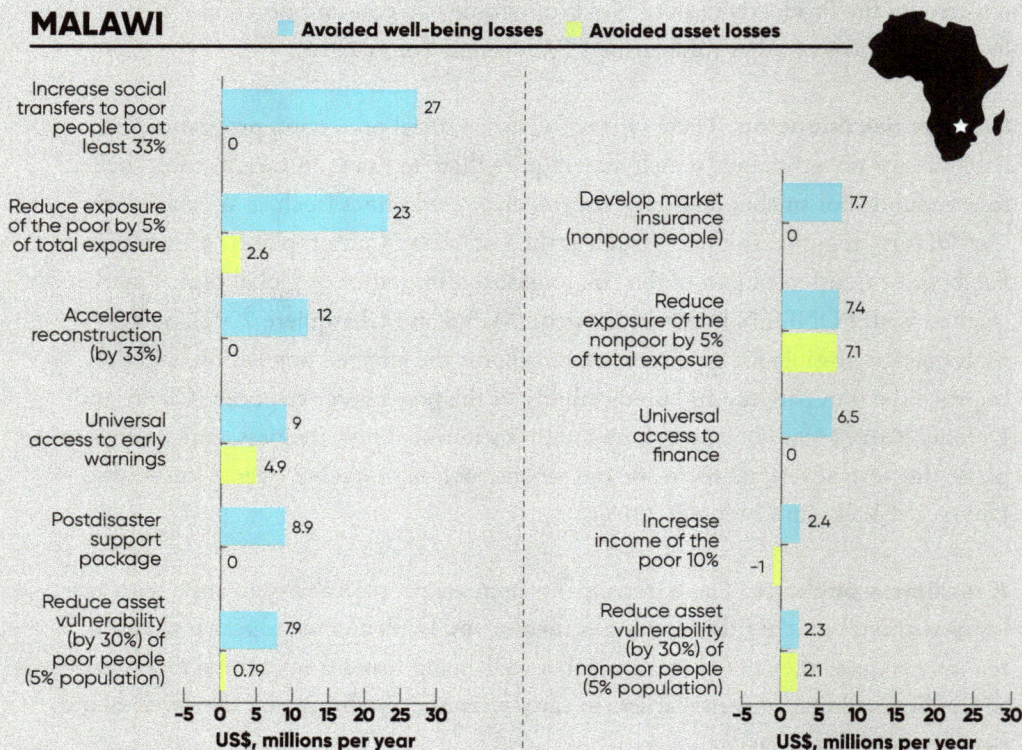

MALAWI

█ Avoided well-being losses   █ Avoided asset losses

Action	Avoided well-being losses	Avoided asset losses
Increase social transfers to poor people to at least 33%	27	0
Reduce exposure of the poor by 5% of total exposure	23	2.6
Accelerate reconstruction (by 33%)	12	0
Universal access to early warnings	9	4.9
Postdisaster support package	8.9	0
Reduce asset vulnerability (by 30%) of poor people (5% population)	7.9	0.79

US$, millions per year (scale: −5, 0, 5, 10, 15, 20, 25, 30)

Action	Avoided well-being losses	Avoided asset losses
Develop market insurance (nonpoor people)	7.7	0
Reduce exposure of the nonpoor by 5% of total exposure	7.4	7.1
Universal access to finance	6.5	0
Increase income of the poor 10%	2.4	−1
Reduce asset vulnerability (by 30%) of nonpoor people (5% population)	2.3	2.1

US$, millions per year (scale: −5, 0, 5, 10, 15, 20, 25, 30)

Source: World Bank estimates.
Note: U.S. dollars are measured in terms of purchasing power parity (PPP). Poor people are defined as the poorest 20 percent in terms of consumption in the country.

To identify promising policy options and help design consistent strategies, this report proposes disaster management profiles for the 117 analyzed countries. The profile for Malawi shows the potential benefits of different actions on well-being and asset losses (figure BO.1.1).

In Malawi, building up social protection systems so that poor people receive a larger share of their income from transfers would increase resilience and reduce the effect of natural disasters on well-being. Even if their income does not change, increasing the share of social transfers in poor people's income to 33 percent would increase resilience, thereby reducing disaster well-being losses by an average $27 million a year. Furthermore, making social protection more adaptive and enhancing the government's ability to provide postdisaster support—by combining financial instruments and delivery mechanisms—should generate well-being gains of nearly $8.9 million a year.

Meanwhile, reducing poor people's exposure so that total exposure is reduced by 5 percent would prevent asset losses of $2.6 million a year and generate well-being gains of $23 million a year. By contrast, reducing the exposure of nonpoor people would prevent much higher asset losses ($7.1 million a year), but would provide much lower well-being benefits ($7.4 million a year).

If only floods are considered, reducing poor people's exposure would cut asset losses by $2.2 million a year, generating well-being gains equivalent to $19 million a year. This finding suggests that a government could be ready to pay up to $3,800 per poor person either protected by a dike or resettled in a safe area (with a 6 percent discount rate).

Designing interventions at the country level would require far more detailed analyses. Still, these estimates could help inspire policy makers everywhere to discuss new ways to reduce disaster impacts by identifying actions that cost less than the estimated benefits and suit a country's context and capacity.

First, disaster risk reduction can generate growth and benefits—beyond avoided losses—by promoting investment. Evaluations of the World Food Programme's R4 Rural Resilience Initiative and Mexico's CADENA program have shown that insurance is helping farmers increase their investments in productive assets, boosting their productivity (Madajewicz, Tsegay, and Norton 2013; de Janvry, Ritchie, and Sadoulet 2016). Such additional benefits from disaster risk management due to changes in people's investment and saving behaviors make risk reduction investment more profitable than avoided losses suggest.

Second, the package of resilience-building policies discussed here would deliver benefits that extend beyond the context of natural disasters: financial inclusion, access to health and nonhealth insurance, and stronger social protection shield people against all sort of shocks, facilitate investment and innovation, and promote development and poverty reduction. Again, there are obvious synergies between efforts to reduce poverty and build resilience.

Although much can be achieved by reducing asset losses from natural disasters, risk can never be eliminated. Flood protection can fail in the face of exceptional tsunamis or storm surges, and huge earthquakes can wreak massive devastation even in the face of the strictest building norms. And then there is climate change: its uncertain effects make it even more likely that some hazards will overwhelm protection infrastructure or hit where they are not expected. In this uncertain world, a more resilient population is critical to break the cycle of poverty-inducing disasters.

NOTES

1. The estimate for the 2015 losses is from Swiss Re. The estimate of average annual losses is from the *United Nations Global Assessment Report on Disaster Risk Reduction* (UNISDR 2015). This later estimate deviates from observations because the model and data are imperfect and because the average annual losses include the average losses from low-probability, high-impact events that have not occurred and the underreported losses from high-probability, low-impact events such as recurrent floods. All dollar amounts are U.S. dollars unless otherwise indicated.

2. The average annual losses are slightly higher than the ones published in the 2015 GAR report because revised estimates of the stock of capital were used in this analysis.

REFERENCES

Baez, J., L. Lucchetti, M. Salazar, and M. Genoni. 2016. "Gone with the Storm: Rainfall Shocks and Household Wellbeing in Guatemala." *Journal of Development Studies.* DOI:10.1080/00220388.2016.1 224853.

Bandyopadhyay, S., and E. Skoufias. 2012. "Rainfall Variability, Occupational Choice, and Welfare in Rural Bangladesh." Policy Research Working Paper 6134, World Bank, Washington, DC.

Barrett, C. B., and M. A. Constas. 2014. "Toward a Theory of Resilience for International Development Applications." *Proceedings of the National Academy of Sciences* 111: 14625–30.

Bustelo, M. 2011. "Bearing the Burden of Natural Disasters: Child Labor and Schooling in the Aftermath of the Tropical Storm Stan in Guatemala." University of Illinois at Urbana-Champaign.

Caruso, G., and S. Miller. 2015. "Long Run Effects and Intergenerational Transmission of Natural Disasters: A Case Study on the 1970 Ancash Earthquake. *Journal of Development Economics* 117: 134–50.

Clarke, D., and S. Dercon. 2016. *Dull Disasters? How Planning Ahead Will Make a Difference.* Oxford: Oxford University Press.

Cole, S., X. Gine, J. Tobacman, P. Topalova, R. Townsend, and J. Vickery. 2013. "Barriers to Household Risk Management: Evidence from India." *American Economic Journal: Applied Economics* 5: 104–35. doi:10.1257/app.5.1.104.

Dang, H. A., P. F. Lanjouw, and R. Swinkels. 2014. "Who Remained in Poverty, Who Moved Up, and Who Fell Down? An Investigation of Poverty Dynamics in Senegal in the Late 2000s." Policy Research Working Paper 7141, World Bank, Washington, DC.

de Janvry, A., A. del Valle, and E. Sadoulet. 2016. "Insuring Growth: The Impact of Disaster Funds on Economic Reconstruction in Mexico." Policy Research Working Paper 7714, World Bank, Washington, DC.

de Janvry, A., E. Ritchie, and E. Sadoulet. 2016. "Weather Index Insurance and Shock Coping: Evidence from Mexico's CADENA Program." Policy Research Working Paper 7715, World Bank, Washington, DC.

del Ninno, C., S. Coll-Black, and P. Fallavier. 2016. *Social Protection Programs for Africa's Drylands: Social Protection Programs.* Washington, DC: World Bank.

Dercon, S. 2004. "Growth and Shocks: Evidence from Rural Ethiopia." *Journal of Development Economics* 74: 309–29.

Dercon, S., and C. Porter. 2014. "Live Aid Revisited: Long-Term Impacts of the 1984 Ethiopian Famine on Children." *Journal of European Economic Association* 12: 927–48. doi:10.1111/jeea.12088.

Engle, N. L., A. de Bremond, E. L. Malone, and R. H. Moss. 2013. "Towards a Resilience Indicator Framework for Making Climate-Change Adaptation Decisions." *Mitigation and Adaptation Strategies for Global Change* 19: 1295–1312.

Gentle, P., R. Thwaites, D. Race, and K. Alexander. 2014. "Differential Impacts of Climate Change on Communities in the Middle Hills Region of Nepal." *Natural Hazards* 74: 815–36. doi:10.1007/s11069-014-1218-0.

Hallegatte, S., M. Bangalore, L. Bonzanigo, M. Fay, T. Kane, U. Narloch, J. Rozenberg et al. 2016. *Shock Waves: Managing the Impacts of Climate Change on Poverty.* Climate Change and Development Series. Washington, DC: World Bank.

Hallegatte, S., M. Bangalore, and A. Vogt-Schilb. Forthcoming. "Socioeconomic Resilience to Multiple Hazards—An Assessment in 117 Countries." Background paper prepared for this report, World Bank, Washington, DC.

Kousky, C. 2016. "Impacts of Natural Disasters on Children." *Future of Children* 73–92.

Madajewicz, M., A. H. Tsegay, and M. Norton. 2013. *Managing Risks to Agricultural Livelihoods: Impact Evaluation of the Harita Program in Tigray, Ethiopia, 2009–2012.* London: Oxfam.

Mahul, O., and F. Ghesquiere. 2007. "Sovereign Natural Disaster Insurance for Developing Countries: A Paradigm Shift in Catastrophe Risk Financing." Policy Research Working Paper 6058, World Bank, Washington, DC.

ODI (Overseas Development Institute) and GFDRR (Global Facility for Disaster Reduction and Recovery). 2015. "Unlocking the Triple Dividend of Resilience—Why Investing in DRM Pays Off." http://www.odi.org/tripledividend.

Rozenberg, J., and S. Hallegatte. Forthcoming. "Model and Methods for Estimating the Number of People Living in Extreme Poverty Because of the Direct Impacts of Natural Disasters." Background paper prepared for this report, World Bank, Washington, DC.

UNISDR (United Nations Office for Disaster Risk Reduction). 2015. *United Nations Global Assessment Report on Disaster Risk Reduction.* Geneva: UNISDR.

White, E. J., and C. Porter. 2016. "Potential for Application of a Probabilistic Catastrophe Risk Modelling Framework to Poverty Outcomes: General Form Vulnerability Functions Relating Household Poverty Outcomes to Hazard Intensity in Ethiopia." Policy Research Working Paper 7717, World Bank, Washington, DC.

1 INTRODUCTION

>> **Natural hazards return
and keep people in poverty.**

D isasters are an obstacle to development and poverty reduction. They affect and kill many people every year, and recent events have been particularly devastating—for example, the 2004 tsunami in South Asia and the 2010 earthquake in Haiti. And beyond their immediate and visible impacts, their effects on people's health, wealth, and ability to save and accumulate assets can be devastating, returning people to or keeping them in poverty.

These effects were recently described in the World Bank report *Shock Waves: Managing the Impacts of Climate Change on Poverty* by Hallegatte et al. (2016). Natural hazards such as droughts, floods, and earthquakes have socioeconomic consequences that go beyond their most obvious impacts; they can affect the lives of their victims for years. Job losses and falling incomes can have significant impacts on people's well-being and long-term prospects, especially those of the poorest, who live close to subsistence levels. Assets and savings accumulated over years such as homes and livestock can be wiped out in a few minutes by a flood or an earthquake. And incomes, especially from agriculture, can be depressed for years by a long drought— for example, when Ethiopia went through a terrible drought in 1984 and 1985, the impacts were long-lived. A decade passed before affected Ethiopians were able to return to their pre-disaster wealth (Dercon 2004).

The importance of these secondary impacts is demonstrated by the visible consequences for children: after Hurricane Mitch hit Nicaragua in 1998, the probability of child undernourishment in regions hit by the hurricane increased by 8.7 percent, and child labor force participation increased by 5.6 percent (Baez and Santos 2007).

The international community is increasingly viewing efforts to reduce people's vulnerability to natural hazards as a policy priority, as illustrated by four recent international conferences (box 1.1). An increasing number of countries have been developing and implementing national strategies to reduce the impact of natural disasters. From this momentum around risk management and resilience has emerged an unprecedented need for better understanding of the link among natural hazards, development, and poverty; better data and indicators to measure resilience; and better tools to identify priorities for action at the country level. This report seeks to contribute such knowledge and tools, focusing on socioeconomic resilience and the two-way relationship between poverty and natural disasters.

In this report, we use the term natural disaster to describe a natural hazard that has notable negative impacts on people. Such natural disasters are not purely natural events; they are caused by the interaction between a natural event—such as heavy rainfall or an earthquake—and socioeconomic vulnerability (World Bank and United Nations 2010). For example, a massive flood is not enough to cause a disaster; a disaster occurs only if the flood takes place where people live and are vulnerable to an inundation.

How is the study described in this report different? In this study, we move beyond monetary losses and focus on the impacts of natural disasters on people's well-being. Traditionally, the economic impact of natural disasters has been measured using the value of the damages disasters cause to assets such as buildings, infrastructure, and equipment, or to agricultural production. These are the numbers that are reported annually by research organizations, reinsurance firms, and the media. Similarly, anyone conducting risk assessment usually focuses on three things: hazard (the probability that an event occurs), exposure (the population and assets located in the affected area), and asset vulnerability (the fraction of asset value lost when affected by a hazard). These factors constitute the risk to assets, in monetary terms, which is the average value of the damages that natural disasters such as floods or earthquakes inflict on assets (often measured in their replacement or repair value). For drought, risk assessments include lost agricultural production as an additional impact.

Although the monitoring of total economic losses and assessments of expected economic losses are useful in providing an aggregate figure of the risk a city or

DISASTER RISK MANAGEMENT HAS BECOME A CENTRAL PART OF THE INTERNATIONAL DEVELOPMENT AGENDA

The Third UN World Conference on Disaster Risk Reduction in March 2015 led to the adoption of the Sendai Declaration and the Sendai Framework for Disaster Risk Reduction 2015–2030. This framework seeks "the substantial reduction of disaster risk and losses in lives, livelihoods and health and in the economic, physical, social, cultural and environmental assets of persons, businesses, communities and countries." This goal is translated into multiple targets for 2030 such as reducing global disaster mortality and direct disaster economic loss in relation to the global gross domestic product and increasing the availability of and access to multihazard early warning systems and disaster risk information and assessments.

Only a few months later, the United Nations' Sustainable Development Goals were approved by the international community. They also include targets related to disaster risk, including Target 1.5 ("By 2030, build the resilience of the poor and those in vulnerable situations and reduce their exposure and vulnerability to climate-related extreme events and other economic, social and environmental shocks and disasters") and Target 13.1 ("Strengthen resilience and adaptive capacity to climate-related hazards and natural disasters in all countries"). The targets on food security and urban development are also relevant to disaster risk reduction.

The Paris Agreement was approved in December 2015 at the 21st Conference of the Parties of the United Nations Framework Convention on Climate Change. The agreement includes many objectives and decisions to support more resilient development. In particular, Article 7 establishes "the global goal on adaptation of enhancing adaptive capacity, strengthening resilience and reducing vulnerability to climate change, with a view to contributing to sustainable development." In part through the Warsaw International Mechanism for Loss and Damage (Article 8), parties to the agreement also plan to seek more action and cooperation on a few priority areas such as early warning systems, emergency preparedness, comprehensive risk assessment and management, and risk insurance facilities, climate risk pooling, and other insurance solutions. The agreement reiterates previous commitments related to finance instruments and financial flows from developed to developing countries to support these goals, and it emphasizes that climate financing should be balanced between adaptation and mitigation.

Finally, the World Humanitarian Summit held in March 2016 highlighted the need to do more to prevent humanitarian crises instead of just managing them. Doing so requires better management of natural disasters and more resilient societies and economies, including through the use of social protection instruments.

country faces, they miss an important implication for people's well-being: $1 in losses does not mean the same thing to a rich person and a poor person.[1] The same loss affects the livelihoods of poor and marginalized people more substantially because they rely on fewer and more vulnerable assets, their consumption is closer to subsistence levels, and they may need more time to recover and rebuild. Moreover, a flood or earthquake can be disastrous for poor people, while having a negligible impact on the gross domestic product (GDP) if it affects people who own almost nothing and have a very small income.

In this report, we move beyond monetary losses and focus on the impacts of natural disasters on well-being, taking into account their distributional impacts within countries and the specific vulnerabilities of poor people as determined by the local socioeconomic context (figure 1.1). This focus provides a different view of natural disasters—one that better accounts for the vulnerability of poor people than the usual reporting.

But it also highlights opportunities. For example, it becomes possible to investigate not only disaster risk management measures that reduce the losses of asset—such as dikes and building norms—but also the resilience-building measures that reduce the impact of disasters on well-being without affecting asset losses—such as social protection, financial inclusion, or insurance. The objective is to explore this full range of measures in an integrated framework and to identify priorities for actions at the country level, with the goal of using disaster risk management and resilience as an instrument to reduce poverty.

In the next chapter, we review the existing literature to show how poor people suffer disproportionately from the effects of natural hazards, not only because they are often more exposed to hazards, but also because they lose more when they are affected and receive less support to recover. In undertaking this review, we find that poverty is a major determinant of a population's vulnerability to natural disasters.

In turn, we find that natural disasters are a driver of poverty. This finding is based on a review in chapter 3 of the growing number of case studies covering all continents, but also a new estimate of the impact of natural disasters on the global poverty headcount.

In chapter 4, we estimate the effects that disasters have on well-being. To do so, we start from estimates of asset losses at the national level, as assessed in the *United Nations Global Assessment Report on Disaster Risk Reduction* (UNISDR 2015), and estimate their impact on people's well-being in 117 countries.

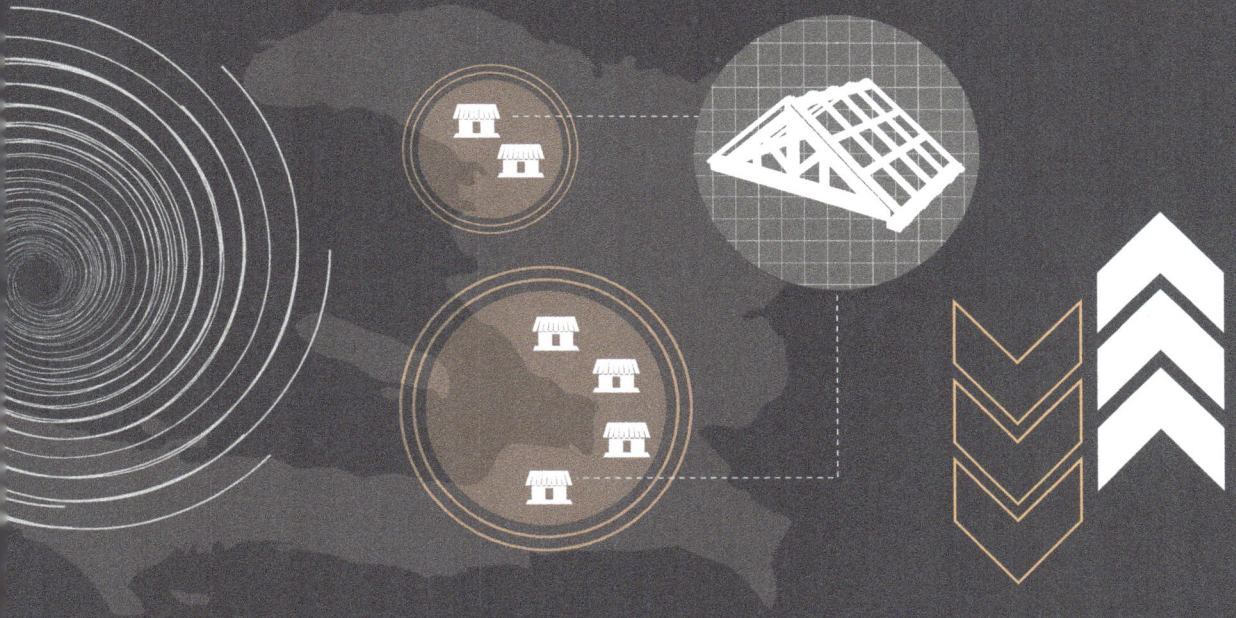

FIGURE 1.1
THIS REPORT GOES BEYOND MONETARY LOSS
AND FOCUSES ON WELL-BEING

ASSET LOSSES

1. Hazard   2. Exposure   3. Vulnerability

WELL-BEING LOSSES

1. Hazard   2. Exposure   3. Vulnerability   4. Socioeconomic resilience

Finally, we use these estimates to assess various policy options to reduce the effects of natural hazards on well-being, looking at the options that can avoid disasters and reduce the asset losses they cause (chapter 5) and the options that make the population better able to cope with these losses (chapter 6). In the final chapter, we demonstrate how this approach can be applied in one country to identify risk management options that are particularly promising and deserve more in-depth analysis.

NOTES

1. In this report, all dollar amounts are U.S. dollars unless otherwise indicated.

REFERENCES

Baez, J. E., and I. V. Santos. 2007. *Children's Vulnerability to Weather Shocks: A Natural Disaster as a Natural Experiment.* New York: Social Science Research Network.

Dercon, S. 2004. "Growth and Shocks: Evidence from Rural Ethiopia." *Journal of Development Economics* 74: 309–29.

Hallegatte, S., M. Bangalore, L. Bonzanigo, M. Fay, T. Kane, U. Narloch, J. Rozenberg et al. 2016. *Shock Waves: Managing the Impacts of Climate Change on Poverty.* Climate Change and Development Series. Washington, DC: World Bank.

UNISDR (United Nations Office for Disaster Risk Reduction). 2015. *United Nations Global Assessment Report on Disaster Risk Reduction.* Geneva: UNISDR.

World Bank and United Nations. 2010. *Natural Hazards, Unnatural Disasters: The Economics of Effective Prevention.* Washington, DC: World Bank.

2 ON THE FRONT LINE

>> **Poor people suffer disproportionately from natural hazards.**

I n July 2005, Mumbai, India, experienced unprecedented floods, causing 500 fatalities and direct economic damage of $2 billion, especially among low-income and marginalized people. In 2015 floods in Malawi affected more than 600,000 people, largely those living in districts with high poverty. And in May 2015, a major heat wave swept across India, with temperatures hitting highs of 48°C in some parts. Official statistics reported more than 1,100 deaths (Al Jazeera 2015). Elderly people, as in most heat waves, were among the most vulnerable, along with low-income workers, especially those employed outdoors in jobs from rubbish collection to farming and construction.

In such natural disasters, poor people suffer more than their richer neighbors. In this chapter, we look more closely at whether disasters affect the poor more than the rest of the population: whether poor people are more often affected (exposure), whether they lose more when affected (vulnerability), and whether they have less ability to cope and recover (which results in higher losses in well-being). We follow the framework presented in chapter 1, which adds to the traditional risk assessment a fourth component—the socioeconomic capacity to cope with asset losses, a critical driver of the risk natural disasters pose for well-being. Our main finding here is that poverty is a major driver of people's vulnerability to natural hazards and natural disasters. An important implication is that poverty reduction and development—provided they do not create excessive new risk—make people less vulnerable and contribute to disaster risk management and reduction.

Poor people are more often affected by natural hazards

Areas at risk of natural hazards have always attracted people and investment. Globally, there has been a trend toward increased risk taking: from 1970 to 2010 the world population grew by 87 percent, while the population in flood plains increased by 114 percent and in cyclone-prone coastlines by 192 percent. Furthermore, the gross domestic product (GDP) exposed to tropical cyclones increased from 3.6 percent to 4.3 percent of global GDP over the same period (UNISDR 2011). The same trends hold true at the country level (Jongman et al. 2014; Pielke et al. 2008). A recent assessment of global damages from natural disasters suggests that annual total damage (averaged over a 10-year period) increased tenfold between 1976–1985 and 2005–2014, from $14 billion to more than $140 billion (GFDRR 2016).

Poor people often have to settle in risky areas

At-risk areas offer opportunities. At-risk areas may be more attractive—in spite of the risk—when they offer economic opportunities, public services or direct amenities, and higher productivity and incomes (Hallegatte 2012b). In some rural areas, proximity to water offers cheaper transport, and regular floods increase agricultural productivity (Loayza et al. 2012). People may settle in risky coastal areas to benefit from job opportunities with industries driven by exports. Agglomeration externalities— the benefits that firms and people obtain by locating near each other—may attract people to cities, even if the cities are more exposed than rural areas and newcomers have no choice but to settle in risky places. For example, households in regularly flooded areas of Mumbai report that they are aware of the flood risks but accept them because of the opportunities offered by the area such as access to jobs, schools, health care facilities, and social networks (Patankar 2015).

Within a country or region, the attractiveness of risky places means that the people living there need not be poorer than the rest of the population. However, on a more local scale and especially in urban areas, land and housing markets often push poorer people to settle in riskier areas, especially where land is scarce. In Ho Chi Minh City, Vietnam, qualitative surveys suggest flooded areas can be much cheaper than nonflooded areas for the same quality of accommodation (World Bank and Australian AID 2014). Indeed, a meta-analysis of the literature suggests that a 1 percentage point increase in the yearly probability of flooding is associated with a 0.6 percent decrease in housing prices (Daniel, Florax, and Rietveld 2009). Reduced housing prices, then, make it possible for poor people to access housing opportunities that would be out of reach in the absence of risk (Husby et al. 2015). In developing countries with informal markets, land scarcity can be particularly acute and land markets function poorly (Durand-Lasserve, Selod, and Durand-Lasserve 2013). In these places, it may not be the prices that push poor people into risky places but simply the availability of land with appropriate access to jobs and services. Informal settlements are often located in hazard-prone locations such as on hillsides, close to riverbanks, or near open drains and sewers—Pune (India), Dhaka, Caracas, Rio de Janeiro, and Mumbai have many such settlements (Lall and Deichmann 2012; Lall, Lundberg, and Shalizi 2008; World Bank 2007).

Poor people benefit less from protection against hazards. Another important issue is the availability of protective infrastructure such as dikes and drainage systems. FLOPROS (FLOod PROtection Standards), a global open and collaborative database, has illustrated the lack of infrastructure to protect poor people. It estimates flood protection at the subnational level based on expert knowledge collection on de facto protection if available, de jure legislation and performance standards otherwise, or simple economic modeling if de jure and de facto information are not available (Scussolini et al. 2016). The resulting protection levels are displayed in figure 2.1, which shows that people in low-income countries—especially those with GDP per capita of less than $5,000 in purchasing power parity (PPP) exchange rates —are significantly less protected than those in richer countries. This difference in protection alone can explain a factor of 100 in flood risks between poor and rich countries before population vulnerability is considered.

And there are differences within countries as well, even if we cannot quantify them at this stage. Too often, investments—including those in disaster risk reduction—are directed toward the relatively wealthier areas at the expense of poorer neighborhoods. This effect can amplify the exposure gap between poor and nonpoor households and generate pockets of high risk. The lack of protection for the poor within countries may be related to the decision-making frameworks. For example, a cost-benefit analysis of flood management investments would favor projects that protect higher-value assets rather than less productive ones. Without an explicit focus on the poor and vulnerable, such an efficiency criterion may fail to help poor communities and instead concentrate support and resources on the better-off. Explicit choices to support poor communities are thus necessary to ensure that risk management policies support communities with the least adaptive capacities. This, however, should not be done at the expense of efficiency in the use of scarce public resources. Chapter 5 of this report proposes a methodology to balance the need for efficient use of public resources with the imperative to protect the poor and vulnerable.

Figure 2.1: People in poor countries are less protected against floods than people in rich countries

Protection level as a function of GDP per capita

Source: Scussolini et al. 2016,

Note: Figure shows protection level from FLOPROS as a function of GDP per capita. A 100-year protection level means that the protection can prevent all floods that are more frequent than the 100-year flood (that is, all floods with an annual probability of occurrence higher than 1 percent). Each dot represents a country. The y-axis is truncated at 200 years. A few countries in the database have higher protection levels such as the Netherlands (more than 4,000 years).

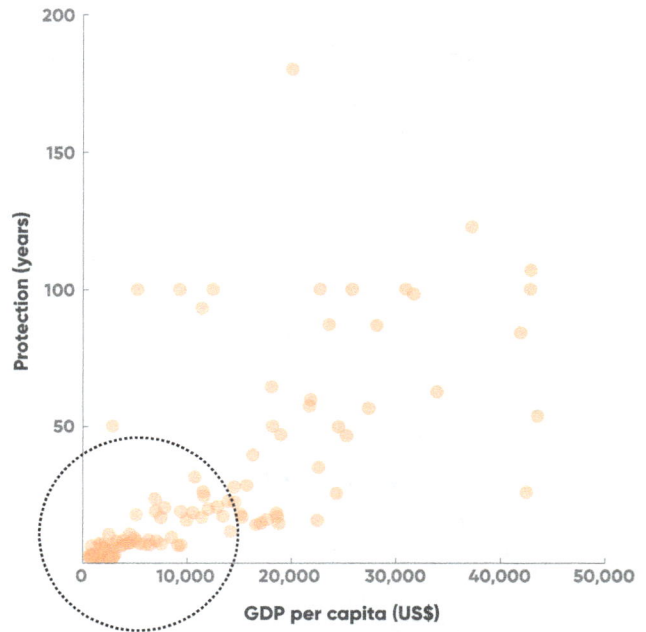

The bottom line is that the "opportunity effect" attracts both the rich and poor to risky areas, but land markets push poor people into riskier areas within a city, and lack of investments compounds the overexposure of poor people. Whether the poor are more or less exposed than the nonpoor is thus an empirical question. The next section explores the differential exposure of poor and nonpoor people, drawing on national studies and local surveys. It builds on the review provided in the *Shock Waves* report (Hallegatte et al. 2016), adding new case studies, especially on geological hazards.

Poor people are more often found among disaster victims or in at-risk areas

At the local level and based on past disasters, poor people seem more likely to be affected by natural disasters. After Cyclone Aila hit Bangladesh in 2009, a postdisaster survey of 12 villages on the southwest coast found that 25 percent of poor households in these villages were exposed to the cyclone, whereas only 14 percent of nonpoor households were (Akter and Mallick 2013). In Vietnam, a similar pattern emerges for the Mekong Delta: 38 percent of the region's poor but only 29 percent of the region's nonpoor live in frequently flooded areas (Nguyen 2011).

However, this pattern is not universal. After the 2011 floods in Kenya, almost everyone in the Bunyala District—poor and nonpoor—was affected (Opondo 2013). And in at least two documented cases, poor people were less exposed: after Hurricane

Mitch struck Honduras in 1998, more than 50 percent of nonpoor households but only 22 percent of poor households were affected (Carter et al. 2007), and a similar pattern was observed after the 2011 floods in Thailand (Noy and Patel 2014).

Our conclusion is that most studies find that poor people are more exposed (figure 2.2). However, the relationship between poverty and disaster exposure depends on the type of hazard, local geography, institutions, and other mechanisms, as illustrated in the following examples drawn from Mumbai (India), Latin America, Vietnam, Malawi, Colombia, and the United States and India.

Figure 2.2: When disasters hit in the past, poor people were more likely to be affected
Percent of poor and nonpoor affected by natural hazards, selected cases

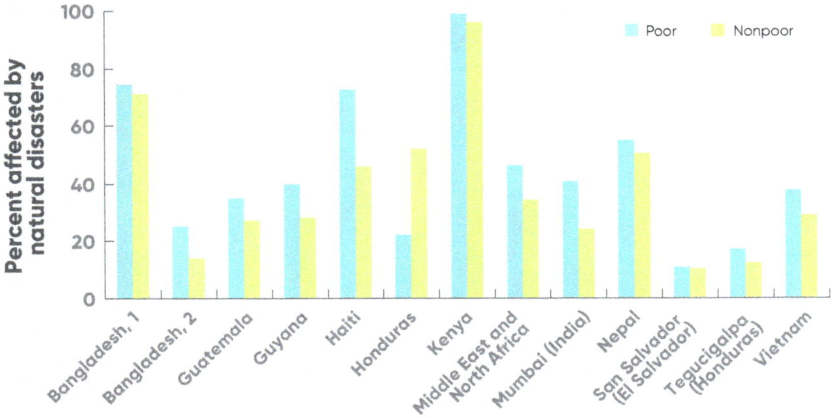

Sources: Bangadesh 1: Akter and Mallick 2013; Bangladesh 2: del Ninno et al. 2001; Guatemala: Tesliuc and Lindert 2003; Guyana: Pelling 1997; Haiti: Fuchs 2014; Honduras: Carter et al. 2007; Kenya: Opondo 2013; Middle East and North Africa: Wodon et al. 2014; Mumbai: Baker et al. 2005, Ranger et al. 2011; Nepal: Gentle et al. 2014; San Salvador and Tegucigalpa: Fay 2005; Vietnam: Nguyen 2011.

Note: Each study has a different definition of "poor" and "nonpoor" people. The definition of exposure differs based on the type of hazard and context in which it occurs.

Floods in Mumbai, India. In July 2005, Mumbai experienced unprecedented floods that produced 500 fatalities and direct economic damage of $2 billion (Ranger et al. 2011). The floods took a toll on low-income and marginalized people; their losses were estimated at about $245 million, of which almost $235 million was from household asset losses and the rest from informal business losses (Hallegatte et al. 2010).

Are Mumbai's poor more exposed than its nonpoor to current and future floods? To answer this question, we explore the exposure of poor and nonpoor people to similar floods in the Mithi River Basin flood zone, drawing on a city-level household survey (containing each household's location and income) and a flood map generated for the study by Risk Management Solutions, Inc. Households in lower-income levels are disproportionately exposed, with 75 percent of those exposed reporting a monthly income of 7,500 rupees (Rs) or less. The richest households are almost completely absent from at-risk areas (table 2.1). When climate change is included in the assessment—looking at 2080 in a high-emission scenario—the fraction of exposed poor people does not change, but the absolute number of people exposed is found to increase significantly (see Ranger et al. 2011).

Table 2.1: Poor people in Mumbai tend to be more exposed to floods

Distribution of income levels in the surveyed population and in the population exposed to floods, in 2005 and 2080

Household income (Rs per month)	Share of population in survey	Share of population exposed in 2005	Share of population exposed in 2080
<5,000	27	44	43
5,000–7,500	28	33	34
7,501–10,000	22	16	17
10,001–15,000	12	5	5
15,001–20,000	6	1	1
>20,000	6	1	1

Source: Based on Baker et al. 2005 and Ranger et al. 2011. Note: Rs = rupees.

Landslides and floods in Latin America. Across Latin America, the evidence suggests that poorly functioning land markets, urban sprawl, and poor transportation on the edge of cities push low-income households to settle in risky areas. In Medellin, Colombia, the informal settlements that house the majority of the city's informal population are perched on steep slopes and near water bodies at the periphery of the city (Restrepo Cadavid 2011). These informal settlements are more exposed to either floods or landslides because of their location and more vulnerable because of the low-quality materials used for housing. And landslides are no small risk: in Venezuela in 1999, 30,000 deaths were attributable to landslides (Fay 2005).

In metropolitan San Salvador, the capital of El Salvador, and Tegucigalpa, the capital of Honduras, a fifth of poor people reported having suffered damage from landslides in the past five years, and 10 percent of poor residents of San Salvador and 17 percent of poor residents in Tegucigalpa reported suffering from floods (Fay 2005). These percentages are much higher than those for richer groups (figure 2.3).

Figure 2.3: Poor people are more exposed to floods and landslides in San Salvador (El Salvador) and Tegucigalpa (Honduras)

A. Population suffering physcial damage from floods
B. Population suffering physical damage from landslides

A. Damage from floods

B. Damage from landslides

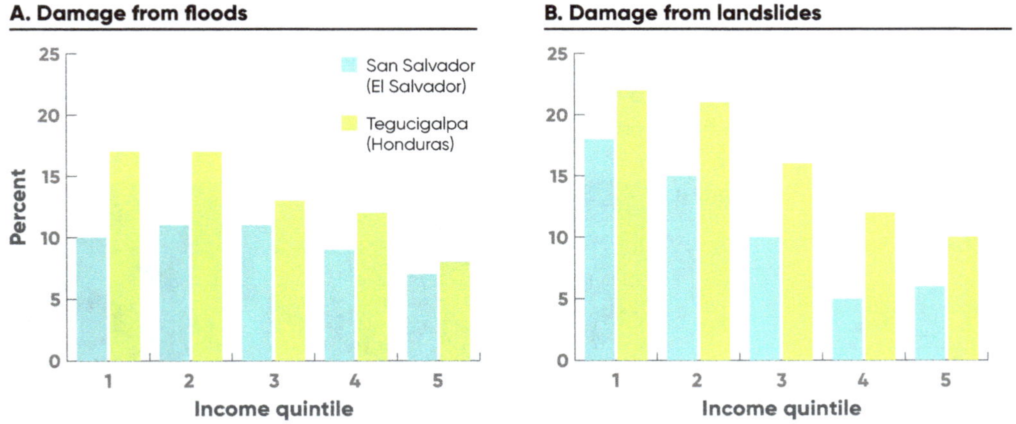

Source: Fay 2005.

And the same may be true in Santo Domingo in the Dominican Republic. Santo Domingo's central city slum is not homogeneous in its vulnerability to flooding and landsides, also as documented by Fay (2005). When it rains, the risk of flooding ranges from 6 percent for households on higher, consolidated ground to 45 percent for households near the river or along the drainage systems. And it is well-known which areas are at risk of landslides: rents, which reflect location safety, are almost twice as high in safer areas as those along the river. Undoubtedly, it is the poor people who reside in the low-cost, risky locations.

Floods in Vietnam (especially Ho Chi Minh City). In Vietnam, the poor are not more exposed to floods and drought than the nonpoor at the national level (Bangalore, Smith, and Veldkamp 2016), but the poor still face high levels of flood risks. For a 25-year return period flood (the flood that has a 4 percent chance of occurring every year), 30 percent of today's poor population is exposed, and this number increases by 16–28 percent in a climate change scenario. For a 50-year return period under a high climate change scenario, 40 percent of today's poor people in Vietnam are exposed to flooding.

Remarkably, Narloch and Bangalore (2016) find that in Vietnam the overexposure of poor people to floods is limited to urban households (figure 2.4). Indeed, rural poor people seems to be less exposed than their richer neighbors. This finding is fully consistent with those in the Shock Waves report. In that report, Hallegatte et al. (2016) find that the overexposure of poor people to floods seems to exist mostly in the urban environment, where land scarcity (and high housing prices) can push the poor toward the high-risk areas that richer households prefer to avoid. In rural areas, more abundant land (and possibly the benefits of floods for agricultural production) may explain why poor people are not systematically overexposed.

Figure 2.4: Poor people are overexposed to floods in urban areas, not in rural areas

Flood risk for different consumption percentiles: rural and urban areas of Vietnam, 2014

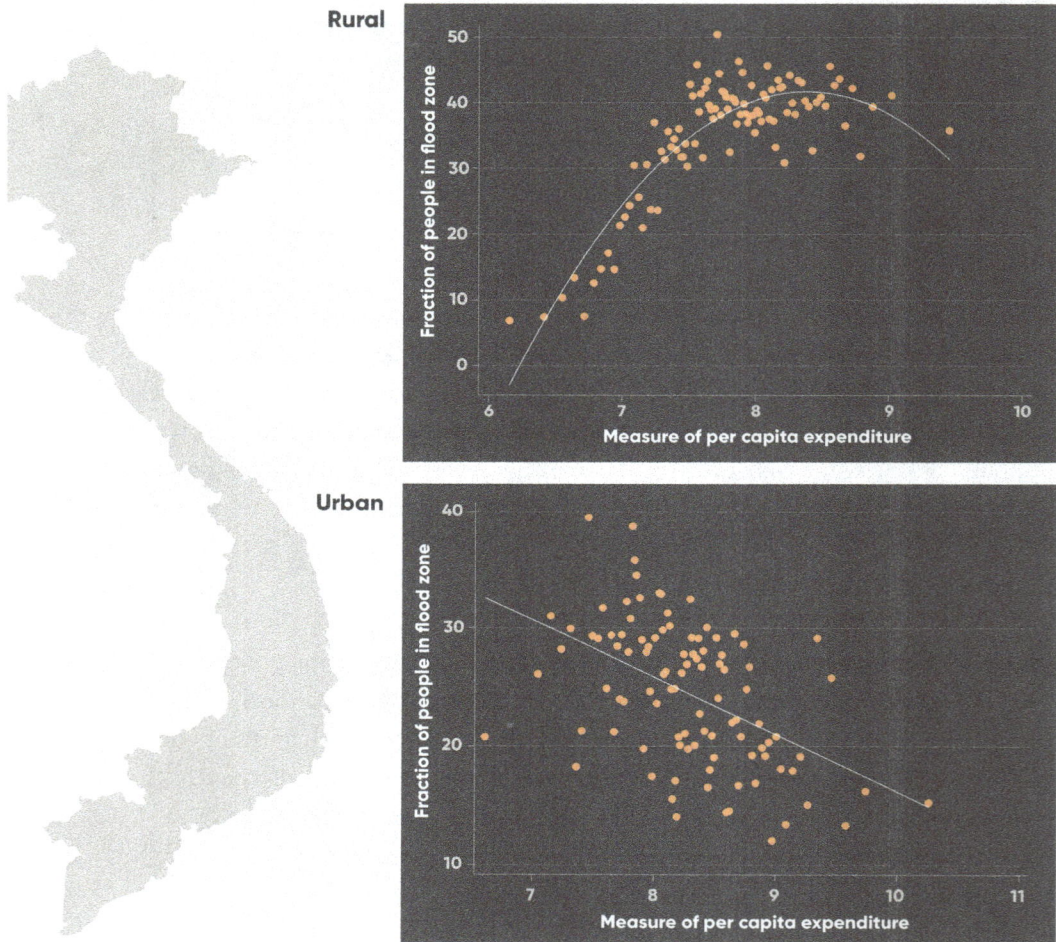

Source: Narloch and Bangalore 2016.

Note: The x-axis in both panels shows the percentiles of logged per capita expenditure among households in 2014. The y-axis in both panels indicates the level of flood exposure. The dots show the binned scatterplots—that is, the mean flood exposure for each consumption level. The white line is the line of best fit.

Bangalore, Smith, and Veldkamp (2016) have examined the exposure of informal settlements to floods in Ho Chi Minh City (figure 2.5). They use high-resolution flood maps and proxy for poverty using the spatial location of potential slums from the World Bank's Platform for Urban Management and Analysis (PUMA) data set. Their finding is that a relatively high percentage of the potential slum areas are exposed to floods, ranging from 69 percent for a 10-year return period up to 80 percent for a 100-year return period (figure 2.5). This exposure is higher than that in the Ho Chi Minh City urban area as a whole: 63 percent for a 10-year return period and up to 66 percent for a 100-year return period.

This overexposure is likely to increase as population and climate change over time. The same study finds that 70 percent of urban expansion areas is prone to flooding. This is consistent with the idea that urbanization takes place first in safer areas and then extends toward riskier areas as urban population growth increases land scarcity (Hallegatte 2014).

Figure 2.5: People living in slum areas of Ho Chi Minh City are more exposed to floods than the rest of the population

Fraction of area exposed to floods: Ho Chi Minh City, Vietnam, 10-year and 100-year return periods (RPs)

Source: Bangalore, Smith, and Veldkamp 2016.

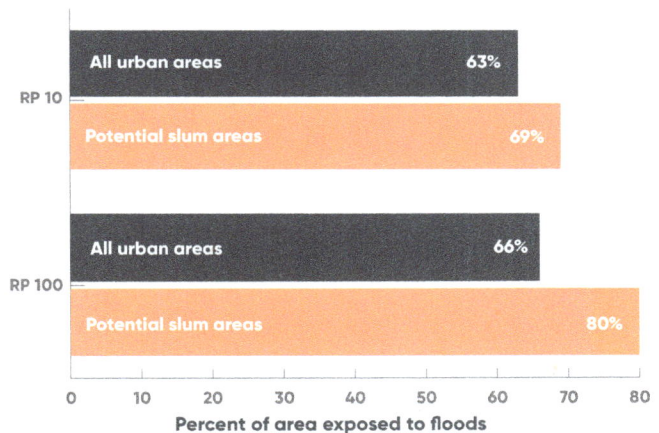

Floods in Malawi. In 2015 floods in Malawi reached unprecedented levels. Beginning in early January, heavy rains triggered significant flooding in the southern and eastern districts of the country. The districts that experienced the largest impacts were Nsanje and Chikwawa in the south and Phalombe and Zomba in the east. The flooding affected more than 600,000 people, displaced over 170,000, and damaged agricultural crops covering more than 60,000 hectares. Although these aggregate numbers and economic costs indicate the seriousness of the event, it is critical to look at exactly who was affected in the country—and it appears that the poorest were on the front line.

Overlaying the poverty map of Malawi with satellite and spatial data on the flood inundation zones reveals that the regions most affected by the floods have poverty rates of 75 percent or more, measured as $1.25 per day using the 2005 purchasing power parity (PPP) exchange rates (map 2.1). The average rate in Malawi is about 40 percent. These trends suggest that populations in flood-prone areas tend to be poorer.

Map 2.1: In Malawi, the 2015 floods hit mostly poor districts

Poverty incidence and flood extent, Malawi

Source: Hallegatte, Bangalore, and Nkoka 2015.

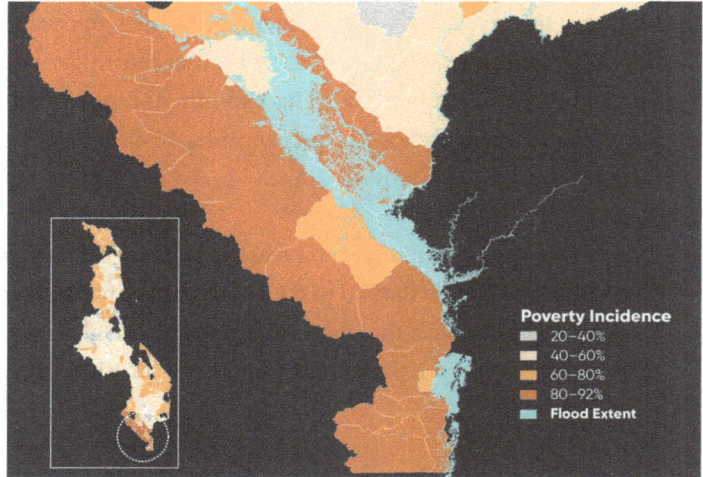

Poverty Incidence
- 20–40%
- 40–60%
- 60–80%
- 80–92%
- Flood Extent

Earthquakes in Bogotá, Colombia. The "sorting" of poor people into low-rent but high-risk locations is particularly acute in cities in developing countries where there is a divide between formal and informal markets for land. Although formal developments may adhere to land-use regulations, informal settlements are often located on hill slopes, riverbanks, or near open drains and sewers—all areas prone to natural hazards (Lall and Deichmann 2012).

Lall and Deichmann (2012) test this hypothesis by means of a case study on poverty and the risk of earthquakes in Bogotá, Colombia. After collecting data on property location and income levels, as well as spatial data on earthquake risk, the authors find evidence that poor people face a disproportionately high burden because they sort in high-density and low-rent properties in higher-risk locations. Poor households tend to settle in the western and southern parts of the city, areas at a higher risk of earthquake. On average, poor people within the city live in areas where the risk of earthquake is twice as high as in areas where richer households live. Compounding this exposure, the housing of poor people is also more vulnerable to earthquakes.

Heat waves in the United States and India. In May 2015, a major heat wave swept across India, with temperatures hitting highs of 48°C in some parts, causing more than 1,100 deaths (Al Jazeera 2015). In the state of Andhra Pradesh, which experienced the greatest effects of the heat wave, a majority of the 900 victims were elderly or low-income workers (Al Jazeera 2015; Vice News 2015). Homeless people unable to find shelter were also among the most vulnerable; according to a Delhi-based nongovernmental organization, of the 186 people who died in the capital, 80 percent were homeless (Vice News 2015). But these figures may underestimate the death toll because reliable statistics are difficult to find (The Economist 2015).

This pattern is also observed in rich countries. In Chicago, lack of air-conditioning was a critical risk factor in the 1995 heat wave, which resulted in over 700 deaths, concentrated among the poor and elderly populations (Whitman et al. 1997). People who did not have a working air-conditioner, access to an air-conditioned lobby, or an air-conditioned place to visit were 20–30 percent more likely to die than people with access to air-conditioning (Semenza et al. 1996). In fact, more than 50 percent of the deaths related to the heat wave could have been prevented if each home had had a working air-conditioner. A meta-analysis of heat wave studies finds working home air-conditioning reduces the odds of death by 23–34 percent (Bouchama et al. 2007).

Often, but not everywhere, poor people are more exposed to floods, drought, and high temperatures

The *Shock Waves* report by Hallegatte et al. (2016) examined poverty-specific exposure to floods, drought, and extreme temperatures in 52 countries (Park et al. 2015; Winsemius et al. 2015). Understanding whether the poor are more exposed than the nonpoor to these hazards requires "geo-referenced" information (where people live, their income levels) and hazard maps, which have only recently become available at the global level and at high resolution for floods (Ward et al. 2013; Winsemius et al. 2013) and drought (Prudhomme et al. 2014; Schewe et al. 2014). The flood and drought hazard data used in the *Shock Waves* study were taken from a global model (GLOFRIS) that produces gridded indicators of inundation depth (for flood, 1-kilometer resolution) and water scarcity (for drought, 5-kilometer resolution). For temperature, it used the observed data on the maximum monthly temperature for each grid cell (at 1-kilometer resolution) from the Climatic Research Unit of the University of East Anglia, from 1960 onward.

These state-of-the-art hazard data were combined with spatially explicit poverty data using a global data set of household surveys in 52 countries from the Demographic and Health Survey (DHS). This survey contains data on each household's location and wealth status. By calculating the flood, drought, and temperature indicators at the household level, it is possible to examine whether and how this exposure is different for poor and nonpoor households. Poor people are defined as those in the lowest quintile of the population in terms of the "wealth index" provided in the surveys, which is a measure of the assets owned by a household.

Once the hazard and socioeconomic data have been combined, a poverty exposure bias can be used to measure whether poor people are more exposed than nonpoor people to a hazard. For a given area, the poverty exposure bias is the share of poor people exposed to a hazard, divided by the share of the total population exposed, minus 1. A positive bias means poor people are more exposed than average; a negative bias implies poor people are less exposed than average.

Floods. For river floods at the country level, we find mixed results as illustrated in panels a, b, and c of map 2.2, which show the poverty exposure bias for floods with a 10-year return period (or 10 percent annual probability of occurrence); other return periods show similar results. In Latin America and the Caribbean and Asia, no pattern emerges: some countries exhibit a positive bias (poor people more exposed than average), and others exhibit no bias or a negative one (poor people less exposed than average). But in Africa, regional patterns appear. Countries in the southwest exhibit strong overexposure of poor people, as do those in the west with larger rivers such as Benin, Cameroon, and Nigeria. Among the countries analyzed, about half (representing 60 percent of the analyzed population) live in countries where poor people are more exposed than average to floods.

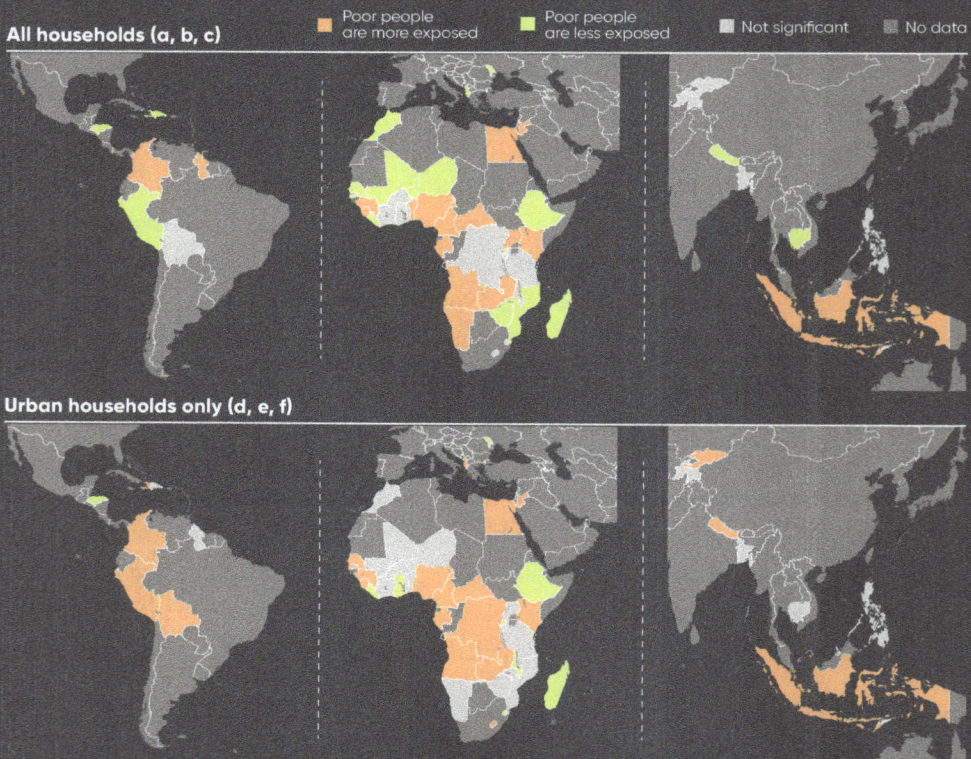

Map 2.2: In many countries, and especially in cities, poor people are more exposed than average to floods

Poverty exposure to floods, 52 countries: all households (a, b, c);

All households (a, b, c) | Poor people are more exposed | Poor people are less exposed | Not significant | No data

Urban households only (d, e, f)

Source: Winsemius et al. 2015.
Note: Maps are based on Demographic Household Survey.

What if we focus only on urban households? Land scarcity is more acute in urban areas than in rural areas and thus might create a stronger incentive for poor urban dwellers to settle in risky areas because of lower prices. The results for urban households reveal a clear difference between the exposure of poor and nonpoor people, as can be seen in panels d, e, and f of map 2.2. In most countries (about 73 percent of the analyzed population), poor urban households are more exposed to floods than the average urban population. There is no such pattern for rural households, suggesting that land scarcity is a driver of flood risk in urban areas.

In a new analysis for this report, we assess whether poor people are exposed to flood risk using an alternative method. The hazard maps remain the same, but instead of deriving poverty from the DHS we use "poverty maps" produced by the World Bank and national statistical agencies. These poverty maps are based on a methodology of small-area estimation from Elbers, Lanjouw, and Lanjouw (2003). They combine household surveys with census data to provide estimates of the number of poor people per subnational unit. The maps present subnational poverty data at the admin1 (provincial) and admin2 (district) level.

As part of the forthcoming report "Exploring Hidden Dimensions: Environmental and Natural Resource Aspects of Poverty," the World Bank's Environment and Natural Resources Global Practice and Poverty Global Practice have developed a database of the World Bank's poverty maps. The database covers 58 countries with poverty maps at the provincial level and 32 countries with poverty maps at the district level (20 countries are included at both admin levels). Different poverty lines are used in different countries, so that the definition of "poor" in this study is country-specific. Our study relies on this database for 69 countries, using the lowest administrative unit available.

The data reveal that across 69 countries 56 million poor people are exposed to the 10-year return period floods (7 percent of the 810 million poor people living in these countries). The 10 countries with the highest number of poor people exposed to floods are India, Bangladesh, Arab Republic of Egypt, Vietnam, Indonesia, Democratic Republic of Congo, Nigeria, Mexico, Iraq, and Sudan. According to this analysis, like in the previous one, the poor are not on average more likely to be affected by the 10-year flood event than the nonpoor. But some countries exhibit a strong bias. In six countries (Panama, Zimbabwe, Egypt, Gambia, Democratic Republic of Congo, and Kenya) the poor are 50 percent more likely to be flooded than the nonpoor. And in four countries (Rwanda, Sudan, Moldova, and Slovak Republic), the poor are at least 20 percent less likely to be flooded than the nonpoor.

Map 2.3 shows the countries in which poor people are overexposed. Although the previous assessment based on the DHS and this new analysis based on poverty maps give contradictory results in some countries such as Morocco, they are in agreement in many countries and indicate that in many countries poor people are more exposed to floods than the rest of the population. And the scale of the analysis means that the differential is not visible within many cities, where risks and incomes are very heterogeneous.

Map 2.3: **Poverty maps confirm poor people are more exposed than average in many countries**

Poverty exposure bias to floods, 69 countries

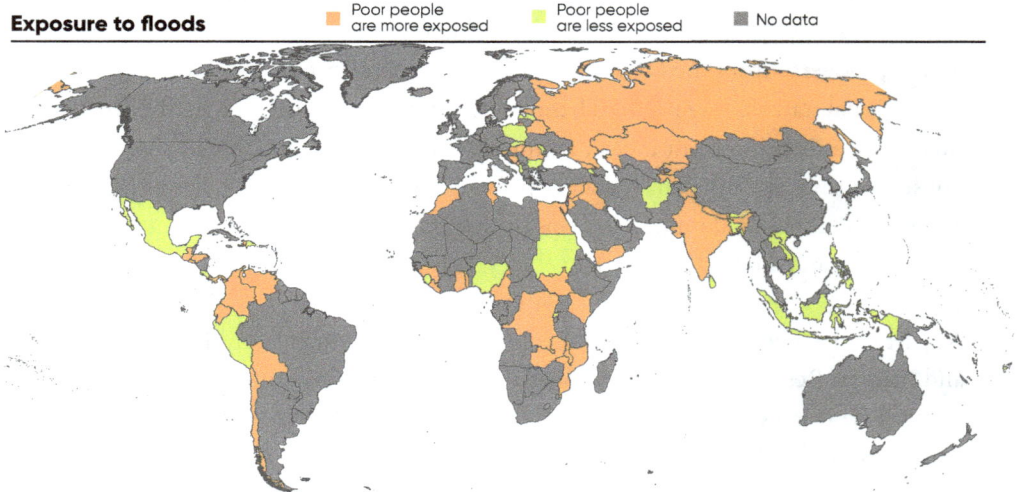

Source: World Bank estimates.

Drought. Based on the DHS surveys, results for drought at the country level reveal a poverty exposure bias, as illustrated in map 2.4. In most Asian countries and in southern and eastern Africa, poor households are more exposed to drought (the definition of drought used here is based only on surface flows and does not include groundwater and artificial water storage). In western Africa, coastal countries (Benin, Cameroon, Ghana, Nigeria, and Togo) exhibit a positive bias, with the exception of Niger. In Latin America, poor people appear underexposed in Bolivia and Peru, but overexposed in Colombia, Guyana, and Honduras. As for the total population, the poverty exposure bias is evident: 85 percent of the analyzed population lives in countries in which poor people are overexposed to drought.

High temperatures. Poor people are often more exposed to high temperatures: 37 out of 52 countries (representing 56 percent of the population) exhibit a positive bias (map 2.5). In Africa, most countries have a positive poverty exposure bias, with regional patterns similar to those found for floods and drought. The positive bias is particularly strong in western

Africa (Benin, Cameroon, and Nigeria) and southern Africa (Angola, Namibia, and Zambia). In Asia, the results for temperature are regionally consistent, with most countries exhibiting zero or negative bias. In Central America, the results are again sporadic.

Also worrying is that many of the 37 countries that exhibit a poverty exposure bias for temperature are already hot. And the hotter countries have a higher exposure bias. Cooler countries exhibit a smaller bias, and in some cool countries a negative bias because in these cool countries the nonpoor tend to settle in areas with higher temperatures, which are climatically more desirable. The results for temperature suggest a sorting of the population into desirable and less desirable areas within a country, with wealthier households typically living in desirable areas and poorer households in less desirable ones.

Map 2.4: In Asia and Sub-Saharan Africa, poor people tend to be more exposed to drought than the average population

Poverty exposure bias to drought by country, 52 countries

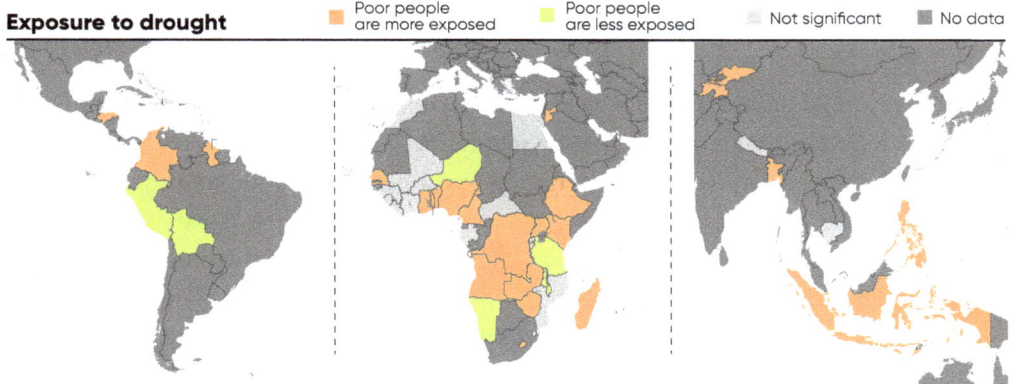

Source: Winsemius et al. 2015.

Map 2.5: In most of Africa, poor people are more exposed than average to high temperatures

Poverty exposure bias to high temperatures by country, 52 countries

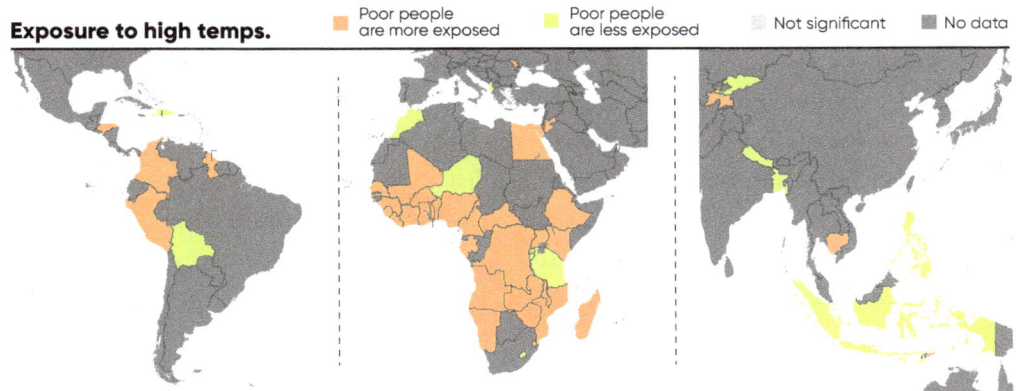

Source: Park et al. 2015.

Recurrent hazards affect poor people, with large hidden costs

Large-scale events make the news, but repeated small adverse events such as regular floods often have serious implications for poor people, even though little data exist on them and their consequences. And although poor and nonpoor people may decide to live in places that are sometimes affected by natural hazards—to enjoy other benefits—only poor people live in dwellings that are frequently flooded or in areas in which landslides are common. To convey a better sense of such events, and their cost, this section describes three case studies.

Recurrent floods in Mumbai, India. Mumbai is prone to recurrent floods during the monsoon season, with significant impacts on poor people (Patankar 2015). The authorities have identified 40 chronic flood spots (low-lying areas) and 200 localized flood spots, where waterlogging stems from inadequate drainage and poor land-use planning. Many low-income slum dwellers report floodwaters entering their homes several times during the monsoon season.

A survey of 200 households has yielded two key insights. First, floods cause problems with transport, drinking water, power supply, and food and fuel availability. Affected households lose workdays—on average 2.5 a year because of poor infrastructure (more than 50 percent of surveyed people cite the unavailability of transport or flooded roads)—implying a loss of income, productivity, and sometimes jobs. Second, floods cause diarrhea in 40 percent of households each year, malaria in 64 percent, and viral fever in 86 percent. Between 2001 and 2011, the number of reported cases of malaria increased by 217 percent in Mumbai, mainly because of lack of sanitation in the slums and water accumulation during the monsoon season.

Recurrent floods in Ho Chi Minh City, Vietnam. A survey of three flood-prone districts in Ho Chi Minh City found the health impacts of recurrent floods to be pervasive (World Bank and Australian AID 2014). Regular floods in a heavily polluted environment have led to many ailments, including skin and intestinal diseases, rheumatism, bronchitis, and chronic coughing, especially among children under 5. Every year, more than two-thirds of survey respondents report they are experiencing health issues, with more than half suffering from a waterborne (55 percent) or respiratory (52 percent) disease directly related to local flood conditions. These impacts also take a significant toll on employment and income, especially that of poor people (table 2.2).

Table 2.2: **Poor people in Ho Chi Minh City suffered disproportionately from recurrent floods in 2014**

Percent of households, poor and nonpoor, affected by impacts of floods:
Ho Chi Minh City, Vietnam, 2014

	Poor (n = 36)	Nonpoor (n = 210)
Households whose health was affected	86	64
Households whose employment was affected	69	56
Households whose income was affected	67	40

Source: World Bank and Australian AID 2014.

Recurrent floods in Metro Manila, the Philippines. Porio (2011) conducted a survey in 2009 to examine the impact of recurrent floods on 300 households in urban poor communities in Metro Manila. Respondents reported large health impacts from the recurrent floods because of improper sanitation, lack of potable water, and inadequate health systems. It is no surprise that health shocks are a significant burden: households affected by flooding reported that they or their household members were sick for an average of 12 days during the last rainy season. And only a small fraction (13 percent) of those who were sick were able to obtain free medicine; all others had to pay out of pocket. On average, households spent 1,930 pesos on medical care, and some households reported spending more than 10,000 pesos.

Respondents also reported four days of work lost a year. Income loss of about 1,000 pesos was reported because of lower productivity when working from home or an inability to get to work. Almost half of respondents reported they could not exit their house, cross the street, or obtain transport to get to work. In addition to lost earnings, households reported damages to household appliances, furniture, and housing stock. On average, this loss amounted to 4,615 pesos each season. And children suffer; a third of households reported the absence of children from school—on average five days a year.

Poor people lose more when hit by a disaster

Exposure is only one component of risk; vulnerability is another. Vulnerability is defined here as the fraction of wealth lost by people when they are hit by a shock.

Do poor people lose more than the nonpoor as a result of a disaster? Answering this question is challenging because of data limitations. Although global data are sufficient for examining exposure, they cannot provide an estimate of vulnerability because that also depends on asset portfolios and livelihoods. Thirteen local case studies have examined exposure to a disaster by poverty status, and five (in Bangladesh, Honduras, and Mumbai) have examined the losses of the poor and nonpoor separately (calculated as income losses, asset losses, or both). Described here, these case studies provide insight into the differences in vulnerability.

In absolute terms, wealthier people lose more assets or income from a flood or storm, which is expected because they have more assets and higher incomes. In relative terms, however, poor people always lose more than the nonpoor from floods and storms (figure 2.6). It is these relative losses rather than the absolute numbers that matter more for livelihoods and well-being.

Figure 2.6: When hit by a disaster, poor people lose relatively more than nonpoor people

Percent of assets or income lost due to a disaster, poor and nonpoor: Bangladesh, Honduras, and Mumbai, India

Sources: Bangladesh, 1: del Ninno et al. 2001; Bangladesh, 2: Brouwer et al. 2007; Bangladesh, 3: Rabbani, Rahman, and Mainuddin 2013; Honduras: Carter et al. 2007; Mumbai: Patankar and Patwardhan 2016.

Note: Each study uses a different definition of "poor" and "nonpoor" for its sample. The three Bangladesh studies use percentage of income loss as a metric, and the Honduras and Mumbai studies use asset loss.

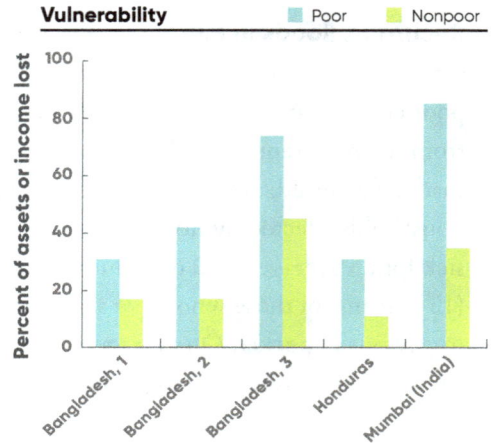

In Mumbai, for example, the 2005 floods not only caused direct losses of household assets but also led to lost income and large expenditures on home repairs or reconstruction (Patankar and Patwardhan 2016). According to a survey of 1,168 households, the nonpoor had higher absolute losses, but the poor lost more as a percentage of income across all three loss categories (table 2.3). When income, assets, and repairs were combined, the total losses from the event reached 85 percent of the average annual income of the poorest people.

Table 2.3: Poor people in Mumbai suffered higher relative losses after the 2005 floods

Losses from floods by income level: Mumbai, India, 2005

Average annual income (Rs)	N	Total loss (Rs)	(as % of yearly income)			
			Income loss	Asset loss	Repair loss	Total loss
<60,000	192	46,478	16	29	40	85
120,000	806	58,378	10	20	22	52
270,000	124	78,477	6	13	12	31
450,000	15	113,020	3	7	21	32
>540,000	10	87,750	8	4	8	19

Source: Based on Patankar and Patwardhan 2016.
Note: Rs = rupees.

Why is it that poor people lose relatively more? For one thing, poor people invest less in risk reduction and have little access to early warning. They also hold lower-quality assets and keep the assets in a more vulnerable form. As for income loss, poor people tend to be more dependent on lower-quality assets and infrastructure and natural capital to earn an income. They also are vulnerable to rises in food prices. The following sections review these vulnerabilities.

Poor people invest less in preparedness and risk reduction

Poor people, with fewer resources, tend to invest less in preventing and mitigating the adverse effects of natural hazards and environmental changes. In China, Indonesia, the Philippines, Thailand, and Vietnam, wealthier households are more likely to invest in proactive ex ante adaptation measures (Francisco et al. 2011). In addition, poorer individuals, lacking resources for long-term investments and proactive risk management, often rely on short planning horizons (Lawrance 1991). However, wealth is not the only determinant of preparedness: policies favoring training in disaster preparedness and higher education can help both rich and poor households (Francisco et al. 2011).

Capital losses can be reduced significantly by early warning systems (Hallegatte 2012). However, surveys conducted in developing countries suggest that access to early warning systems is low and biased against poor people. In the subdistrict of Shyamnagar in Bangladesh, only 15 percent of nonpoor people and 6 percent of poor people attend cyclone preparedness training. The levels of access to early warning are higher, but still biased against poor people: 41 percent for the nonpoor and 26 percent for the poor (Akter and Mallick 2013). In the Lamjung district of Nepal, the penetration of early warning systems in flood- and landslide-prone communities is lower than 1 percent (Gentle et al. 2014). These shortfalls highlight the challenges and the opportunities associated with building hydrometeorological institutions and systems that could produce actionable warnings (Rogers and Tsirkunov 2013).

In 2010 the Hyogo Framework for Action (HFA) identified priorities for action on disaster risk management, and it created a monitoring system whereby countries could report on their actions and progress. The second priority for action in the HFA is providing populations with access to early warning, and the monitoring system offers insights into the current situation in the world. More precisely, Core Indicator P2-C3 for this priority for action is "early warning systems are in place for all major hazards, with outreach to communities," and countries report a score of from 0 to 5 for this indicator, self-assessing their ability to warn their population. Self-assessment and self-reporting do have many issues—in particular, it is difficult to ensure that the criteria used for the assessment are consistent across countries—but these data provide a view of the availability of early warning in different countries.

Comparing high-income countries with developing countries, figure 2.7 illustrates the lag in early warning in developing countries. Most likely, the self-reporting underestimates this lag because we observed a large discrepancy in self-reporting and information from household surveys. For example, India reports a score of 4 for access to early warning systems, whereas in Mumbai only 10 percent of the surveyed households reported receiving some form of early flood warning (Patankar and Patwardhan 2016).

Figure 2.7: Developing countries are lagging in terms of access to early warning

Distribution of scores, Hyogo Framework for Action Core Indicator P2-C3, high-income and developing countries

Source: Hyogo Framework for Action.

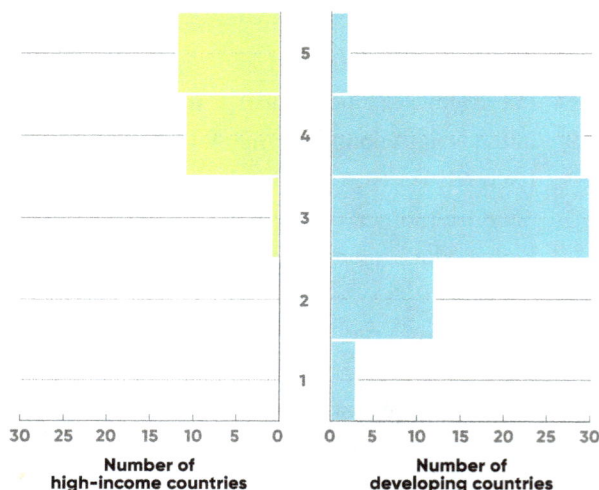

Access to and utilization of insurance is another tool that would help developing countries better manage risk. For example, Peter, Dahlen, and Saxena (2012) find that low- and middle-income countries suffer more and recover more slowly from natural disasters when uninsured. However, the current rates of coverage are paltry; a recent review by Lloyd's found that most low-income markets in the developing world remain undiscovered by insurers and that less than 5 percent of people on low incomes have access to insurance (Lloyd's Risk Insight 2013).

Poor people hold lower-quality assets

The typical asset portfolio of a poor person and a nonpoor person is very different (figure 2.8). Poor people tend to have less diversified portfolios: they hold a larger percentage of their assets in material form and save "in kind." The first savings of poor urban dwellers often takes the form of investments in their home, which may be vulnerable to natural hazards such as floods or landslides (Moser and Felton 2007). Many rural poor use livestock as savings, despite their vulnerability to drought (Nkedianye et al. 2011). The nonpoor, who have higher financial access, are able to spatially diversify and save in financial institutions, and their savings are thus better protected from natural hazards. This factor of vulnerability suggests that financial inclusion, especially targeting poor people through microfinance and products designed for their needs, could be a powerful risk reduction strategy. This finding mirrors similar conclusions reached for nonnatural risks (World Bank 2013).

Figure 2.8: Poor people less often have savings at financial institutions, especially in poor countries

Percent of poor and nonpoor with savings in financial institutions as function of GDP per capita

Source: Global Findex, World Bank.

Note: Each country is represented by two dots, one for households in the bottom 40 percent in terms of consumption and one for households in the top 60 percent.

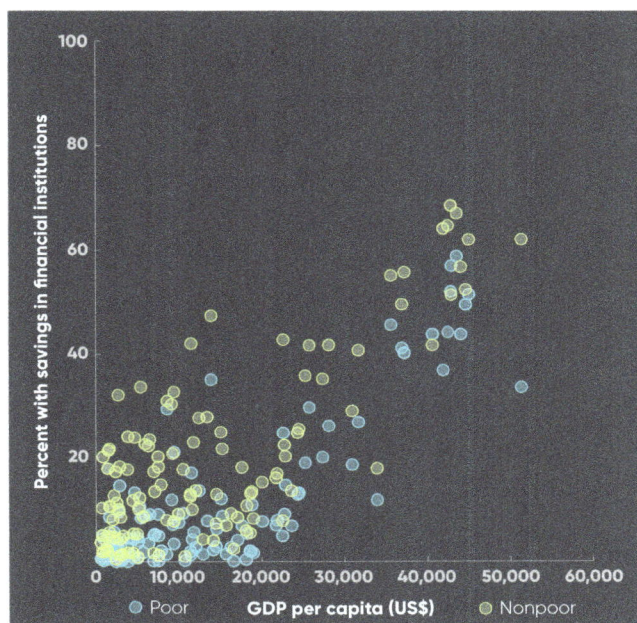

In addition to the portfolio composition effect, the quality of assets owned by poor people is lower. An example is housing stock. Households living in slums or informal settlements constructed of wood, bamboo, and mud and occupying steep slopes will suffer more damage from a natural disaster than households whose homes are made of stone or brick. In coastal communities in southwest Bangladesh following Cyclone Aila, 76 percent of households in kacha houses (traditional homes built of mud and bamboo) reported structural damage—far above the 47 percent for those in pucca houses (built of concrete and wood). In terms of economic damage, the average for kacha houses, $400, was also well above the $133 for pucca ones. Furthermore, households in kacha houses were significantly more likely to experience a fatality or physical injury—on average, 0.28 people per kacha house were injured or killed by the cyclone, compared with 0.13 per pucca house (Akter and Mallick 2013).

Going beyond the available case studies, we estimated how the vulnerability of the housing of the poor and nonpoor differs at the global level by conducting a global analysis. Even though the methodology is simple, it provides a crude estimate of the vulnerability differential between the poor and nonpoor. The Global Building Inventory database from PAGER (U.S. Geological Survey, USGS) provides a distribution of building types (buildings only, not contents) within countries across the world (Jaiswal, Wald, and Porter 2010). This typology was developed to assess vulnerability to earthquakes, but it is used here for all natural hazards.

We aggregated the 106 building types in PAGER into three categories, by vulnerability level: (1) fragile (the most vulnerable buildings), (2) median, and (3) robust—see Hallegatte, Bangalore, and Vogt-Schilb (forthcoming) for details on the categories. The PAGER data do not indicate who is living in buildings of different categories, and so it is assumed here that the poorest live in the most vulnerable buildings, which is a reasonable assumption in most cases and confirmed in one case study in the Philippines. In the 207 countries for which we have data, the poorest 20 percent in terms of consumption are 1.8 times more likely than the average person to live in dwellings in the "fragile" category (figure 2.9). Meanwhile, the situation is very diverse across countries for the nonpoor. Overall, however, housing vulnerability decreases with income. Within countries, dispersion also decreases when income increases, meaning that, on average, the overvulnerability of poor people decreases with national income.

Besides losses of private income and assets, natural disasters cause significant disruption to public infrastructure. Even though all people depend to some extent on electricity, working roads, and running water, poorer people tend to be less able to protect themselves from the consequences of disruptions in infrastructure services. And poor people must often rely on more fragile or undermaintained infrastructure such as unpaved roads, which are impractical during the rainy season, or drainage systems that are insufficient or clogged by solid waste.

Figure 2.9: Many people—and most poor people—live in fragile buildings

Fraction of poor and nonpoor residing in buildings of varying robustness to disasters, 209 countries

Poor

Nonpoor

- Fragile
- Medium
- Robust

Source: Hallegatte, Bangalore, and Vogt-Schilb, forthcoming.
Note: Here poor people are defined as the bottom 20 percent in terms of income or consumption in each country.

Poor people depend more on vulnerable agricultural income and ecosystems

Poor people, especially in rural areas without functioning markets, are highly dependent on agricultural income and ecosystems, and they are therefore vulnerable to the impacts of natural disasters on yields and the health and functioning of ecosystems. Large-scale events can wreak havoc on natural capital and threaten these sources of income. In 2008 Cyclone Nargis hit southwest Myanmar, killing an estimated 140,000 people, and recovery is still far from complete (World Bank 2015a). A major reason is the damage inflicted on embankments and streams by the cyclone, which resulted in a reinforcing chain of events for the affected farmers. Erosion and the loss of embankments made fields more prone to flooding. Furthermore, after Nargis the duration of daily and monthly tides became longer, making fields more saline and prone to pest infestation. Without funds for repair, affected farming villages became more prone to these external events—flooding, saline intrusion, and pest infestation. As a result, yields fell, as did incomes. Households have attempted to borrow money, but this has led only to more indebtedness.

On the other hand, natural capital also often serves as a safety net after a disaster when not depleted (Barbier 2010). In Bangladesh after Cyclone Aila hit in 2009, households living closest to the coast, while more exposed and vulnerable to the storm (and poorer), had more resilient income because the proximity to mangrove reserves offered higher income generation opportunities than those available to inland inhabitants (Akter and Mallick 2013). However, the effects of climate change on these ecosystems may impair their ability to serve as a safety net and to smooth consumption in the face of shocks (Noack et al. 2015).

In developing countries, livelihood diversification is becoming a crucial part of dealing with natural hazards. Occupational choice is one way in which households can diversify their income and increase resilience (Barrett, Reardon, and Webb 2001). For example, for households located in tourism regions, engaging with tourists can serve as a means of livelihood diversification (Mbaiwa and Sakuze 2009). Empirical evidence from Bangladesh suggests that household income diversification is more likely in areas with high local rainfall variability as households seek to become less vulnerable to the rainfall variability risks (Bandyopadhyay and Skoufias 2012). Crop choice and other forms of agricultural diversification are another option for rural households. In Ethiopia, risk-averse farmers have utilized crop diversification as a form of insurance against various agricultural risks (Mesfin, Fufa, and Haji 2011).

This said, opportunities to diversify differ between better-off and poor households, and diversification can be costly (see chapter 3). Barrett, Reardon, and Webb (2001), who have reviewed the entry barriers that prevent poor households from diversification, suggest that greater access to credit and financial capital, advantages in the labor market, and other ex ante endowments provide richer households with more diversification opportunities. Similarly, Ellis (2004) observes that even though both types of households may diversify at the same level, the better-off households experience greater returns.

Poor people have more vulnerable consumption patterns and often are food-insecure

In rural areas, lack of access to markets can create food security issues: if local production is lost to a drought or a flood, isolated communities cannot rely on production from other areas. Safir, Piza, and Skoufias (2013) found a 4 percent decrease in food consumption in areas of the Philippines with low precipitation, but this effect disappears in areas close to highways. This finding suggests that well-connected areas are less vulnerable to the food security consequences of natural disasters.

Even in well-connected areas, natural disasters can result in food price spikes as a result of supply shocks. Disasters can destroy crops and seed reserves, destroying in turn productive assets in agricultural communities and sparking food price shocks, as occurred after the unprecedented 2010 floods in Pakistan (Cheema et al. 2015). The floods destroyed 2.1 million hectares of agricultural land, decimating production and sending the price of wheat up to more than 50 percent above the preflood level.

Blanc and Strobl (2016) assess the impact of typhoons on rice production in the Philippines using satellite data on storm tracks and rice field location. Their analysis suggests significant rice production impacts in a country in which agriculture accounts for 12 percent of GDP; since 2001, losses are estimated to be up to 12.5 million tons. It is estimated that 2013 Cyclone Haiyan alone caused production losses of about 260,000 tons.

Poor people are more vulnerable than the rest of the population to increases in food prices. Those in developing countries spend on average between 40 and 60 percent of their household budget on food—far more than the 25 percent spent by the nonpoor (figure 2.10). However, net food producers could gain from higher food prices if they can maintain their production levels.

Finally, the very fact that they are poor makes poor people less able to cope with income losses. Losing half of its income has very different consequences for a household living on $30,000 a year and a household living on $1,000 a year (see chapter 4). In particular, poorer households cannot cut back on luxury consumption or delay consumption the way wealthier households can, and in many countries they are close to the subsistence level, which means that reducing consumption can have immediate negative impacts on health (if food intake is reduced or medical care becomes unaffordable), education (if children are taken out of school), or economic prospects (if essential assets have to be sold).

Figure 2.10: Poor people spend more on food, making them more vulnerable to spikes in food prices

Percent of total household expenditure devoted to food and beverages by income category: developing countries by region, 2010

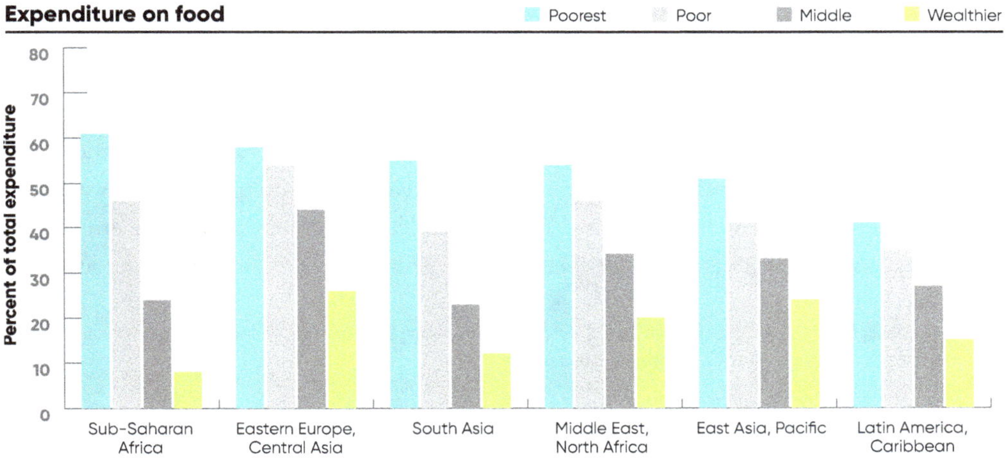

Expenditure on food ▪ Poorest ▪ Poor ▪ Middle ▪ Wealthier

Source: Global Consumption Database, World Bank.

Note: Calculated based on total consumption value in 2010 (U.S. dollars, purchasing power parity–adjusted values) in developing countries. Consumption groups are based on global income distribution data: poorest = less than $2.97 per capita per day; poor = between $2.97 and $8.44 per capita per day; middle = between $8.44 and $23.03 per capita per day; wealthier = above $23.03 per capita per day.

Higher productivity of capital and transfers may mitigate losses for poor people

All this said, poor people do have sources of resilience. For one thing, as discussed by Hallegatte and Vogt-Schilb (forthcoming), physical capital is scarce in many developing countries, and production is more labor-intensive. For example, a restaurant in a poor country is less likely to have all of the equipment and material that can be found in a rich-country restaurant, even at the same production level, but it is likely to have more staff. The productivity of capital thus tends to be higher in low-income countries. With less physical capital to damage, the asset losses from natural disasters are smaller when compared with production, and reconstruction is a smaller effort. In other words, a smaller share of consumption needs to be redirected toward reconstruction, reducing the impact on well-being and the duration of the reconstruction phase. As a result, reconstruction in developing countries is often quicker than what can be observed in rich countries, reducing the overall losses. (However, this distinction across countries is not valid within countries: even an individual who makes 100 percent of his or her income from labor in fact depends on the capital used to produce this labor income, even if the capital is owned by other people.)

Another source of the resilience of poor people is the share of their income made up of transfers from government or family. Figure 2.11 uses data from the ASPIRE database to calculate the fraction of income that poor and nonpoor households receive from public and private transfers, as a proxy for the geographical diversification of their income. In most countries, a large share of the income of poor people is composed of transfers, and especially from social protection (cash transfers, work programs, subsidies, contributory pensions and health insurance, and unemployment compensation). Thus if their labor income is reduced or interrupted by a disaster, the relative effect on total income is smaller, assuming that transfers are unchanged (if, for example, the social assistance transferred is maintained by the government) or even increases (see next section on postdisaster support).

Figure 2.11: Poor households tend to receive a large share of their income from transfers, except in low-income countries

Percent of income of poor and nonpoor from social protection, pensions, and remittances as function of GDP per capita

Source: ASPIRE database, World Bank.

Note: Each country is represented by two dots, one for the average poor household and one for the average nonpoor household.

This pattern is not observed, however, in low-income countries: below $5,000 in GDP per capita (PPP-adjusted), the difference in the income structure of the poor and nonpoor is small, and the share of income from transfers in these countries is very low, usually less than 15 percent. Therefore, the entire population of these countries is dependent on labor income, which is vulnerable to natural disasters.

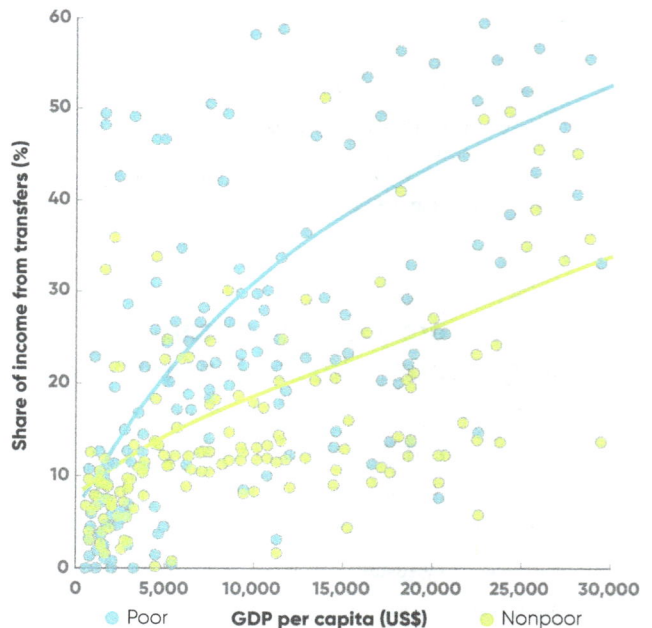

And the picture is different when looking in absolute terms. Poor people—the bottom 20 percent in each country—receive every year transfers from social protection and remittances that are worth only one-third of what the top 80 percent receive (according to the ASPIRE database, based on 106 countries). If transfers are not affected, a nonpoor individual who loses his or her labor income due to a disaster will thus receive three times more income than a poor individual in the same situation.

Poor people receive less support to cope and recover

Poor people are particularly exposed and vulnerable to the physical impacts of disasters. However, these direct impacts tell only part of the story. The overall impact on well-being and quality of life also depends on how well people cope and adapt, which depends in turn on the support they receive.

After they are hit by a shock, poor people receive less support than nonpoor people from financial instruments, social protection schemes, and private remittances. For example, in response to the flooding and landslides in communities in Nepal in 2011, only 6 percent of the very poor sought government support, compared with almost 90 percent of the well-off (Gentle et al. 2014). Besides suffering from larger immediate shocks than the wealthier, poor people also tend to be more alone in the struggle to cope and recover.

Postdisaster support often does not reach the poor, or is too small to make a difference

Even when poor households receive support, the amounts received are often too small to enable better coping strategies. In Bangladesh following the 1998 Great Flood, 66 percent of households in the bottom quintile received transfers, compared with 33 percent in the top quintile, and 53 percent of the flood-exposed households received transfers, compared with 34 percent of nonflood-exposed households (del Ninno et al. 2001). Although the targeting was relatively good, the transfer amounts were small: only 4 percent of the total household monthly expenditure for poor households and 2 percent for all households. Household borrowing highlights this limit: poor households affected by the flood borrowed six to eight times more than the level of government transfers.

Postdisaster support often fails to provide the poorest with enough resources because of their lack of voice and influence. When poor people are excluded from governance and have no say in the decision-making process, support is unlikely to be provided in a timely and adequate manner. In particular, different categories of the population compete for help after a disaster, and those with better connections are likely to get more, or faster, support. In two case studies on Thailand, it was found that the majority of government support after a flood benefited the well-off, with 500 baht per capita (about $14) going to the richest quartile, compared with 200 baht per capita for the poorest quartile (Noy and Patel 2014).

Nondisaster programs and horizontal safety net programs can play a key role, but the poor are often not covered

After a shock, when income and wealth are reduced and people's health is affected, broad safety net programs may automatically scale up if they are designed to respond to changes in household situations. Deryugina (2016) describes the role of nondisaster safety nets in hurricanes in the United States. After a hurricane makes landfall, nondisaster programs such as Medicare and unemployment insurance increase their support to the affected populations. Even without disaster-related triggers, means-tested social protection can be "adaptive" and respond to natural disasters.

In the United States, postdisaster support through nondisaster programs is more than five times larger than the dedicated transfers that follow federal disaster declarations. Nondisaster transfers per capita in affected counties increase by about $1,000 (compared with $150 for dedicated postdisaster support). Most of these transfers are from Medicare (especially disability) and unemployment insurance.

Strong social programs thus increase people's resilience even in the absence of explicit disaster-related triggers. In fact, safety nets that capture all shocks together are likely to be more useful for households than shock-specific risk management tools (World Bank 2013). One important consequence is that most of the fiscal costs of hurricanes for the U.S. government originate in higher nondisaster social expenditures, not in explicit postdisaster aid, which needs to be taken into account in the budgetary planning processes.

But there are obvious limits to what nondisaster programs can achieve in the aftermath of a disaster. First, budgetary constraints or the design of the programs can make it impossible for transfers to increase enough or to increase fast enough. Even in the United States, transfers from nondisaster programs are larger than earning losses for weak hurricanes (categories 1 and 2), but much lower for stronger ones (category 3 and higher)—see Deryugina (2016). In developing countries with liquidity constraints, the ability to scale up is even more limited in the absence of a dedicated financial mechanism, especially when countries have to rely on donor resources to finance a disaster response.

Second, the coverage of social protection programs is limited in developing countries, and these programs are therefore not always able to support the affected population (see figure 2.12, panel a). And transfers to poor people are usually smaller than those to richer people (figure 2.12, panel b). Conditional and unconditional cash transfers specifically target poor households and are increasingly associated with good coverage among households in the bottom quintile. But the two other types of transfers—social insurance and labor market policies—reach poor and nonpoor households in about the same proportion. This does not necessarily mean that those schemes are poorly designed; some programs such as contributory pensions are designed for those who can afford to contribute.

Poor people are often excluded from programs that should benefit them. Some programs are tied to formal employment, whereas most poor people work in the informal economy. Also, poor people in remote rural areas can be difficult to reach. However, the conditional and unconditional cash transfer programs that have revolutionized social protection over the last decade are easier to deploy in rural areas than in urban areas because of the challenge of targeting the poor in cities where they often live next door to the wealthier (Gentilini 2015). As a result, even social assistance shows a wide range of coverage for poor people: in many countries, coverage does not exceed 50 percent, meaning that half of poor people within a country do not receive any social assistance, and even less than 10 percent in many low-income countries. For people with no coverage, labor is the only source of income, and a disaster can easily put a halt to that if a harvest or manufacturing equipment is lost.

Figure 2.12: Coverage of poor people by social protection is often under 50 percent, and they often receive lower transfer amounts

Coverage of poor and nonpoor by social protection and total public transfers received, most recent value

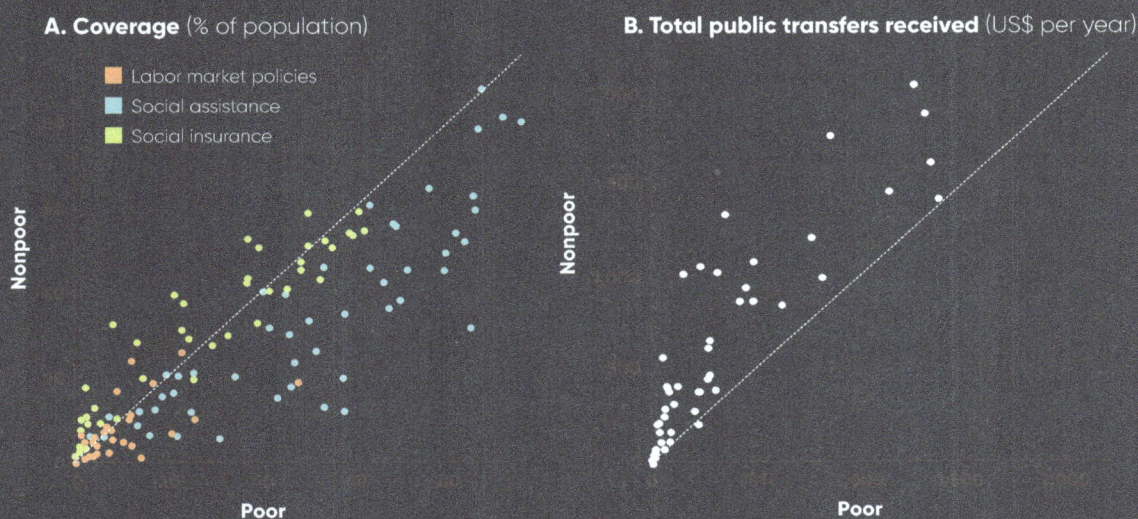

A. Coverage (% of population)

- Labor market policies
- Social assistance
- Social insurance

B. Total public transfers received (US$ per year)

Source: ASPIRE database, World Bank. Note: Each dot represents a country for which data exist.

There is a third limit to what nondisaster programs can achieve in the aftermath of a disaster. Targeting methods used by social assistance programs are often based on data that are costly and hard to collect, making it difficult for these programs to adjust quickly to the changing conditions of households (Bastagli 2014; Gentilini 2015; Kuriakose et al. 2013). After a large shock, most programs are unable to adjust transfers in a few weeks, as would be needed to prevent the negative coping behaviors in the aftermath of a disaster such as reduced food intake. Chapter 6 discusses policy options and solutions to make social protection more responsive to sudden shocks.

Domestic and global remittances increase recipients' resilience, but mostly benefit the better-off

Remittances—that is, the private transfer of money by foreign workers to individuals in their home country—were estimated at $584 billion worldwide in 2014. They are a vital resource for developing countries and significantly exceed official development assistance and foreign direct investment everywhere except China.

International remittance flows are a stable source of finance that is generally not correlated with capital flows and that can help hedge against shocks (Bugamelli and Paterno 2009; World Bank 2015b). After natural, economic, financial, and political shocks, these flows have been found to either remain stable or increase (Clarke and Wallsten 2004; Fagen 2006; Mohapatra, Joseph, and Ratha 2009; World Bank 2015b).

Remittances can help smooth consumption and finance recovery and reconstruction. After the 1998 flood in Bangladesh, consumption was higher in remittance-receiving households (Mohapatra, Joseph, and Ratha 2009). In the Philippines, it was estimated that remittances compensated for nearly 65 percent of lost income after rainfall shocks in 1997 (Yang and Choi 2007). And despite disruptions in transfer channels and financial services, remittances remained relatively stable after disasters hit Pakistan in 2005 and Indonesia in 2004, and they were an important factor in recovery and reconstruction (Suleri and Savage 2006; Wu 2006). In Indonesia, households that received remittances in the Aceh region recovered faster from the 2004 tsunami, despite disruptions in financial services and informal transfer channels (Wu 2006).

However, international and domestic remittances tend to benefit the better-off within a country (figure 2.13). And sometimes they lower government spending through a substitution effect between the private insurance provided by remittances and the public insurance provided through government expenditures (Kapur and Singer 2006).

Figure 2.13: Within a country, remittances tend to be higher for the better-off

Remittance transfers, poor and nonpoor, in US$, PPP-adjusted

Source: ASPIRE database, World Bank.

Note: PPP = purchasing power parity. Each dot represents a country for which adequate data exist.

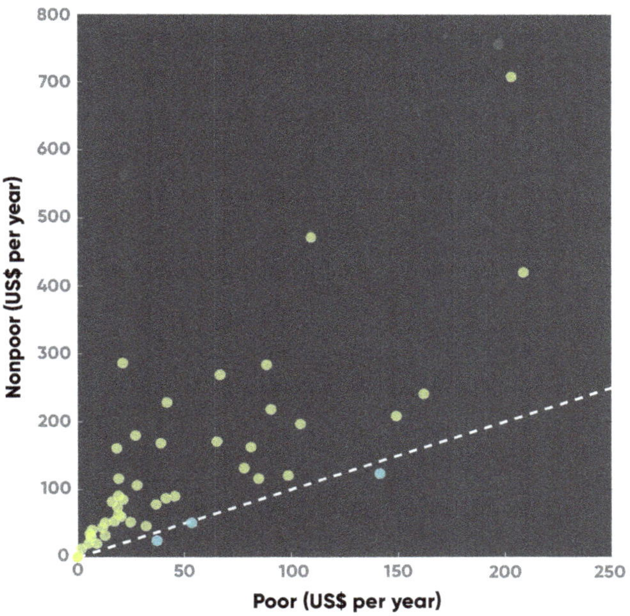

People in conflict-prone areas are more likely to be poor and less likely to receive support

A weakened capacity to respond to a natural hazard, at whatever the level of government, is one reason natural disasters have worse impacts in an area that is already riddled by conflict.[1] Generally, the vulnerability to climate shocks is highest in more fragile and conflict-affected areas (UNISDR 2009). And because many poor people live in such fragile areas, they usually receive less support when they are hit by a hazard. This determinant of the vulnerability of the poor will become increasingly important: by 2030, almost half of the world's poor are expected to live in countries affected by fragility, conflict, and violence.

Countries in the throes of a violent conflict and governance issues are less likely to successfully support local communities in their struggles to cope with the aftermath of natural disasters (IPCC 2012). In Somalia, the government does not have full control of its territory, and so it cannot respond successfully to natural disasters (Ferris 2010). In Chad, the civil war from 2005 to 2010 helped to undermine the governance and capacity of the central government. At the end of the five-year war, the government lacked the logistical capacity to help remote areas during the food crisis of 2010 (Gubbels 2011). And conflicts sometimes displace people to areas that are hazardous. In the Mindanao area in the Philippines, for example, camps of internally displaced people (IDPs) were flooded in 2008, affecting people who were already in a dire situation (Harris, Keen, and Mitchell 2013).

In summary, this chapter has described how poor people are more often affected by hazards, lose more than the nonpoor when they are affected by a shock, and receive less support to recover. A conclusion from this analysis is that vulnerability to natural hazards and disasters can be reduced through development and poverty reduction that makes people better able to settle in safe places, makes their livelihoods and assets less vulnerable, and provides them with tools and support to cope with shocks. Policies that contribute to reducing poverty can therefore be considered a tool in the disaster risk management toolbox. But the connection between poverty and disaster risk goes both ways: for poor people, disaster losses add up, making it more difficult for them to escape poverty, as discussed in the next chapter.

NOTES

1.   This section was contributed by Martin Heger.

REFERENCES

Akter, S., and B. Mallick. 2013. "The Poverty–Vulnerability–Resilience Nexus: Evidence from Bangladesh." *Ecological Economics* 96: 114–24. doi:10.1016/j.ecolecon.2013.10.008.

Al Jazeera. 2015. "Poor Bear Brunt as India Heatwave Death Toll Tops 1,000." May 27.

Baker, J., R. Basu, M. Cropper, S. V. Lall, and A. Takeuch. 2005. "Urban Poverty and Transport: The Case of Mumbai." Policy Research Working Paper 3693, World Bank, Washington, DC.

Bandyopadhyay, S., and E. Skoufias. 2012. "Rainfall Variability, Occupational Choice, and Welfare in Rural Bangladesh." Policy Research Working Paper 6134. World Bank, Washington, DC.

Bangalore, M., A. Smith, and T. Veldkamp. 2016. "Exposure to Floods, Climate Change, and Poverty in Vietnam." Policy Research Working Paper 7765, World Bank, Washington, DC.

Barbier, E. B. 2010. "Poverty, Development, and Environment." *Environment and Development Economics* 15: 635–60. doi:10.1017/S1355770X1000032X.

Barrett C. B., T. Reardon, and P. Webb. 2001. "Nonfarm Income Diversification and Household Livelihood Strategies in Rural Africa: Concepts, Dynamics, and Policy Implications." *Food Policy* 26: 315–31.

Bastagli, F. 2014. "Responding to a Crisis: The Design and Delivery of Social Protection." Overseas Development Institute, London.

Blanc, E., and E. Strobl. 2016. "Assessing the Impact of Typhoons on Rice Production in the Philippines." *Journal of Applied Meteorology and Climatology* 55: 993–1007. doi:10.1175/JAMC-D-15-0214.1.

Bouchama, A., M. Dehbi, G. Mohamed, F. Matthies, M. Shoukri, and B. Meanne. 2007. "Prognostic Factors in Heat Wave–Related Deaths: A Meta-analysis." *Archives of Internal Medicine* 167: 2170–76. doi:10.1001/archinte.167.20.ira70009.

Brouwer, R., S. Akter, L. Brander, and E. Haque. 2007. "Socioeconomic Vulnerability and Adaptation to Environmental Risk: A Case Study of Climate Change and Flooding in Bangladesh." *Risk Analysis* 27: 313–26. doi:10.1111/j.1539-6924.2007.00884.x.

Bugamelli, M., and F. Paterno. 2009. "Do Workers' Remittances Reduce the Probability of Current Account Reversals?" *World Development* 37: 1821–38.

Carter, M. R., P. D. Little, T. Mogues, and W. Negatu. 2007. "Poverty Traps and Natural Disasters in Ethiopia and Honduras. *World Development* 35: 835–56. doi:10.1016/j.worlddev.2006.09.010.

Cheema, I., S. Hunt, M. Jakobsen, M. Marzi, S. O'Leary, and L. Pellerano. 2015. "Citizen's Damage Compensation Programme: Impact Evaluation Report." Oxford Policy Management, Oxford, U.K.

Clarke, G., and S. Wallsten. 2004. *Do Remittances Protect Households in Developing Countries against Shocks? Evidence from a Natural Disaster in Jamaica.* Washington, DC: World Bank.

Daniel, V. E., R. J. G. M. Florax, and P. Rietveld. 2009. "Flooding Risk and Housing Values: An Economic Assessment of Environmental Hazard." *Ecological Economics* 69 (2): 355–65.

del Ninno, C., P. A. Dorosh, L. C. Smith, and D. K. Roy. 2001. "The 1998 Floods in Bangladesh: Disaster Impacts, Household Coping Strategies, and Response." Research Report No. 122, International Food Policy Research Institute, Washington, DC.

Deryugina, T. 2016. "The Fiscal Cost of Hurricanes: Disaster Aid Versus Social Insurance." National Bureau of Economic Research, Cambridge, MA.

Durand-Lasserve, A., H. Selod, and M. Durand-Lasserve. 2013. "A Systemic Analysis of Land Markets and Land Institutions in West African Cities: Rules and Practices—The Case of Bamako, Mali." Policy Research Working Paper 6687, World Bank, Washington, DC.

Elbers, C., J. O. Lanjouw, and P. Lanjouw. 2003. "Micro-level Estimation of Poverty and Inequality." *Econometrica* 71: 355–64. doi:10.1111/1468-0262.00399.

Ellis, F. 2004. "Occupational Diversification in Developing Countries and the Implications for Agricultural Policy." Programme of Advisory and Support Services to DFID (PASS), UK Department for International Development, London.

Fagen, P. W. 2006. "Remittances in Conflict and Crises: How Remittances Sustain Livelihoods in War, Crises and Transitions to Peace." Policy Paper, International Peace Academy, New York, February.

Fay, M. 2005. "The Urban Poor in Latin America." Directions in Development–General, World Bank, Washington, DC.

Ferris, E. 2010. "Natural Disasters, Conflict, and Human Rights: Tracing the Connections." Brookings Institution–University of Bern Project on Internal Displacement, March 3.

Francisco, H. A., C. D. Predo, A. Manasboonphempool, P. Tran, R. Jarungrattanapong, L. M. Penalba, N. Tuyen et al. 2011. "Determinants of Household Decisions on Adaptation to Extreme Climate Events in Southeast Asia." Economy and Environment Program for Southeast Asia (EEPSEA).

Fuchs, A. 2014. "Shocks and Poverty in Haiti." Presentation at the Poverty and Climate Change in the Latin America and Caribbean Region Workshop, September 14.

Gentilini, U. 2015. "Safety Nets in Urban Areas: Emerging Issues, Evidence and Practices." In *The State of Social Safety Nets,* 62–72. Washington, DC: World Bank.

Gentle, P., R. Thwaites, D. Race, and K. Alexander. 2014. "Differential Impacts of Climate Change on Communities in the Middle Hills Region of Nepal." *Natural Hazards* 74: 815–36. doi:10.1007/s11069-014-1218-0.

GFDRR (Global Facility for Disaster Reduction and Recovery). 2016. "The Making of a Riskier Future: How Our Decisions Are Shaping Future Disaster Risk." World Bank, Washington, DC.

Gubbels, P. 2011. "Escaping the Hunger Cycle: Pathways to Resilience in the Sahel." *Oxfam Policy Practice: Agriculture, Food, and Land* 11: 165–288.

Hallegatte, S. 2012a. "A Cost Effective Solution to Reduce Disaster Losses in Developing Countries: Hydro-Meteorological Services, Early Warning, and Evacuation." Policy Research Working Paper 6058, World Bank, Washington, DC.

_____. 2012b. "An Exploration of the Link between Development, Economic Growth, and Natural Risk." Policy Research Working Paper 6216, World Bank, Washington, DC.

_____. 2014. *Natural Disasters and Climate Change.* Basel: Springer International Publishing.

Hallegatte, S., M. Bangalore, L. Bonzanigo, M. Fay, T. Kane, U. Narloch, J. Rozenberg et al. 2016. *Shock Waves: Managing the Impacts of Climate Change on Poverty.* Climate Change and Development Series. Washington, DC: World Bank.

Hallegatte, S., M. Bangalore, and F. S. Nkoka. 2015. "Recent Floods in Malawi Hit the Poorest Areas: What This Implies." *Voices—Perspectives on Development.* http://blogs.worldbank.org/voices/recent-floods-malawi-hit-poorest-areas-what-implies.

Hallegatte, S., M. Bangalore, and A. Vogt-Schilb. Forthcoming. "Socioeconomic Resilience to Multiple Hazards—An Assessment in 117 Countries." Background paper prepared for this report, World Bank, Washington, DC.

Hallegatte, S., F. Henriet, A. Patwardhan, K. Narayanan, S. Ghosh, S. Karmakar, U. Patnaik et al. 2010. *Flood Risks, Climate Change Impacts and Adaptation Benefits in Mumbai: An Initial Assessment of Socio-economic Consequences of Present and Climate Change Induced Flood Risks and of Possible Adaptation Options.* Paris: OECD Publishing.

Hallegatte, S., and A. Vogt-Schilb. Forthcoming. "Are Losses from Natural Disasters More Than Just Asset Losses? The Role of Capital Aggregation, Sector Interactions, and Investment Behaviors." Background paper prepared for this report, World Bank, Washington, DC.

Harris, K., D. Keen, and T. Mitchell. 2013. "When Disasters and Conflicts Collide: Improving Links between Disaster Resilience and Conflict Prevention." Overseas Development Institute (ODI), London.

Husby, T., H. L. de Groot, M. W. Hofkes, and T. Filatova. 2015. "Flood Protection and Endogenous Sorting of Households: The Role of Credit Constraints." *Mitigation and Adaption Strategies for Global Change.* doi:10.1007/s11027-015-9667-7

IPCC (Intergovernmental Panel on Climate Change). 2012. "Special Report on Managing the Risks of Extreme Events and Disasters to Advance Climate Change Adaptation: Summary for Policymakers: A Report of Working Groups I and II of the IPCC." Geneva.

Jaiswal, K., D. Wald, and K. Porter. 2010. "A Global Building Inventory for Earthquake Loss Estimation and Risk Management." *Earthquake Spectra* 26 (3): 731–48.

Jongman, B., S. Hochrainer-Stigler, L. Feyen, J. C. J. H. Aerts, R. Mechler, W. J. W. Botzen, L. M. Bouwer et al. 2014. "Increasing Stress on Disaster-Risk Finance due to Large Floods." *Nature Climate Change* 4: 264–68. doi:10.1038/nclimate2124.

Kapur, D., and D. A. Singer. 2006. "Remittances, Government Spending and the Global Economy." Paper presented at annual meeting of American Economic Association, San Diego, CA.

Kuriakose, A. T., R. Heltberg, W. Wiseman, C. Costella, R. Cipryk, and S. Cornelius. 2013. "Climate-Responsive Social Protection." *Development Policy Review* 31: o19–o34. doi:10.1111/dpr.12037.

Lall, S. V., and U. Deichmann. 2012. "Density and Disasters: Economics of Urban Hazard Risk." *World Bank Research Observer* 27: 74–105.

Lall, S. V., M. K. A. Lundberg, and Z. Shalizi. 2008. "Implications of Alternate Policies on Welfare of Slum Dwellers: Evidence from Pune, India." *Journal of Urban Economics* 63: 56–73. doi:10.1016/j.jue.2006.12.001.

Lawrance, E. C. 1991. "Poverty and the Rate of Time Preference: Evidence from Panel Data." *Journal of Political Economy* 54–77.

Lloyd's Risk Insight. 2013. *Insurance in Developing Countries: Exploring Opportunities for Microinsurance.* London: Lloyd's.

Loayza, N. V., E. Olaberria, J. Rigolini, and L. Christiaensen. 2012. "Natural Disasters and Growth: Going Beyond the Averages." *World Development.*

Mbaiwa, J. E., and L. K. Sakuze. 2009. "Cultural Tourism and Livelihood Diversification: The Case of Gcwihaba Caves and XaiXai Village in the Okavango Delta, Botswana." *Journal of Tourism and Cultural Change* 7 (1): 61–75.

Mesfin, W., B. Fufa, and J. Haji. 2011. "Pattern, Trend and Determinants of Crop Diversification: Empirical Evidence from Smallholders in Eastern Ethiopia." *Journal of Economics and Sustainable Development* 2 (8): 78-89.

Mohapatra, S., G. Joseph, and D. Ratha. 2009. "Remittances and Natural Disasters: Ex-Post Response and Contribution to Ex-Ante Preparedness." Policy Research Working Paper 4972, World Bank, Washington, DC.

Moser, C., and A. Felton. 2007. "Intergenerational Asset Accumulation and Poverty Reduction in Guayaquil, Ecuador, 1978–2004." In *Reducing Global Poverty: The Case for Asset Accumulation,* ed. C. Moser, 15–50. Washington, DC: Brookings.

Narloch, U. G., and M. Bangalore. 2016. "Environmental Risks and Poverty: Analyzing Geo-spatial and Household Data from Vietnam." Policy Research Working Paper 7763, World Bank, Washington, DC.

Nguyen, van K. 2011. "Building Livelihood Resilience in Changing Climate." Paper presented at Asia Regional Conference, Kuala Lumpur, Malaysia.

Nkedianye, D., J. de Leeuw, J. O. Ogutu, M. Y. Said, T. L. Saidimu, S. C. Kifugo, D. S. Kaelo, and R. S. Reid. 2011. "Mobility and Livestock Mortality in Communally Used Pastoral Areas: The Impact of the 2005–2006 Drought on Livestock Mortality in Maasailand." *Pastoralism* 1: 1–17. doi:10.1186/2041-7136-1-17.

Noack, F., S. Wunder, A. Angelsen, and J. Boerner. 2015. "Responses to Weather and Climate: A Cross-Section Analysis of Rural Incomes." Policy Research Working Paper 7478, World Bank, Washington, DC.

Noy, I., and P. Patel. 2014. "Floods and Spillovers: Households after the 2011 Great Flood in Thailand." Working Paper Series No. 3609, School of Economics and Finance, Victoria University of Wellington.

Opondo, D. O. 2013. "Erosive Coping after the 2011 Floods in Kenya." *International Journal of Global Warming* 5: 452–66. doi:10.1504/IJGW.2013.057285.

Park, J., S. Hallegatte, M. Bangalore, and E. Sandhoefner. 2015. "The Deck Is Stacked (and Hot)? Climate Change, Labor Productivity, and Developing Countries." Policy Research Working Paper 7479, World Bank, Washington, DC.

Patankar, A. 2015. "The Exposure, Vulnerability and Adaptive Capacity of Households to Floods in Mumbai." Policy Research Working Paper 7481, World Bank, Washington, DC.

Patankar, A., and A. Patwardhan. 2016. "Estimating the Uninsured Losses due to Extreme Weather Events and Implications for Informal Sector Vulnerability: A Case Study of Mumbai, India." *Natural* Hazards 80: 285. doi:10.1007/s11069-015-1968-3.

Pelling, M. 1997. "What Determines Vulnerability to Floods: A Case Study in Georgetown, Guyana." *International Journal of Environmental Problems* 9: 203–26.

Peter, G. von, S. von Dahlen, and S. C. Saxena. 2012. "Unmitigated Disasters? New Evidence on the Macroeconomic Cost of Natural Catastrophes." BIS Working Paper No. 394, Bank for International Settlements, Basel, Switzerland.

Pielke, R., J. Gratz, C. Landsea, D. Collins, M. Saunders, and R. Musulin. 2008. "Normalized Hurricane Damage in the United States: 1900–2005." *Natural Hazards Review* 9: 29–42. doi:10.1061/(ASCE)1527-6988(2008)9:1(29).

Porio, E. 2011. "Vulnerability, Adaptation, and Resilience to Floods and Climate Change-Related Risks among Marginal, Riverine Communities in Metro Manila." *Asian Journal of Social Science* 39 (4): 425–45.

Prudhomme, C., I. Giuntoli, E. L. Robinson, D. B. Clark, N. W. Arnell, R. Dankers, B. M. Fekete et al. 2014. "Hydrological Droughts in the 21st Century, Hotspots and Uncertainties from a Global Multimodel Ensemble Experiment." *Proceedings of the National Academy of Sciences* 111: 3262–67. doi:10.1073/pnas.1222473110.

Rabbani, G., S. H. Rahman, and L. Faulkner. 2013. "Impacts of Climatic Hazards on the Small Wetland Ecosystems (Ponds): Evidence from Some Selected Areas of Coastal Bangladesh." *Sustainability* 5: 1510–21. doi:10.3390/su5041510.

Ranger, N., S. Hallegatte, S. Bhattacharya, M. Bachu, S. Priya, K. Dhore, F. Rafique et al. 2011. "An Assessment of the Potential Impact of Climate Change on Flood Risk in Mumbai." *Climate Change* 104: 139–67.

Restrepo Cadavid, P. 2011. "The Impacts of Slum Policies on Households' Welfare: The Case of Medellin (Colombia) and Mumbai (India)." Ecole Nationale Superieure des Mines de Paris.

Rogers, D. P., and V. V. Tsirkunov. 2013. *Weather and Climate Resilience: Effective Preparedness through National Meteorological and Hydrological Services.* Washington, DC: World Bank.

Safir, A., S. F. A. Piza, and E. Skoufias. 2013. "Disquiet on the Weather Front: The Welfare Impacts of Climatic Variability in the Rural Philippines." Policy Research Working Paper 6579, World Bank, Washington, DC.

Schewe, J., J. Heinke, D. Gerten, I. Haddeland, N. W. Arnell, D. B. Clark, R. Dankers et al. 2014. "Multimodel Assessment of Water Scarcity under Climate Change." *Proceedings of the National Academy of Sciences* 111: 3245–50. doi:10.1073/pnas.1222460110.

Scussolini, P., J. Aerts, B. Jongman, L. Bouwer, H. C. Winsemius, H. de Moel, and P. J. Ward. 2016. "FLOPROS: An Evolving Global Database of Flood Protection Standards." *Natural Hazards and Earth System Science* 16 (5): 1049–61. doi:10.5194/nhess-16-1049-2016.

Semenza, J. C., C. H. Rubin, K. H. Falter, J. D. Selanikio, W. D. Flanders, H. L. Howe, and J. L. Wilhelm. 1996. "Heat-Related Deaths during the July 1995 Heat Wave in Chicago." *New England Journal of Medicine* 335: 84–90. doi:10.1056/NEJM199607113350203.

Suleri, A. Q., and K. Savage. 2006. "Remittances in Crises: A Case Study from Pakistan." Sustainable Development Policy Institute, Islamabad, Pakistan.

Tesliuc, E., and K. Lindert. 2003. "Vulnerability: A Quantitative and Qualitative Assessment." Working Paper 36209, World Bank, Washington, DC.

The Economist. 2015. "Why India's Heatwaves Are So Deadly." May 27.

UNISDR (United Nations Office for Disaster Risk Reduction). 2009. *United Nations Global Assessment Report on Disaster Risk Reduction.* Geneva: UNISDR.

———. 2011. *United Nations Global Assessment Report on Disaster Risk Reduction.* Geneva: UNISDR.

Vice News. 2015. "Poor People Are Most Affected as Hundreds Die in Blistering Indian Heatwave." May 25.

Ward, P. J., B. Jongman, F. S. Weiland, A. Bouwman, R. van Beek, M. F. P. Bierkens, W. Ligtvoet et al. 2013. "Assessing Flood Risk at the Global Scale: Model Setup, Results, and Sensitivity." *Environmental Research Letter* 8: 44019. doi:10.1088/1748-9326/8/4/044019.

Whitman, S., G. Good, E. R. Donoghue, N. Benbow, W. Shou, and W. Mou. 1997. "Mortality in Chicago Attributed to the July 1995 Heat Wave." *American Journal of Public Health* 87: 1515–18.

Winsemius, H., B. Jongman, T. Veldkamp, S. Hallegatte, M. Bangalore, and P. J. Ward. 2015. "Disaster Risk, Climate Change, and Poverty: Assessing the Global Exposure of Poor People to Floods and Droughts." Policy Research Working Paper 7480, World Bank, Washington, DC.

Winsemius, H. C., L. P. H. Van Beek, B. Jongman, P. J. Ward, and A. Bouwman. 2013. "A Framework for Global River Flood Risk Assessments." *Hydrology and Earth System Sciences* 17: 1871–92. doi:10.5194/hess-17-1871-2013.

Wodon, Q., A. Liverani, G. Joseph, and N. Bougnoux. 2014. *Climate Change and Migration: Evidence from the Middle East and North Africa*. Washington, DC: World Bank.

World Bank. 2007. "Bangladesh—Dhaka: Improving Living Conditions for the Urban Poor (No. 35824)." World Bank, Washington, DC.

_____. 2013. *World Development Report 2014: Risk and Opportunity—Managing Risk for Development.* Washington, DC: World Bank.

_____. 2015a. "Another Nargis Strikes Everyday: Post-Nargis Social Impacts Monitoring Five Years On." Washington, DC.

_____. 2015b. *Can Remittances Help Promote Consumption Stability? (Global Economic Prospects).* Washington, DC: World Bank.

World Bank and Australian AID, 2014. "'Where Are We During Flooding?' A Qualitative Assessment of Poverty and Social Impacts of Flooding in Selected Neighborhoods of HCMC." Washington, DC.

Wu, T. 2006. "The Role of Remittances in Crisis: An Aceh Research Study." Overseas Development Institute, London.

Yang, D., and H. Choi. 2007. "Are Remittances Insurance? Evidence from Rainfall Shocks in the Philippines." *World Bank Economic Review* 21: 219–48.

VICIOUS CIRCLES

Natural disasters keep people in poverty.

Poverty reduction is not a one-way street out of poverty, and natural disasters are one of the reasons why. Between 2006 and 2011 in Senegal, 45 percent of poor households escaped poverty, whereas 40 percent of nonpoor households fell into poverty (Dang et al. 2014). Similar mobility in and out of poverty is found in other countries as well (Baulch 2011; Beegle, De Weerdt, and Dercon 2006; Krishna 2006; Lanjouw, McKenzie, and Luoto 2011). Surveys reveal that natural disasters are partly responsible for the flow of households into poverty.

In Senegal, a household affected by a natural disaster was 25 percent more likely to have fallen in poverty over the 2006-2011 period (Dang et al. 2014). In India, among the 12 percent of households in 36 Andhra Pradesh communities that fell into poverty over a 25 year period, 44 percent cited "drought, irrigation failure, or crop disease" as one of the reasons for their income losses (Krishna 2006). In Bangladesh, Sen (2003) found that 15 percent of the 379 rural households surveyed cited natural disasters and 18 percent cited loss of natural assets as the main reasons for falling into poverty.

The previous chapter showed how poverty is a factor increasing vulnerability to disasters. Here, we explore how disasters are a driver of poverty. The main finding of this chapter is that natural disasters have observable impacts on poverty through multiple channels, including their direct effects on income and wealth, education, and health, but also their indirect effects through people's savings and investment behaviors. Looking at a subset of these channels, we provide a conservative estimate of the number of people who are in extreme poverty today because of natural disasters, showing that the poverty implications of natural disasters are high enough to consider disaster risk management an essential component of poverty reduction policies.

Disasters have visible impacts on poverty

Poverty increases in the direct aftermath of a disaster. In Bolivia, the incidence of poverty climbed by 12 percent in Trinidad City after the 2006 floods, a fivefold increase compared with the national average (Perez-De-Rada and Paz 2008). Examining the ex post impacts of Hurricane Mitch, which struck Nicaragua in 1998, Jakobsen (2012) found that poorer households faced a larger *absolute* decline in productive assets immediately after Mitch. Furthermore, among those households affected by Mitch, the share of asset-poor households (those who own less than a given asset-poverty line) increased from 75 percent in 1998 to 80 percent in 2001. Among households hit by Tropical Storm Agatha in 2010 in Guatemala, consumption per capita fell 5.5 percent, increasing poverty by 14 percent (Baez et al. 2016). Whereas previous studies typically focused on the impacts of Agatha in rural areas, Baez et al. (2016) document the sharp impacts of Agatha in urban areas of Guatemala, where poverty increased by 18 percent, mainly because of higher food prices. Meanwhile, Ishizawa and Miranda (2016) find that an increase of one standard deviation in the intensity of a hurricane in Central America increases moderate and extreme poverty levels by 1.5 percentage points. Finally, a recent meta-analysis of 38 such studies found that incomes are consistently reduced by natural disasters (Karim and Noy 2014).

Households affected by the El Niño floods of 1997–98 in Ecuador suffered a decline in total income, total consumption, and food consumption (Rosales-Rueda 2014). On average, total income fell by 8 percent in 1998 and 11 percent in 1999, total consumption by 6 percent in 1998 and 10 percent in 1999, and food expenditures by 10 percent in 1999. In Colombia after the 2011–12 La Niña, the total consumption expenditure fell by 850 pesos ($0.40) for each day of exposure to La Niña, and households cut their expenditures on health and education by 350 pesos for each day of exposure (Brando and Santos 2015). In the Philippines, the El Niño season that began in September 1997 increased the poverty headcount by 4–5 percent (Datt and Hoogeveen 2003). The 2015 El Niño season was considered by many to be one of the worst on record, with impacts on poverty across many continents (box 3.1).

>>>

BOX 3.1

THE 2015 EL NIÑO SEASON BROUGHT HARDSHIP TO POOR PEOPLE

El Niño weather patterns, which entail a warming of the Pacific Ocean waters, cause drought conditions in some regions while exacerbating flooding in others.

In early 2016, drought and excessive rainfall threatened the food security of more than 60 million people in southern Africa, East Africa, Central America, and the Pacific Islands (UNOCHA 2016). The majority of food-insecure people reside in southern Africa, and so the number of people affected in the region, 32 million, could double by the end of 2016 (World Food Programme 2016).

In Lesotho, more than 500,000 people, or about 25 percent of the population, were found to be at risk of food insecurity in early 2016, in part due to drought, with poor households experiencing a 44 percent decline in their food consumption and cash income (MDAT 2016). In Madagascar, almost 2 million people are food-insecure, and poor households are engaging in detrimental coping strategies such as selling animals (World Food Programme 2016). Poor households have also turned to desperate strategies to smooth their food consumption, with reports of increased consumption of cactus leaves and unripe fruits (FEWS NET 2015).

The impact of El Niño on health has also been severe. The Democratic Republic of Congo has experienced a mix of drought and floods with severe impacts on health. Floods have affected over 700,000 people and inundated over 5,500 hectares of cropland. Outbreaks of waterborne diseases have been reported, with a 16 percent increase in cholera cases in the first quarter of 2016 compared with the same period in 2015 (UNOCHA 2016).

Beyond the immediate impact after a disaster, evidence suggests that natural disasters increase poverty over the medium and long term. Glave, Fort, and Rosemberg (2008) studied exposure to disasters and poverty from 2003 to 2008 at the provincial level in Peru. They found that one extra disaster per year increased poverty rates by 16–23 percent. At the municipal level in Mexico, Rodriguez-Oreggia and his colleagues (2013) found that floods and droughts increased poverty levels between 1.5 and 3.7 percent between 2000 and 2005. And in Ecuador, Calero, Maldonado, and Molina (2008) found that from 1970 to 2007 exposure to drought increased the incidence of poverty by 2 percent on average.

The impact of natural disasters on poverty is not homogeneous; it depends on local capacity. In Burkina Faso, Reardon and Taylor (1996) found that drought conditions in the 1980s increased poverty levels by 17 percent in the Sahelian zone (poorest climate, least household diversification) and by 3 percent in the Sudanian zone, but not in the

Guinean zone (best climate, most household diversification). In Madagascar, cyclone risk increases poverty in rural areas (Andrianarimanana 2015): the average cyclone decreases total consumption by 12 percent and increases the probability of being poor by 7.4 percent. But no such impact has been found in urban areas.

In Asia, Akter and Mallick (2013) surveyed households in coastal communities affected by Cyclone Aila in 2010 in the southwest of Bangladesh. Unemployment skyrocketed, from 11 percent in 2009 to 60 percent in 2010, and the poverty headcount rate increased from 41 percent before the storm to 63 percent afterward. In a recent analysis of the 2011 floods in Bangkok, Thailand, Noy and Patel (2014) report a large decrease in the agricultural and total income of poor households, compared with those with greater wealth. And even households that were not directly affected by the floods experienced a significant decrease in income—a spillover effect of the flood. In their study in the Philippines, Safir, Piza, and Skoufias (2013) found that low precipitation (below one standard deviation) decreases consumption by 4 percent, and all of the decrease occurs in food consumption, suggesting potential health impacts through undernutrition.

This large and growing body of empirical evidence suggests that household well-being and poverty status are largely susceptible to natural disasters, at least in the short term. But what are the drivers of these impacts?

Disasters increase poverty by reducing economic growth

Aggregate economic growth is the main driver of poverty reduction over time (Dollar, Kleineberg, and Kraay 2013; Dollar and Kraay 2002), and so any impact of disasters on economic growth has direct implications for poverty. Evidence suggests that disasters slow down economic growth, at least over the short term.

Disasters reduce growth over the short term, but the long-term impacts remain unclear. Researchers agree that disasters, especially high-intensity ones, have negative short-term impacts on economic growth (Cavallo and Noy 2009). For example, according to Rasmussen (2004), a natural disaster leads to a median reduction of about 2 percentage points in the growth rate of the gross domestic product (GDP) the year it occurs. In a recent analysis of Central America, Ishizawa and Miranda (2016) find that an increase of one standard deviation in the intensity of a hurricane leads to a decrease in total per capita GDP growth of between 0.9 and 1.6 percent and a decrease in total income by 3 percent. And Felbermayr and Gröschl (2014) find that disasters in the top decile of magnitude result on average in a 3 percent reduction in GDP growth. The loss is only 1.5 percent for disasters in the top 15 percent of magnitude and 0.8 percent for disasters in the top 20 percent. For smaller disasters, they detect no impact. Impacts are also visible at the subnational level. Strobl (2010) has investigated the impact of hurricane landfall on county-level economic growth in the United States. Growth in a county struck by at least one hurricane over a year is reduced on average by 0.79 percentage points.

There is little doubt, then, that such short reductions in economic activity, GDP, or economic growth have a direct impact on short-term poverty and poverty reduction. By contrast, the long-term impacts of natural disasters on growth remain less clear. Although early studies, notably by Albala-Bertrand (1993) and Skidmore and Toya (2002), suggested natural disasters have a positive influence on long-term economic growth, a few recent studies find negative impacts on long-term economic growth.

Using a data set of natural disasters from 1960 to 2011, Peter, Dahlen, and Saxena (2012) find that a typical natural disaster causes a drop in long-term economic growth of 0.6–1.0 percent and results in a permanent output loss of two to three times this magnitude, with higher estimates for larger natural disasters. Examining global exposure to cyclones from 1950 to 2008, Hsiang and Jina (2014) find that significant income losses spread across 15 years following a disaster. The authors suggest that a 90th percentile event reduces per capita income by more than 7 percent after two decades, "effectively undoing 3.7 years of average development."

And what was the impact in 1992 of Hurricane Iniki, the strongest storm to hit Hawaii in decades? Coffman and Noy (2012) compare the impacts on the island of Kauai to those on unaffected Hawaiian islands. Eighteen years after the event, Kauai's economy had yet to recover. The island's population in 2010 was 12 percent smaller than it would have been without the hurricane, and its aggregate per capita income and employment were proportionally lower.

Although these three studies find long-term impacts, most existing studies find a return to normal economic conditions after a few years. In a recent meta-analysis using more than 750 estimates, Klomp and Valckx (2014) confirm that natural disasters appear to have a negative effect on growth, particularly in developing countries. However, the impact is in the short term; long-term GDP per capita returns to its original growth path.

To examine the impacts on economic activity of the large-scale floods that occurred in 1,800 cities from 2003 to 2008, Kocornik-Mina et al. (2015) use flood maps and night light data. The authors find that when cities are hit by large floods, economic activity recovers rapidly and is fully restored within a year of the flood. Bertinelli and Strobl (2013) also use night light data as a proxy for economic activity and examine how hurricanes in the Caribbean have affected local economic growth. On average, hurricane strikes reduce income growth by about 1.5 percent at the local level, but much like Kocornik-Mina et al. (2015), they find no effect beyond the year of the strike. Applying the same method to China, Elliott, Strobl, and Sun (2015) find that typhoons have a significant negative impact on local activity (with expected annual losses of $0.54 billion), but the impact is again only short term. These results should be considered with caution because, although night light data provide a good proxy for average economic activity, it is unclear whether they can also capture a reconstruction process in which light may come back before economic activity returns to its predisaster level. Meanwhile, worker panel data also suggest that the impact of Hurricane Katrina on incomes disappeared after a few years, with some workers even benefiting from increased labor scarcity in the affected areas (Deryugina, Kawano, and Levitt 2014; Groen, Kutzbach, and Polivka 2016).

Using the same counterfactual methodology as Coffman and Noy (2012) and comparing across countries and decades, Cavallo et al. (2013) find that natural disasters do not have any significant effect on subsequent long-term economic growth. The largest disasters (such as those in the 99th percentile) have some long-term impacts on growth, but this effect disappears entirely when controlled for political change: the long-term impact occurs only when the disaster is followed by political instability. This result suggests that the secondary impacts of natural disasters through political instability and conflicts could play a major role in determining their long-term effects.

Disasters may affect development by exacerbating or alleviating conflict.

The 2004 Indian Ocean tsunami, one of the deadliest natural disasters ever recorded, provides insights into the impacts of a disaster on conflict.[1] The tsunami struck 14 countries. The two worst affected, Indonesia and Sri Lanka, were both in a state of civil war, but had very different responses to the tsunami. In Aceh, a territory in Indonesia, the natural disaster brought peace to a region that had been in the throes of a civil war for nearly 30 years. The tsunami crucially contributed to the cessation of violence between the Indonesian army and the Acehnese rebels and to the signing of a peace treaty. In Sri Lanka, the tsunami may have had the opposite effect. The floods appear to have stoked the flames of war and rekindled violence and armed conflict.

Overall, the Indian Ocean tsunami brought peace to Indonesia (Aspinall 2005; Heger, forthcoming). A few scholars have argued that the peace process was already well under way and likely would have occurred even if there had been no tsunami (Waizenegger 2007). But most studies suggest that the tsunami was the essential catalyst in bringing about lasting peace—see, for example, Aspinall (2005).

When the tsunami floods engulfed much of the Acehnese coastline, they brought a halt to the violence between the Free Aceh Movement rebels and the Indonesian army. The floods made way for a massive humanitarian response and unprecedented cooperation between the central government and the rebels as they sought a unified response to the disaster. Jakarta first responded by lifting military emergency law, which paved the way for reconstruction.

Figure 3.1: Casualties from the separatist conflict in Aceh, Indonesia, fell dramatically after the 2004 tsunami

Number of deaths from separatist conflict and unrelated violence: Aceh, Indonesia, 1999–2012

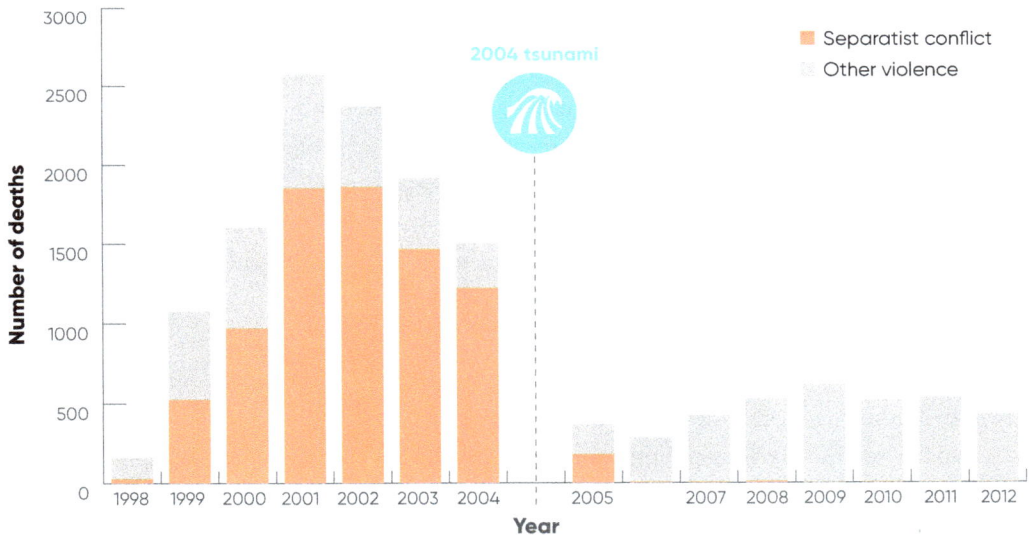

Source: Heger, forthcoming.

Note: "Separatist conflict" refers to deaths caused by the armed conflict, and "other violence" refers to deaths unrelated to the civil war.

Before the tsunami struck Aceh in late 2004, many deaths were due to the separatist conflict, but, as shown in figure 3.1, those casualties fell dramatically when the tsunami struck Aceh's shores on December 26, 2004. On August 15, 2005, a peace accord was signed in Helsinki. Under the agreement, the Free Aceh Movement disarmed, and, in turn, most government troops withdrew from Acehnese territory. Moreover, Aceh was granted special autonomous status within the Republic of Indonesia. It is widely believed that the tsunami was the principal reason for the cessation of violent conflict in Aceh.

By contrast, the Indian Ocean tsunami seems to have brought more violence and armed conflict to Sri Lanka. The tsunami's role in the ongoing conflict in Sri Lanka is less clear than the one in Aceh. Nonetheless, the evidence points to dynamics that were a total opposite of those in Aceh—that is, the tsunami actually contributed to a renewal of the fighting (Kuhn 2009). The aid funds allowed the rebels to strengthen the fight for their freedom because the funds contributed to their financial independence and military expansion (Keen 2009; Mampilly 2009).

What about the impacts of natural disasters on conflict-free areas? They may bring political upheaval and turmoil or increase the risk of violent civil conflict in both the short and medium term, as revealed by Nel and Righarts (2008), who studied the postdisaster situation in 187 countries. This effect is particularly pronounced in countries with a lower GDP, more inequality, and less democracy (Nel and Righarts 2008; Olson and Drury 1997).

In 2013 the Overseas Development Institute (ODI) issued a special report summarizing the literature on the natural disaster and conflict nexus (Harris, Keen, and Mitchell 2013). Weighing cases on both sides of the spectrum—disasters contributing to conflict versus disasters alleviating conflict—the report concluded that more often disasters exacerbate existing conflicts because they add to existing grievances, reduce opportunities in the immediate aftermath, and lead to a power vacuum, which may be filled by criminal groups.

The outcome depends on how the authorities react. A natural disaster may give way to grievances that could translate into conflict if they are not addressed properly. It may even threaten the political order if the establishment is unable to respond to the challenges it has created—for example, if the government fails to provide food and shelter as a response to crops lost, supply chains disrupted, and houses destroyed. Guatemala (1976), Nicaragua (1976), and Iran (1979) are all examples of countries in which natural disasters (earthquakes) contributed to the fall of governments because the governments responded inadequately (Bhavani 2006; Cavallo et al. 2013). Another example is the 1970 typhoon in East Pakistan. The failed response of the central government in West Pakistan contributed to the civil war and the struggle for independence, which eventually led to the creation of Bangladesh. In these cases, popular discontent with the disaster response was the reason the government was overthrown (Bhavani 2006).

Disasters also affect poverty directly, even in the absence of visible impacts on GDP

Although aggregate growth is the main driver of poverty reduction over time, the impact of natural disasters on poverty is not necessarily due to their effect on economic growth. Disasters may affect poverty directly in many ways. Even when losses from disasters are small on average, some victims may lose everything during an event, including their health and, in the case of children, their chances of escaping poverty through education. As discussed in this section, such circumstances can result in millions of people falling into poverty every year worldwide, notwithstanding the fact that the impacts of disasters measured in monetary terms are small—or even negligible when disasters affect those who do not have significant wealth or earnings.

Even when average losses seem small, poor people suffer disproportionately from the impacts of disasters. Because poor people suffer disproportionately from natural disasters (chapter 2), these events increase inequalities, reducing the wealth and income of poor people more than that of the nonpoor. And if poor people are losing more than average, then even a small aggregate decrease in income—a decrease that may not be visible in aggregate statistics such as GDP—may have significant consequences for poor people's income and well-being.

This effect is magnified by the fact that the impacts of disasters are highly heterogeneous. By means of various case studies, table 3.1 shows that the median losses are always significantly less than the average losses because of the large losses of some households. The average losses may underestimate the effects of large losses on some individuals, especially those who are close to the subsistence level.

Table 3.1: Disaster losses are highly heterogeneous

Mean loss and median loss, selected hazards

Country	Hazard	Year	Mean loss	Median loss	Source
Bangladesh	Flood	2005	$198	$95	Brouwer et al. 2007
Germany	Flood	2002	€58,428	€32,000	Thieken et al. 2005
India	Tsunami	2004	Rs 24,261	Rs 10,891	Arlikatti et al. 2010
Mumbai (India)	Flood	2005	Rs 13,700	Rs 9,300	Patankar and Patwardhan 2016
Pakistan	Flood	2012	Rs 535	Rs 250	Kurosaki et al. 2012

Note: Rs = rupees. Pakistani and Indian rupees have different values.

Large losses by some households can have long-term consequences. After Ethiopia's 1984–85 famine, it took a decade on average for asset-poor households to bring livestock holdings back to prefamine levels (Dercon 2004). One explanation offered by Carter and Barrett (2006) is that if household assets go below a certain critical value—the Micawber threshold—it becomes difficult or almost impossible to rebuild the asset stock, and people may end up locked in poverty traps. For example, herders with only a few animals left after a natural disaster are probably unable to regrow their herd quickly after the event. If a drought or a flood drives households below this minimum asset threshold, then impacts could become permanent.

The existence of such a threshold—which has been debated (see Barnett, Barrett, and Skees 2008; Carter et al. 2007; Kraay and McKenzie 2014; Maccini and Yang 2009)—would also explain why some households do not use their savings to smooth consumption losses. Carter and Barrett (2006) suggest that poor households tend not to use their savings or sell their assets to maintain consumption; they instead decide to reduce consumption to maintain their asset stock above the critical threshold. But such a choice also has consequences for their prospects, as discussed shortly.

Some people—especially children—suffer from irreversible impacts on health and education. Some responses to disaster situations can be particularly damaging in the long term, especially for children, who are disproportionately vulnerable (Kousky 2016). As discussed in the previous chapter, recurrent events, such as urban floods in informal settlements, have impacts on the health of adults and children and have large cumulative impacts on poor people, even if each event is relatively small. Such events lead in particular to missed days at school for children and missed days at work for adults because traveling to the workplace is impossible or because adults (mostly women) stay home to take care of sick children (Hallegatte et al. 2016, chap. 4).

And after more intense shocks, poor households may be forced to make choices with detrimental long-term effects, such as withdrawing a child from school or reducing health care expenses. For the people experiencing large losses, the possible long-term effects, such as a reduction in food intake, health effects and disability, and exclusion from job markets, can push households into poverty traps.

Impacts on education are prevalent. In Africa, enrollment rates have declined 20 percent in regions affected by drought (Jensen 2000); drought-affected households have delayed starting children in school by 3.7 months on average, and 0.4 fewer grades are completed (Alderman, Hoddinott, and Kinsey 2006); and children younger than 36 months at the apex of the Ethiopia famine were less likely to complete primary school, leading to income losses of 3 percent a year (Dercon and Porter 2014). Such findings are not restricted to Africa; similar postdisaster impacts on health and education have been found in Asia, Latin America, and elsewhere (Baez, de la Fuente, and Santos 2010; Maccini and Yang 2009). In Mexico, once children have been taken out of school, even just for a temporary shock such as a flood, they are 30 percent less likely to proceed with their education, compared with children who remain in school (de Janvry et al. 2006). The impacts of the 1970 Ancash earthquake in Peru on educational attainment can be detected even for the children of mothers affected at birth, demonstrating that the effects of large disasters can extend even to the next generation (Caruso and Miller 2015).

Evidence also suggests that disasters have acute impacts on health, either directly or indirectly, through lower postdisaster consumption. After the 2004 floods in Bangladesh, more than 17,000 cases of diarrhea were registered (Qadri et al. 2005), and the cholera epidemic in West Bengal, India, in 1998 was attributed to the earlier floods (Sur et al. 2000). In Pakistan, the incidence of infectious disease and diarrhea increased as a result of the impact of the 2010 floods on the quality of the water. Ongoing efforts to eradicate polio were also interrupted, further setting back this goal (Warraich, Zaidi, and Patel 2011). Meanwhile, one death can have a large economic impact on other members of the household, stemming not only from the loss itself but also from the reduced household income and funeral expenses. Household surveys in India, Peru, Uganda, and Kenya have found that, in some places, funeral expenses are a significant cause of poverty, sometimes comparable to health expenditures (Krishna 2007).

In Sub-Saharan Africa, asset-poor households respond to weather shocks by reducing the quality of the nutrition provided to their children (Alderman, Hoddinott, and Kinsey 2006; Dercon and Porter 2014; Hoddinott 2006; Yamano, Alderman, and Christiaensen 2005), and they are less likely to take sick children for medical consultations (Jensen 2000). These behaviors have short- and long-term impacts, particularly for children younger than 2. Within this group, in households reducing nutrition, height fell by 0.9 centimeters within six months of a disaster (Yamano, Alderman, and Christiaensen 2005), and the stature of children in these households was permanently lowered by 2–3 centimeters (Alderman, Hoddinott, and Kinsey 2006; Dercon and Porter 2014). These households were also more likely to suffer from illness (Dercon and Porter 2014).

In Central America, major disasters have also reduced investments in human capital. After Hurricane Mitch hit Nicaragua in 1998, the probability of child undernourishment in regions affected by the hurricane increased by 8.7 percent, and child labor force participation increased by 5.6 percent (Baez and Santos 2007). In Guatemala, Storm Stan increased the probability of child labor by 7.3 percent in departments hit by the storm (Bustelo 2011). Natural disasters also increase the multidimensional poverty index through a deterioration of "education conditions" and "child and youth conditions," as demonstrated by Sanchez and Calderon (2014) for Colombia from 1976 to 2005.

Disasters affect birth outcomes as well. Rocha and Soares (2015) find that negative rainfall shocks in semiarid Brazil are correlated with higher infant mortality, lower birthweight, and shorter gestation periods. An increase of one standard deviation in rainfall (28 percent increase from average) leads to a 1.53-point reduction in the infant mortality rate (or 5 percent of the sample average of 30 deaths per 1,000 births). Rocha and Soares (2015) suggest that lack of access to safe drinking water (and the resulting increase in infectious disease) is the main channel, although reduced agricultural production (and the resulting lower nutritional intake) may also play a role. In Ecuador, children exposed in utero to the severe floods from El Niño in 1997–98 were more likely to be born with low birthweight (Rosales-Rueda 2014). These exposed children were shorter in stature five and seven years later (height-for-age decreased by 0.09 standard deviations) and scored lower on cognitive tests (vocabulary test scores fell by 0.13 standard deviations, compared with those of nonaffected children).

In addition, natural disasters can cause high levels of stress and mental disorders, thereby affecting the ability of individuals to make the right choices and to earn an income (Banerjee and Duflo 2012). Anxiety, depression, and post-traumatic stress disorder (PTSD) have been reported in populations affected by flooding and during slow-onset events such as drought (Ahern et al. 2005; Paranjothy et al. 2011).

Natural disasters—especially floods and droughts— have a significant impact on the global poverty headcount

Natural disasters have an impact on poverty through many different channels (economic growth, health, schooling, behaviors) that are difficult to quantify. It is nonetheless possible to assess a fraction of the full effect. Here, we quantify the short-term impacts that natural disasters have on poverty through people's income when they are hit—see Rozenberg and Hallegatte (forthcoming), a background paper prepared for this report.

To do so, we built a counterfactual scenario of what people's income would be today in the developing world in the absence of natural disasters. This scenario uses household surveys of 1.4 million households, which are representative of 1.2 billion households and 4.4 billion people in 89 developing countries. Depending on where they live and work, what they consume, and the nature of their vulnerability, we calculated the additional income that each household in the survey could earn every year on average in the absence of natural disasters. We then assess the average number that are living today with less than $1.90 per day only because they have been affected by a disaster.

The following natural disasters were modeled: floods, droughts, tsunamis, cyclones, storm surges, and earthquakes. Flood and drought hazard data were drawn from a global model (GLOFRIS) that produces gridded indicators of inundation depth (1-kilometer resolution) and water scarcity (5-kilometer resolution)—see Winsemius et al. (2015). Exposure data for earthquakes, windstorms, storm surges, and tsunamis were taken from the *United Nations Global Assessment Report on Disaster Risk Reduction* (UNISDR 2015), and vulnerability parameters were drawn from the literature. Because of the large uncertainty about exposure and vulnerability, three scenarios (based on the low, medium, and high impacts of natural disasters) were explored to provide a range of estimates.

A single 1,000-year return period earthquake or tsunami in a densely populated developing country has the potential to push tens of million people into poverty, and recovery and reconstruction for such events can be very long. The probability of occurrence of these events is low, however, which reduces the average impact on the global scale. Taken together, earthquakes, storm surges, tsunamis, and windstorms are responsible on average every year for the extreme poverty of 730,000 people (figure 3.2, panel a).

Floods and droughts also can have significant impacts on poverty, even when they are only small events that happen every 5–10 years. As a result, on average every year floods and drought together are responsible for the extreme poverty of about 25 million people (figure 3.2, panel b).

Our conclusion is that if all disasters could be prevented next year, the number of people in extreme poverty would be immediately reduced by around 26 million. A systematic analysis of the uncertainty suggests that this impact could lie between 7 million if all the most optimistic assumptions are combined, and 77 million if we retain only the most pessimistic assumptions. This wide range reflects the large uncertainty surrounding disasters' impacts and the challenges faced when moving from the available case studies to global estimates.

Figure 3.2: Natural disasters are responsible for the extreme poverty of millions of people

Simulated impacts of natural disasters on poverty headcount in 2012, 89 countries

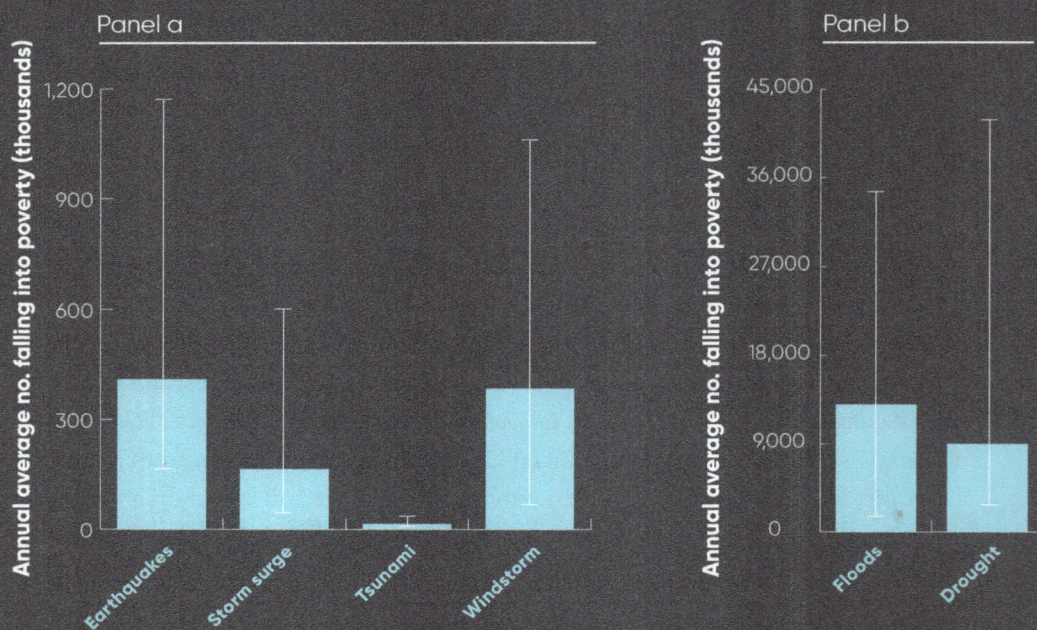

Source: Rozenberg and Hallegatte, forthcoming.

Note: These numbers are an underestimation of the current effects of natural disasters on the poverty headcount, because (1) they do not include frequent events (those that happen more than once every five years); (2) data for all hazard types are not available in all countries; and (3) some mechanisms and the dynamics of poverty reduction have not been taken into account.

That said, these numbers should be used with caution because they largely underestimate the total impacts of disasters on poverty. For one thing, disaster risk data are not available in all countries, and the impacts of disasters are calculated only in the countries and for the disasters for which data are available. Moreover, our analysis does not include the very frequent events (with a return period of less than five years). For another, these estimates do not include any dynamic considerations such as the impacts of disasters on asset accumulation and investment; they represent only the transient poverty due to the immediate shock and not the chronic poverty possibly created by natural hazards. Meanwhile, using the poverty headcount only hides the fact that disasters also affect people who are already in poverty. Paradoxically, this metric may give the impression that disasters do not strongly affect countries in which most of the population lives in poverty, disregarding the fact that disasters worsen the situation by making poor people fall further and increasing the poverty gap.

Finally, because we rely on household surveys that report only household-level consumption, we cannot account for the intrahousehold distributional issues, and especially the fact that children and women may be disproportionately affected by natural disasters. Gender inequality in the face of disasters has been widely reported— see, for example, Hoddinott (2006) and Rose (1999)—and a disproportionate impact on children is well identified—see Kousky (2016)—but these important effects cannot be included in this analysis. The estimates proposed here are therefore a lower bound to the impacts of natural disasters on poverty.

Recurrent risk reduces incentives to invest and keeps people in poverty

Although it is not taken into account in the previous estimates, the losses the poor suffer are not the only way in which disasters and natural risks contribute to ongoing poverty. When people do not have the proper tools to manage natural risk, they tend to spread risk over a large array of lower-risk activities and to reduce their investments, thereby reducing in turn returns to assets and income (Hallegatte, Bangalore, and Jouanjean 2016; ODI and GFDRR 2015; World Bank 2013). For example, smallholders plant low-return, low-risk crops and limit their investment in fertilizers (Cole et al. 2013). In rural Zimbabwe, farmers who are exposed to risk own on average half as much capital as farmers who are not exposed (Elbers, Gunning, and Kinsey 2007). Ex ante reductions in investments account for two-thirds of the difference (the rest stems from the actual destruction of capital because of shocks). In that case, most of the impact of risk on well-being is through reduced investments, not through the damages and losses incurred when a hazard does materialize into an actual event.

Disaster risk reduction can thus generate growth and benefits, beyond avoided losses, by promoting more investment. The *Triple Dividend* report refers to this benefit as the "second dividend of disaster risk reduction" (ODI and GFDRR 2015). (The first dividend is that disaster losses can be avoided, and the third dividend refers to co-benefits such as when a water retention area can also be used as a recreation park or a dike is combined with a road.)

Existence of the second dividend is supported by empirical evidence. Household insurance and social safety net programs have been observed to stimulate savings, investment in productive assets, and increases in agricultural productivity in a number of countries, with subsequent improvements in income levels. In Ethiopia, the R4 Rural Resilience Initiative (previously HARITA) program is providing risk management support, including weather-indexed insurance, to small-scale and subsistence farmers. An evaluation of the program has found that insurance is enabling farmers to increase their savings, which can act as an important reserve in the case of floods or droughts. Moreover, insured farmers increase their investments in productive assets—in particular, oxen, fertilizer, improved seeds, and compost—thereby improving their overall productivity (Madajewicz, Tsegay, and Norton 2013). Similar evidence exists for many African countries (Berhane et al. 2015; Jensen, Barrett, and Mude 2014; Karlan et al. 2011).

Evaluations of the Mexican government's CADENA program have confirmed that weather-indexed insurance not only helps to compensate for drought losses, but also directly increases the productivity of small-scale farmers (de Janvry, Ritchie, and Sadoulet 2016). This insurance program has enabled farmers to overcome credit constraints and has mitigated previously chronic underinvestment in tools and fertilizer. As a result, farmers have been able to increase their agricultural productivity, with an average 6 percent increase in maize yields. Evidence also suggests that insured farmers invest more than their uninsured peers in riskier and higher-yielding cultivation methods, with higher overall planting stage investments, thereby enabling them to reconcile entrepreneurial investment decisions with effective risk management (Emerick et al. 2016).

The second dividend also has implications for future disasters: as countries become richer and able to afford better protection, they will invest in measures that prevent the most frequent events for instance with drainage systems to avoid repeated urban floods and irrigation to manage rainfall variability. As a result, they will see a reduction in the frequency of disasters because only higher-intensity hazards will lead to losses. Reducing the level of risk will also attract additional investment and assets in at-risk areas, especially when these areas benefit from comparative advantages such as cheaper transport costs because of proximity to port and waterways. However, even though these additional investments are positive and desirable—on average, they increase well-being—they also increase the consequences of a protection failure (or of an exceptional event that exceeds the protection design). Thus countries will experience, and have to be prepared for, rarer but larger disasters (Hallegatte 2012; Hallegatte et al. 2013). To do so, they will need to improve their ability to manage crises and respond to disasters—in other words, they will need to strengthen population's resilience.

To summarize, chapter 2 showed how poverty is an essential component of vulnerability to natural disasters and how poverty reduction contributes to disaster risk management. This chapter has in turn described how natural disasters can affect poverty rates and therefore how disaster risk management can be considered a poverty reduction policy. In particular, disaster risk management can facilitate and provide incentives for asset accumulation, with benefits that go beyond the losses that can be avoided. Together, these chapters highlight the alignment and strong synergies that exist between risk management and development.

Going one step further, the next chapter presents an evaluation framework that combines the physical determinants of vulnerability with socioeconomic characteristics to provide an aggregate measure of the impacts of natural disasters on well-being in 117 countries, taking into account the capacity of households, especially the poorest, to cope with a shock. It then defines *socioeconomic resilience* as the ability of an economy to mitigate the impact of asset losses from disasters on losses of well-being.

NOTES

1. This section was contributed by Martin Heger.

REFERENCES

Ahern, M., R. S. Kovats, P. Wilkinson, R. Few, and F. Matthies. 2005. "Global Health Impacts of Floods: Epidemiologic Evidence." *Epidemiologic Reviews* 27: 36–46. doi:10.1093/epirev/mxi004.

Akter, S., and B. Mallick. 2013. "The Poverty–Vulnerability–Resilience Nexus: Evidence from Bangladesh." *Ecological Economics* 96: 114–24. doi:10.1016/j.ecolecon.2013.10.008.

Albala-Bertrand, J. M. 1993. *Political Economy of Large Natural Disasters: With Special Reference to Developing Countries.* New York and Oxford: Clarendon Press and Oxford University Press.

Alderman, H., J. Hoddinott, and B. Kinsey. 2006. "Long Term Consequences of Early Childhood Malnutrition." *Oxford Economic Papers* 58: 450–74. doi:10.1093/oep/gpl008.

Andrianarimanana, D. 2015. "The Role of Inter-Household Transfers in Coping against Post-disaster Losses in Madagascar." In *Disaster Risk Financing and Insurance: Issues and Results*, edited by Daniel Clarke, Alain de Janvry, Elisabeth Sadoulet, and Emmanuel Skoufias. http://www.ferdi.fr/en/publication/ouv-disaster-risk-financing-and-insurance-issues-and-results.

Arlikatti, S., W. G. Peacock, C. S. Prater, H. Grover, and A. S. G. Sekar. 2010. "Assessing the Impact of the Indian Ocean Tsunami on Households: A Modified Domestic Assets Index Approach." *Disasters* 34: 705–31.

Aspinall, E. 2005. "Indonesia after the Tsunami: Journal of an Aceh Volunteer." *Inside Indonesia* 82 (April–June): 28–30.

Baez, J., A. de la Fuente, and I. V. Santos. 2010. "Do Natural Disasters Affect Human Capital? An Assessment Based on Existing Empirical Evidence." Discussion Paper No. 5164, IZA, Bonn Germany.

Baez, J., L. Lucchetti, M. Salazar, and M. Genoni. 2016. "Gone with the Storm: Rainfall Shocks and Household Wellbeing in Guatemala." *Journal of Development Studies.* DOI:10.1080/00220388.2016.1224853.

Baez, J. E., and I. V. Santos. 2007. *Children's Vulnerability to Weather Shocks: A Natural Disaster as a Natural Experiment.* New York: Social Science Research Network.

Banerjee, A., and E. Duflo. 2012. *Poor Economics: A Radical Rethinking of the Way to Fight Global Poverty*, reprint ed. New York: Public Affairs.

Barnett, B. J., C. B. Barrett, and J. R. Skees. 2008. "Poverty Traps and Index-Based Risk Transfer Products." *World Development*, special section: "The Volatility of Overseas Aid." 36: 1766–85.

Baulch, B. 2011. *Why Poverty Persists: Poverty Dynamics in Asia and Africa.* Cheltenham, U.K.: Edward Elgar Publishing.

Beegle, K., J. De Weerdt, and S. Dercon. 2006. *Poverty and Wealth Dynamics in Tanzania: Evidence from a Tracking Survey.* Washington, DC: World Bank.

Berhane, G., S. Dercon, R. V. Hill, and A. Taffesse. 2015. "Formal and Informal Insurance: Experimental Evidence from Ethiopia." Paper presented at 2015 Conference of International Association of Agricultural Economists, Milan, August 9–14 (No. 211331).

Bertinelli, L., and E. Strobl. 2013. "Quantifying the Local Economic Growth Impact of Hurricane Strikes: An Analysis from Outer Space for the Caribbean." *Journal of Applied Meteorology and Climatology* 52: 1688–97.

Bhavani, R. 2006. "Natural Disaster Conflicts." Manuscript, Harvard University, Cambridge, MA.

Brando, J. F., and R. J. Santos. 2015. "La Niña y los niños: Effects of an Unexpected Winter on Early Life Human Capital and Family Responses." *Documento CEDE* (2015–25).

Brouwer, R., S. Akter, L. Brander, and E. Haque. 2007. "Socioeconomic Vulnerability and Adaptation to Environmental Risk: A Case Study of Climate Change and Flooding in Bangladesh." *Risk Analysis* (27): 313–26.

Bustelo, M. 2011. "Bearing the Burden of Natural Disasters: Child Labor and Schooling in the Aftermath of the Tropical Storm Stan in Guatemala." University of Illinois at Urbana-Champaign.

Calero, C., R. Maldonado, and A. Molina. 2008. "Relación entre eventos climáticos y geológicos externos y pobreza." Document prepared for ISDR/RBLAC Research Project on Disaster Risk and Poverty.

Carter, M. R., and C. B. Barrett. 2006. "The Economics of Poverty Traps and Persistent Poverty: An Asset-Based Approach." *Journal of Development Studies* 42: 178–99.

Carter, M. R., P. D. Little, T. Mogues, and W. Negatu. 2007. "Poverty Traps and Natural Disasters in Ethiopia and Honduras." *World Development* 35: 835–56. doi:10.1016/j.worlddev.2006.09.010.

Caruso, G., and S. Miller. 2015. "Long Run Effects and Intergenerational Transmission of Natural Disasters: A Case Study on the 1970 Ancash Earthquake. *Journal of Development Economics* 117: 134–50.

Cavallo, E., S. Galiani, I. Noy, and J. Pantano. 2013. "Catastrophic Natural Disasters and Economic Growth." *Review of Economics and Statistics* 95 (5): 1549–61.

Cavallo, E. A., and I. Noy. 2009. "The Economics of Natural Disasters: A Survey." *SSRN Electronic Journal.* doi:10.2139/ssrn.1817217.

Coffman, M., and I. Noy. 2012. "Hurricane Iniki: Measuring the Long-Term Economic Impact of a Natural Disaster Using Synthetic Control." *Environment and Development Economics* 17: 187–205. doi:10.1017/S1355770X11000350.

Cole, S., X. Gine, J. Tobacman, P. Topalova, R. Townsend, and J. Vickery. 2013. "Barriers to Household Risk Management: Evidence from India." *American Economic Journal: Applied Economics* 5: 104–35. doi:10.1257/app.5.1.104.

Dang, H. A., P. F. Lanjouw, and R. Swinkels. 2014. "Who Remained in Poverty, Who Moved Up, and Who Fell Down? An Investigation of Poverty Dynamics in Senegal in the Late 2000s." Policy Research Working Paper 7141, World Bank, Washington, DC.

Datt, G., and H. Hoogeveen. 2003. "El Niño or El Peso? Crisis, Poverty and Income Distribution in the Philippines." *World Development*, special issue: "Economic Crises, Natural Disasters, and Poverty." 31: 1103–24. doi:10.1016/S0305-750X(03)00060-3.

de Janvry, A., F. Finan, E. Sadoulet, and R. Vakis. 2006. "Can Conditional Cash Transfer Programs Serve as Safety Nets in Keeping Children at School and from Working When Exposed to Shocks?" *Journal of Development Economics* 79: 349–73.

de Janvry, A., E. Ritchie, and E. Sadoulet. 2016. "Weather Index Insurance and Shock Coping: Evidence from Mexico's CADENA Program." Policy Research Working Paper 7715, World Bank, Washington, DC.

Dercon, S. 2004. "Growth and Shocks: Evidence from Rural Ethiopia." *Journal of Development Economics* 74: 309–29.

Dercon, S., and C. Porter. 2014. "Live Aid Revisited: Long-Term Impacts of the 1984 Ethiopian Famine on Children." *Journal of European Economic Association* 12: 927–48. doi:10.1111/jeea.12088.

Deryugina, Tatyana, Laura Kawano, and Steven Levitt. 2014. "The Economic Impact of Hurricane Katrina on Its Victims: Evidence from Individual Tax Returns." Working Paper 20713, National Bureau of Economic Research, Cambridge, MA.

Dollar, D., T. Kleineberg, and A. Kraay. 2013. "Growth Still Is Good for the Poor." Policy Research Working Paper 6568, World Bank, Washington, DC.

Dollar, D., and A. Kraay. 2002. "Growth Is Good for the Poor." *Journal of Economic Growth* 7: 195–225. doi:10.1023/A:1020139631000.

Elbers, C., J. W. Gunning, and B. Kinsey. 2007. "Growth and Risk: Methodology and Micro Evidence." *World Bank Economic Review* 21: 1–20. doi:10.1093/wber/lhl008.

Elliott, R. J., E. Strobl, and P. Sun. 2015. "The Local Impact of Typhoons on Economic Activity in China: A View from Outer Space." *Journal of Urban Economics* 88: 50–66.

Emerick, K., A. de Janvry, E. Sadoulet, and M. H. Dar. 2016. "Technological Innovations, Downside Risk, and the Modernization of Agriculture." *American Economic Review* 106: 1537–61.

Felbermayr, G., and J. Gröschl. 2014. "Naturally Negative: The Growth Effects of Natural Disasters." *Journal of Development Economics*, special Issue: "Imbalances in Economic Development." 111: 92–106. doi:10.1016/j.jdeveco.2014.07.004.

FEWS NET (Famine Early Warning Systems Network). 2015. "Madagascar Food Security Outlook February to September 2015." Washington, DC.

Glave, M., R. Fort, and C. Rosemberg. 2008. "Disaster Risk and Poverty in Latin America: The Peruvian Case Study." Document prepared for the ISDR/RBLAC Research Project on Disaster Risk and Poverty.

Groen, Jeffrey, Mark J. Kutzbach, and Anne Elise Polivka. 2016. "Storms and Jobs: The Effect of Hurricanes on Individuals' Employment and Earnings over the Long Term." Center for Economic Studies Paper No. CES-WP-15-21R, U.S. Census Bureau, Suitland, MD.

Hallegatte, S. 2012. "An Exploration of the Link between Development, Economic Growth, and Natural Risk." Policy Research Working Paper 6216, World Bank, Washington, DC.

Hallegatte, S., M. Bangalore, L. Bonzanigo, M. Fay, T. Kane, U. Narloch, J. Rozenberg et al. 2016. *Shock Waves: Managing the Impacts of Climate Change on Poverty.* Climate Change and Development Series. Washington, DC: World Bank.

Hallegatte, S., M. Bangalore, and M. A. Jouanjean. 2016. "Higher Losses and Slower Development in the Absence of Disaster Risk Management Investments." Policy Research Working Paper 7632, World Bank, Washington, DC.

Hallegatte, S., C. Green, R. J. Nicholls, and J. Corfee-Morlot. 2013. "Future Flood Losses in Major Coastal Cities." *Nature Climate Change* 3: 802–6. doi:10.1038/nclimate1979.

Harris, K., D. Keen, and T. Mitchell. 2013. "When Disasters and Conflicts Collide: Improving Links between Disaster Resilience and Conflict Prevention." Overseas Development Institute (ODI), London.

Heger, M. Forthcoming. "Economic Legacy Effects of Armed Conflict: Insights from the Civil War in Aceh, Indonesia."

Hoddinott, J. 2006. "Shocks and Their Consequences across and within Households in Rural Zimbabwe." *Journal of Development Studies* 42: 301–21.

Hsiang, S. M., and A. S. Jina. 2014. "The Causal Effect of Environmental Catastrophe on Long-Run Economic Growth: Evidence from 6,700 Cyclones." Working Paper No. 20352, National Bureau of Economic Research, Cambridge, MA.

Ishizawa, O. A., and J. J. Miranda. 2016. "Weathering Storms: Understanding the Impact of Natural Disasters on the Poor in Central America." Policy Research Working Paper 7692, World Bank, Washington, DC.

Jakobsen, K. T. 2012. "In the Eye of the Storm¾The Welfare Impacts of a Hurricane." *World Development* 40: 2578–89. doi:10.1016/j.worlddev.2012.05.013.

Jensen, N.D., C. B. Barrett, and A. Mude. 2014. "Index Insurance and Cash Transfers: A Comparative Analysis from Northern Kenya." SSRN 2547660.

Jensen, R. 2000. "Agricultural Volatility and Investments in Children." *American Economic Review* 90: 399–404. doi:10.1257/aer.90.2.399.

Karim, A., and I. Noy. 2014. "Poverty and Natural Disasters: A Meta-analysis." SEF Working Paper 04/2014, University of Wellington.

Karlan, D., E. Kutsoati, M. McMillan, and C. Udry. 2011. "Crop Price Indemnified Loans for Farmers: A Pilot Experiment in Rural Ghana." *Journal of Risk and Insurance* 78 (1): 37–55.

Keen, D. 2009. "Compromise or Capitulation? Report on WFP and the Humanitarian Crisis in Sri Lanka." *In Humanitarian Assistance in Conflict and Complex Emergencies: Conference Report and Background Paper.* Rome: United Nations World Food Programme.

Klomp, J., and K. Valckx. 2014. "Natural Disasters and Economic Growth: A Meta-analysis." *Global Environmental Change* 26: 183–95.

Kocornik-Mina, A., T. K. McDermott, G. Michaels, and F. Rauch. 2015. "Flooded Cities." CEP Discussion Paper, Centre for Economic Policy, London.

Kousky, C. 2016. "Impacts of Natural Disasters on Children." *Future of Children* 26(1): 73–92.

Kraay, A., and D. McKenzie. 2014. "Do Poverty Traps Exist? Assessing the Evidence." *Journal of Economic Perspectives* 28: 127–48. doi:10.1257/jep.28.3.127.

Krishna, A. 2006. "Pathways Out of and into Poverty in 36 Villages of Andhra Pradesh, India." *World Development*, special issue: "Corruption and Development: Analysis and Measurement." 34: 271–88. doi:10.1016/j.worlddev.2005.08.003.

———. 2007. "The Stages-of-Progress Methodology and Results from Five Countries." In *Reducing Global Poverty: The Case for Asset Accumulation,* edited by Carolina Moser, 62–79. Washington, DC: Brookings.

Kuhn, R. 2009. "Tsunami and Conflict in Sri Lanka." Background paper for the Joint World Bank–UN Project on the Economics of Disaster Risk Reduction, Washington DC.

Kurosaki, T., H. Khan, M. K. Shah, and M. Tahir. 2012. "Household-Level Recovery after Floods in a Developing Country: Further Evidence from Khyber Pakhtunkhwa, Pakistan." Institute of Economic Research, Hitotsubashi University, Japan.

Lanjouw, P., D. McKenzie, and J. Luoto. 2011. "Using Repeated Cross-Sections to Explore Movements In and Out of Poverty." Policy Research Working Paper 5550, World Bank, Washington, DC.

Maccini, S., and D. Yang. 2009. "Under the Weather: Health, Schooling, and Economic Consequences of Early-Life Rainfall." *American Economic Review* 99: 1006–26. doi:10.1257/aer.99.3.1006.

Madajewicz, M., A. H. Tsegay, and M. Norton. 2013. *Managing Risks to Agricultural Livelihoods: Impact Evaluation of the Harita Program in Tigray, Ethiopia, 2009–2012.* London: Oxfam.

Mampilly, Z. 2009. "A Marriage of Inconvenience: Tsunami Aid and the Unraveling of the LTTE and the GoSL's Complex Dependency." *Civil Wars* 11: 302–20. doi:10.1080/13698240903157545

MDAT (Multi-Agency Drought Assessment Team). 2016. *Lesotho: Rapid Drought Impact Assessment Report.* Lesotho.

Nel, P., and M. Righarts. 2008. "Natural Disasters and the Risk of Violent Civil Conflict." *International Studies Quarterly* 52: 159–85.

Noy, I., and P. Patel. 2014. "Floods and Spillovers: Households after the 2011 Great Flood in Thailand." Working Paper Series No. 3609, School of Economics and Finance, Victoria University of Wellington.

ODI (Overseas Development Institute) and GFDRR (Global Facility for Disaster Reduction and Recovery). 2015. "Unlocking the Triple Dividend of Resilience—Why Investing in DRM Pays Off." http://www.odi.org/tripledividend.

Olson, R. S., and A. C. Drury. 1997. "Un-therapeutic Communities: A Cross-National Analysis of Post-disaster Political Unrest." *International Journal of Mass Emergencies and Disasters* 15: 221–38.

Paranjothy, S., J. Gallacher, R. Amlôt, G. J. Rubin, L. Page, T. Baxter, J. Wight et al. 2011. "Psychosocial Impact of the Summer 2007 Floods in England." *BMC Public Health* 11: 145.

Patankar, A., and A. Patwardhan. 2016. "Estimating the Uninsured Losses due to Extreme Weather Events and Implications for Informal Sector Vulnerability: A Case Study of Mumbai, India." *Natural Hazards* 80 (1): 285–310. doi:10.1007/s11069-015-1968-3.

Perez-De-Rada, E., and D. Paz. 2008. "Análisis de la relación entre amenazas naturales y condiciones de vida: El Caso de Bolivia." ISDR/RBLAC Research Project on Disaster Risk and Poverty.

Peter, G. von, S. von Dahlen, and S. C. Saxena. 2012. "Unmitigated Disasters? New Evidence on the Macroeconomic Cost of Natural Catastrophes." BIS Working Paper No. 394, Bank for International Settlements, Basel, Switzerland.

Qadri, F., A. I. Khan, A. S. G. Faruque, Y. A. Begum, F. Chowdhury, G. B. Nair, M. A. Salam et al. 2005. "Enterotoxigenic Escherichia Coli and Vibrio Cholerae Diarrhea, Bangladesh, 2004." *Emerging Infectious Diseases* 11: 1104–07. doi:10.3201/eid1107.041266.

Raddatz, C. 2009. "The Wrath of God: Macroeconomic Costs of Natural Disasters." Policy Research Working Paper 5039, World Bank, Washington, DC.

Rasmussen, T. 2004. "Macroeconomic Implications of Natural Disasters in the Caribbean." IMF Working Paper 04/224, International Monetary Fund, Washington, DC.

Reardon, T., and J. E. Taylor. 1996. "Agroclimatic Shock, Income Inequality, and Poverty: Evidence from Burkina Faso." *World Development* 24: 901–14. doi:10.1016/0305-750X(96)00009-5.

Rocha, R., and R. R. Soares. 2015. "Water Scarcity and Birth Outcomes in the Brazilian Semiarid." *Journal of Development Economics* 112: 72–91. doi:10.1016/j.jdeveco.2014.10.003.

Rodriguez-Oreggia, E., A. de la Fuente, R. de la Torre, and H. A. Moreno. 2013. "Natural Disasters, Human Development and Poverty at the Municipal Level in Mexico." *Journal of Development Studies* 49: 442–55. doi:10.1080/00220388.2012.700398.

Rosales-Rueda, M. F. 2014. "Impact of Early Life Shocks on Human Capital Formation: Evidence from El Nino Floods in Ecuador." Working Paper, University of California Irvine.

Rose, E. 1999. "Consumption Smoothing and Excess Female Mortality in Rural India." *Review of Economics and statistics* 81 (1): 41–49.

Rozenberg, J., and S. Hallegatte. Forthcoming. "Model and Methods for Estimating the Number of People Living in Extreme Poverty Because of the Direct Impacts of Natural Disasters." Background paper prepared for this report, World Bank, Washington, DC.

Safir, A., S. F. A. Piza, and E. Skoufias. 2013. "Disquiet on the Weather Front: The Welfare Impacts of Climatic Variability in the Rural Philippines." Policy Research Working Paper 6579, World Bank, Washington, DC.

Sanchez, F., and S. Calderon. 2014. "Natural Disasters and Multidimensional Poverty in Colombia." Paper presented at the Workshop on Climate Change and Poverty in the Latin America Region, World Bank, Washington, DC.

Sen, B. 2003. "Drivers of Escape and Descent: Changing Household Fortunes in Rural Bangladesh." *World Development, Chronic Poverty and Development Policy* 31: 513–34.

Skidmore, M., and H. Toya. 2002. "Do Natural Disasters Promote Long-Run Growth?" *Economic Inquiry* 40: 664–87.

Strobl, E. 2010. "The Economic Growth Impact of Hurricanes: Evidence from U.S. Coastal Counties." *Review of Economics and Statistics* 93: 575–89. doi:10.1162/REST_a_00082.

Sur, D., P. Dutta, G. B. Nair, and S. K. Bhattacharya. 2000. "Severe Cholera Outbreak following Floods in a Northern District of West Bengal." *Indian Journal of Medical Research* 112: 178–82.

Thieken, A. H., M. Müller, H. Kreibich, and B. Merz. 2005. "Flood Damage and Influencing Factors: New Insights from the August 2002 Flood in Germany." *Water Resources Research* 41 (12).

UNISDR (United Nations Office for Disaster Risk Reduction). 2015. *United Nations Global Assessment Report on Disaster Risk Reduction.* Geneva: UNISDR.

UNOCHA (United Nations Office for the Coordination of Humanitarian Affairs). 2016. *El Nino: Overview of Impact, Projected Humanitarian Needs, and Response.* New York: UNOCHA.

Waizenegger, A. 2007. "Armed Separatism and the 2004 Tsunami in Aceh." *Canada Asia Commentary* 43: 1–10.

Warraich, H., A. K. Zaidi, and K. Patel. 2011. "Floods in Pakistan: A Public Health Crisis." *Bulletin of the World Health Organization* 89: 236–37.

Winsemius, H. C., B. Jongman, T. Veldkamp, S. Hallegatte, M. Bangalore, and P. Ward. 2015. "Disaster Risk, Climate Change, and Poverty: Assessing the Global Exposure of Poor People to Floods and Droughts." Policy Research Working Paper 7480, World Bank, Washington, DC.

World Bank. 2013. *World Development Report 2014: Risk and Opportunity—Managing Risk for Development.* Washington, DC: World Bank.

World Food Programme. 2016. *El Nino: Undermining Resilience: Implications of El Nino in Southern Africa from a Food and Nutrition Security Perspective.* Geneva: World Food Programme.

Yamano, T., H. Alderman, and L. Christiaensen. 2005. "Child Growth, Shocks, and Food Aid in Rural Ethiopia." *American Journal of Agricultural Economics* 87: 273–88. doi:10.1111/j.1467-8276.2005.00721.x.

4 A DIAGNOSIS

>> **The global impacts of natural disasters
on well-being are underestimated.**

We now know that disasters have an impact on poverty, and
that the level of poverty matters for the impact of disasters
on well-being. Poor people are often more exposed to
disasters, they lose more from disasters, and they receive less support
when they are hit. Moreover, when they experience the same monetary
loss in consumption as the nonpoor, that loss has a larger impact on their
well-being because they are closer to the subsistence level and so, unlike
wealthier people, cannot cut back on luxury consumption. These multiple
factors combine to make poor people more vulnerable to natural hazards.
But how much more vulnerable?

Here, we propose a tool to quantify the vulnerability of countries to natural hazards,
taking into account the excess in vulnerability caused by poverty. Practically, we
measure the *risk to well-being* as the average loss in well-being caused by natural hazards.

The main conclusion of this analysis is that estimates of disaster consequences based
on asset losses underestimate the impact on well-being. Accounting for the differential
impact on poor and nonpoor people, and their different ability to recover and
reconstruct, we find that the loss of well-being attributable to floods, windstorms,
earthquakes, and tsunamis in 117 countries is equivalent to a $520 billion drop in

annual consumption—a cost that is 60 percent larger than the asset losses that are commonly reported.

The risk to well-being can be calculated with a simple model that considers the four drivers of the loss in well-being as described in chapter 1. For each possible hazard—such as a hurricane making landfall in one particular location on India's coastline—we can estimate the number of people and the value of assets affected by the event (exposure). Then we can assess the damages to these assets based on their vulnerability. However, looking only at asset losses is misleading because a $1 loss in assets has a very different impact on the poor and nonpoor. For that reason, the assessment is carried out separately for poor and nonpoor people. Furthermore, we take into account the distribution of losses in order to capture the fact that losses concentrated in a few individuals have a larger impact than the same losses shared across a large population. And we also consider the different abilities of the poor and the nonpoor to cope with the asset losses by modeling the effect of asset losses on income (accounting for capital productivity) and then on consumption (accounting for diversification of income, social protection, and postdisaster transfers). Well-being loss is expressed as the equivalent loss in national consumption: if the analysis finds that a disaster causes $1 million in well-being losses, it means that the impact of the disaster on well-being is equivalent to a $1 million decrease in country consumption, perfectly shared among the population.

Such an analysis produces the asset and well-being losses caused by a hazard. If all hazards are considered—different types and of different magnitudes— the analysis can also provide the risk to assets (the average annual value of asset losses) and the risk to well-being (the average annual loss of well-being, expressed as an equivalent loss in consumption). From these estimates, *socioeconomic resilience* can be defined as the ratio of *asset* losses to *well-being* losses:

$$\textbf{socioeconomic resilience} = \frac{\text{asset losses}}{\text{well-being losses}}$$

If the socioeconomic resilience is 100 percent, then asset losses and well-being losses are equal, and thus $1 in asset losses from a disaster is equivalent to a $1 consumption loss, perfectly shared across the population. If the socioeconomic resilience is 50 percent, then well-being losses are twice as large as asset losses—that is, $1 in asset losses from a disaster is equivalent to a $2 consumption loss, perfectly shared across the population. In most cases, well-being losses are larger because these losses are not perfectly shared across the population; they are concentrated only in a fraction of the population and mainly on the poorest, who are more vulnerable to any loss in consumption.

Based on this definition, socioeconomic resilience can be considered a driver of the risk to well-being along with the three usual drivers: hazard (the probability an event occurs), exposure (the population and assets located in the affected area), and asset vulnerability (the fraction of asset value lost when affected by a hazard):

$$\text{Risk to well-being} = \frac{\text{expected asset losses}}{\text{socioeconomic resilience}} = \frac{(\text{hazard}) * (\text{exposure}) * (\text{asset vulnerability})}{\text{socioeconomic resilience}}$$

Socioeconomic resilience (sometimes also called socioeconomic capacity) measures the ability of an economy to minimize the impact of asset losses on well-being and is one part of the ability to *resist, absorb, accommodate,* and *recover* from the effects of a hazard *in a timely and efficient manner* (the qualitative definition of resilience by the United Nations).

We illustrate our approach by looking first at the 2005 floods in Mumbai, India. We then turn to a global estimate, looking at multiple hazards and events of different likelihood.

The impact of the 2005 floods in Mumbai on well-being, and options for action, can be estimated

The July 2005 floods in Mumbai affected 4.2 million people and 350 billion rupees (Rs) in assets, leading to Rs 35 billion in asset losses (Ranger et al. 2011). Here we describe how the well-being losses from that disaster can be assessed. Hallegatte, Bangalore, and Vogt-Schilb (forthcoming) provide all the equations with detailed explanations, the full code, and data. We use standard economics to estimate the consumption and well-being losses resulting from these asset losses. Doing so implies the series of steps shown in figure 4.1.

Figure 4.1: The chain from a natural hazard to its impacts on well-being involves many drivers

Hazard	Exposure	Asset losses	Income losses	Consumption losses	Well-being losses
• Flood level	• Location of people and assets	• Housing and infrastructure quality	• Diversification of income	• Social protection	• Marginal utility of consumption
• Wind speed	• Occupation	• Livestock and other assets	• Link between assets and income	• Savings and borrowing	• Income distribution
• Hard and soft protection		• Early-warning systems	• How long will the shock last?	• Insurance and remittances	• Non-consumption poverty
• Temperature					
• Precipitations					

Source: Hallegatte, Bangalore, and Vogt-Schilb, forthcoming.

Starting from asset losses, we first estimate income losses, which depend on the average productivity of the assets that have been lost or damaged, on the diversification of income sources, and on the speed of recovery and reconstruction. Importantly, how asset losses translate into income losses depends on livelihood and income sources (Barrett, Reardon, and Webb 2001). Over the short term, income from labor decreases in proportion to each individual's asset losses (Hallegatte and Vogt-Schilb, forthcoming). A pastoralist losing one-third of his or her herd is likely to lose one-third of the income derived from it. By contrast, transfers such as pensions or cash transfers are diversified at the country level (such as through the government budget or the financial system). As a result, higher diversification leads to lower income losses (figure 4.2).[1]

These income losses can then be translated into consumption losses, accounting for the response to the disaster, especially for formal and informal insurance (Kunreuther 1996; Skoufias 2003), remittances (Le De, Gaillard, and Friesen 2013), ad hoc postdisaster transfers, and the scaling up of social protection (Siegel and de la Fuente 2010). These mechanisms can replace some of the lost income after a disaster and reduce the resulting consumption losses. In Mumbai, insurance is largely absent, but after the 2005 floods the government provided postdisaster support to households, which, according to household surveys, amounted to approximately 10 percent of their asset losses. We estimate that the floods caused Rs 39 billion in discounted consumption losses, which was about 10 percent larger than the asset losses.

Figure 4.2: The income of affected people after a disaster depends on share of transfers and the response to the shock

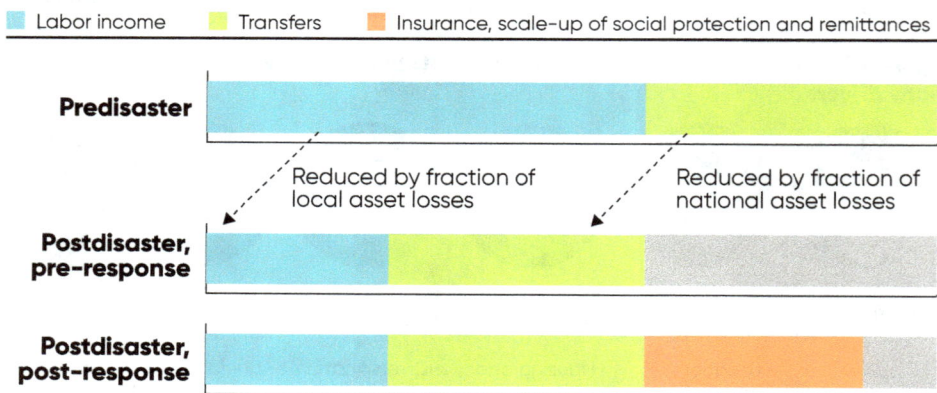

Source: Hallegatte, Bangalore, and Vogt-Schilb, forthcoming.

We then examine the distribution of this aggregate consumption loss across individuals to account for the fact that the same aggregate loss has a higher impact on well-being if it disproportionately affects a small fraction of the population, and especially if it affects people close to the subsistence level. Analyses of household location and flood hazard in Mumbai show poor households (with incomes of less than Rs 5,000 per month) were 71 percent more likely to have been flooded than the average household (Patankar and Patwardhan 2016). We also account for the difference in the magnitude of asset losses when a poor or a nonpoor person is flooded. In Mumbai, household surveys have shown poor people lost about 60 percent more than nonpoor people relative to their estimated wealth (Patankar and Patwardhan 2016). Taking into account these differences, our calculations indicate losses at the time of the 2005 floods in Mumbai were about 11 percent of the predisaster consumption level for the affected poor and 8 percent for the affected nonpoor. Findings from household surveys after the floods are consistent with these results (Patankar and Patwardhan 2016).

To explore the effects of such consumption losses on well-being, we translate them into *equivalent consumption losses*, defined as the decrease in aggregate consumption in the city of Mumbai (optimally shared across the population) that would lead to the same decrease in well-being as the individual losses from the disaster (box 4.1).

BOX 4.1

WELFARE ECONOMICS PROVIDES TOOLS TO TRANSLATE CONSUMPTION LOSSES INTO WELL-BEING IMPACTS

In welfare economics, the fact that $1 is worth more for a poor person than a richer person is usually measured by means of a utility function, which represents how the well-being of one individual depends on his or her consumption (Arrow 1965; Fleurbaey and Hammond 2004). The marginal utility of consumption is the additional well-being derived from $1 more in consumption (or the loss in well-being from a $1 reduction in consumption). Of course, the marginal utility of consumption is lower for people with higher consumption ($1 more in consumption increases more significantly the well-being of a poor individual than a richer one). This difference can be measured with the elasticity of the marginal utility of consumption, which describes how the additional well-being from $1 more in consumption changes with income (it is also one of the main determinants of the discount rate). More simply, it can be described by distributional weights, which give a higher value to an additional $1 in consumption of a poor individual than to an additional $1 in consumption of a richer one (Harberger 1978).

Here, we use a classical isoelastic utility function, with a standard value of 1.5 for the elasticity of the marginal utility of consumption. Because this parameter is a normative choice, we explore in the background analysis how results change for different values (Hallegatte, Bangalore, and Vogt-Schilb 2016). Higher values give more importance to poor people, lead to higher estimates of well-being losses, and make it relatively more important to use policy instruments that target poor people.

We estimate that well-being losses from the 2005 floods in Mumbai are equivalent to a loss in aggregate consumption of about Rs 60 billion—almost twice as large as the asset losses—resulting in a socioeconomic resilience of the city of 57 percent. This result means that the effect of the flood on well-being in the city is equivalent to a perfectly shared decrease in income of Rs 60 billion. These well-being consequences are larger than asset or consumption losses because of the overexposure and overvulnerability of poor people and the fact that losses are highly concentrated on a fraction of the population. However, these losses remain an underestimate because we do not include in the analysis the direct and indirect effects of the fatalities caused by the flood.

Beyond this simple estimate, this analysis allows investigation of how various policy options could have reduced well-being losses from the 2005 floods in Mumbai (figure 4.3). It is possible to distinguish policies that act through asset losses from policies that act on the ability to deal with these losses:

- Some policies would have reduced well-being losses by reducing asset losses (such as enacting flood zones, improving asset quality).
- Other options (increasing postdisaster support, accelerating reconstruction, increasing diversification, or improving access to savings) would have reduced well-being losses from unchanged asset losses by enhancing the capacity of the population to manage the asset losses.

Figure 4.3: Policy measures can reduce asset and well-being losses

Simulated effects of policy measures on asset and well-being losses: 2005 floods, Mumbai, India

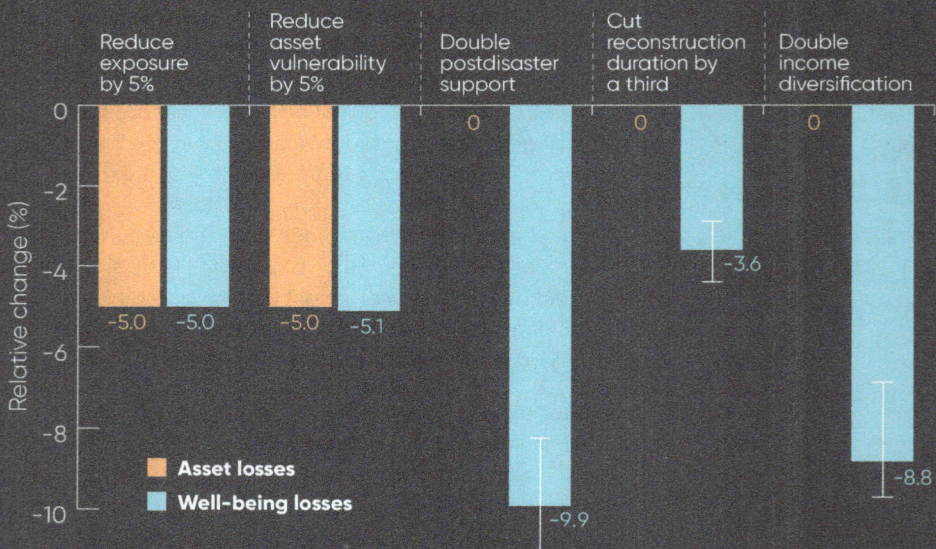

Source: Hallegatte, Bangalore and Vogt-Schilb, 2016.
Note: Error bars reflect the results of an uncertainty analysis.

These findings make it possible to quantify risk management options and policies that are rarely quantified. For example, it is well accepted that rapid reconstruction is critical to reducing disaster impacts. In Mumbai, cutting reconstruction duration by a third would have reduced well-being losses by 3.6 percent. Similarly, income diversification, social protection, and insurance are widely discussed as potential tools for increasing resilience (G7 2015; Surminski, Bouwer, and Linnerooth-Bayer 2016). By estimating the benefits of these tools, we make it possible to compare them with implementation costs and alternative approaches such as land-use planning or retrofitting buildings.

To account for the uncertainty in the exposure to the floods and its consequences and in socioeconomic characteristics (such as diversification), we performed a systematic sensitivity analysis by varying all uncertain parameters 33 percent above and below their central value, and we measured the robustness of our findings (see Hallegatte, Bangalore, and Vogt-Schilb, 2016, for full details). Error bars in figure 4.3 reveal the resulting interquartile uncertainty about the impacts of the various policies on asset and well-being losses, and it shows that our results are robust. We also find that the relative ranking of the policies is stable and not sensitive to the uncertainties.

A simple model provides estimates of the risk to well-being and socioeconomic resilience in 117 countries

Now we use this approach to quantify the risk to well-being in 117 countries. We calculate asset and well-being losses for multiple hazards: river floods, coastal floods due to storm surge, windstorms, earthquakes, and tsunamis. For each of these hazards, we consider several return periods, from 2 to 1,500 years. Socioeconomic resilience is then estimated as the ratio of expected asset losses to expected well-being losses.

Our analysis focuses on the ability of a population to cope with asset losses—that is, on its socioeconomic resilience. We start with the estimates of asset losses in the *United Nations Global Assessment Report on Disaster Risk Reduction,* otherwise known as the GAR report (UNISDR 2015). Its estimates of the asset losses due to river floods, coastal floods caused by storm surge, windstorms, earthquakes, and tsunamis are based on a global catastrophe model. The model represents the interaction of hazards (a set of possible hurricanes, earthquakes, and so forth with their characteristics and probability of occurrence) with a global inventory of exposed assets with their vulnerability. Asset losses can be attributed to each hazard event. Using the probability of occurrence, these asset losses per event can be translated into an exceedance probability curve—that is, a curve giving the probability of exceeding a given amount of asset losses. This curve reveals the asset losses that have a 5 percent chance of occurrence per year (the

20-year return period event), a 1 percent chance of occurrence (the 100-year return period event), and so forth. These estimates serve as the basis of our resilience model. According to the GAR estimates, the average annual asset loss from disasters is $327 billion a year in the 117 countries for which we have data.[2]

For the exposure bias (that is, whether poor people are more often affected than the rest of the population), we use the estimates described in chapter 2 and shown in map 2.3, based on poverty maps and the GLOFRIS flood maps. For countries without poverty maps, we use the results from the *Shock Waves* report (Hallegatte et al. 2016), using geolocalized household surveys (from the Demographic and Health Survey) as described in Winsemius et al. (2015). Countries in which data are not available are assigned the average exposure bias for floods. We assume that there is no exposure bias for the other hazards (wind, earthquake, and tsunami) because of the scale and frequency of these events. This is a simplification, however, because soil characteristics and slopes may contribute to making poor people more exposed to such events (as discussed in chapter 2). But in the absence of global data, we disregard this factor (again making our estimates conservative).

We proxy asset vulnerability and the asset vulnerability bias using a global data set of building types (Jaiswal, Wald, and Porter 2010). As explained in chapter 2, we classify buildings as fragile, medium, and robust—categories we match to simple damage-depth functions (Hallegatte et al. 2013)—and we assume that richer households live in and use higher-quality assets.

What fraction of assets is lost to a disaster also depends on softer measures such as the existence of early warning systems. In addition to being an effective way of reducing casualties and fatalities, such systems allow households to plan for a disaster and move some of their assets outside (or above) the affected zone, thereby reducing asset losses (Hallegatte 2012; Kreibich et al. 2005). Based on previous case studies, we assume that asset losses are reduced by 20 percent when people have access to early warning systems, and we use data from the Hyogo Framework for Action (HFA) monitoring system on early warning to estimate the fraction of population with such access.

For income diversification, social protection, and financial inclusion, we build on global databases such as the World Bank's ASPIRE—The Atlas for Social Protection: Indicators of Resilience and Equity database—and its Global Findex (financial inclusion) database, as well as data provided in the *World Social Protection Report 2014/15* issued by the International Labour Organization (2014). Parameters related to economic inequalities are from the World Bank's World Development Indicators (WDI) database.

Adaptive social protection, in which benefits, beneficiaries, or both are expanded automatically in the aftermath of a disaster, is an efficient tool to reduce the impact of disasters on well-being (Davies et al. 2013; Hallegatte et al. 2016). It is impossible to predict the support that will be provided after a disaster, and so we assume a willingness to share the losses and proxy for the ability to provide such support, depending on institutional capacity and public financial management. To measure a country's ability to manage public finance and reallocate resources in times of crisis, we use sovereign credit ratings and data from the HFA on contingent finance, the existence of plans for emergency responses, and social protection scale-up. More in-depth analyses of the postdisaster *financing gap* have been performed using specific models, investigating the various mechanisms available to finance postdisaster actions, including budget reallocation, domestic and international borrowing, and specific instruments such as catastrophe bonds, insurance contracts, and reserve funds (Cardenas et al. 2007; Hochrainer-Stigler et al. 2014).

The sensitivity analysis presented in Hallegatte, Bangalore, and Vogt-Schilb (2016) concludes that our estimates of socioeconomic resilience and our ranking of policy options are largely independent of our hazard data—that is, the map of the likelihood of floods, storms, earthquakes, and other shocks—and of the aggregate asset exposure and vulnerability. Therefore, our results are robust to the simplification in the GAR assessment of asset losses. Meanwhile, changes in hazards due to climate change are not expected to influence the estimates of resilience, even though they will affect the risk to assets and to well-being.

Our analysis is, however, subject to major limitations that are important to keep in mind when interpreting its results. First, the analysis covers only 117 countries, including 23 developed countries, 50 International Bank for Reconstruction and Development (IBRD) countries, 33 International Development Association (IDA) countries, and 10 blend (IBRD and IDA) countries—see the list in the Appendix at the end of this report. It misses high-vulnerability countries such as small island countries in the Pacific and the Caribbean. Therefore, even though our analysis covers 92 percent of the world's population, priority actions cannot be identified in some of the most vulnerable places on the planet.

Second, we cannot include drought risk in the analysis, and more generally any slow-onset event. We focus on rapid-onset events such as floods and windstorms that inflict damage over a short timeframe. And for all hazards, we do not take into account the impacts through higher food prices or food insecurity. Including drought and food security in this framework is an obvious priority for follow-up work.

In all countries, the impacts of natural disasters on well-being are larger than asset losses

We assess the resilience of 117 countries to natural disasters by calculating the ratio of expected asset losses to expected well-being losses. All the results of our assessment are reproduced in the appendix to this report.

Resilience averages 63 percent across the sample, ranging from 25 percent in Guatemala to 81 percent in Denmark. Resilience in Benin is 50 percent, which means that $1 of asset losses in Benin has the same impact on well-being as a reduction in Benin's national consumption of $2. According to the GAR analysis, risk to assets—that is, the annual average of asset losses in countries—averages 0.63 percent of GDP, ranging from 0.005 percent in Denmark to 4.5 percent in the Philippines. As for the risk to well-being—that is, the equivalent loss in consumption—this risk averages 1.1 percent of GDP across our sample, ranging from 0.006 percent in Denmark to 6.5 percent in the Philippines.

Over the 117 countries covered, asset losses from natural disasters total $327 billion a year. Because disaster losses are concentrated in a fraction of the population and are imperfectly shared, and because they affect more poor people, who have a limited ability to cope with them, we estimate that losses in terms of well-being are equivalent to a loss of consumption that is 1.6 times larger than asset losses, about $520 billion a year. On average, then, each time a disaster causes a $1 loss in the world, the impact on well-being is worth $1.60. Globally, poor people are disproportionately affected by these losses: people in the bottom 20 percent experience only 11 percent of total asset losses but 47 percent of well-being losses. Thus poor people experience asset losses that are only half of the average but well-being losses that are more than twice as large.

Maps 4.1, 4.2, and 4.3 show our estimates of the risk to assets, socioeconomic resilience, and the risk to well-being, respectively. As visible in Maps 4.1 and 4.3, and in figure 4.4, the risk to assets and to well-being, expressed as a percentage of GDP, decreases with a country's income, and this result is very consistent with the evidence reviewed in chapter 2. Indeed, the level of protection against floods is much higher in rich countries thanks to land-use plans and infrastructure such as dikes and sea walls, as already shown in figure 2.1. In addition, infrastructure, buildings, and other assets are much less vulnerable in rich countries. Finally, early warning systems in developed countries make it possible to reduce asset losses by, for example, moving vehicles out of flood zones and safely interrupting industrial processes.

Map 4.1: Risk to assets depends on the hazard, exposure, and asset vulnerability

Risk to assets as percent of GDP per year, 117 countries

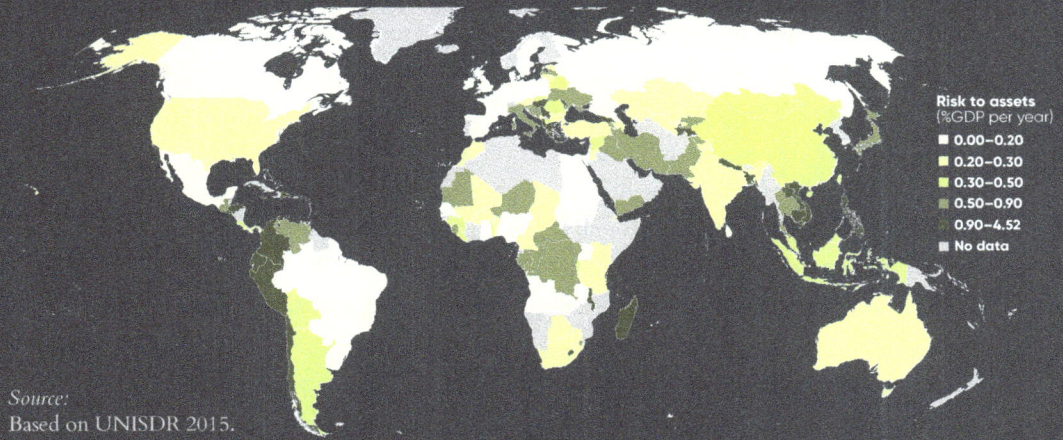

Risk to assets
(%GDP per year)
- 0.00–0.20
- 0.20–0.30
- 0.30–0.50
- 0.50–0.90
- 0.90–4.52
- No data

Source:
Based on UNISDR 2015.

Map 4.2: Socioeconomic resilience measures the ability of a population to cope with asset losses

Socioeconomic resilience (percent), 117 countries

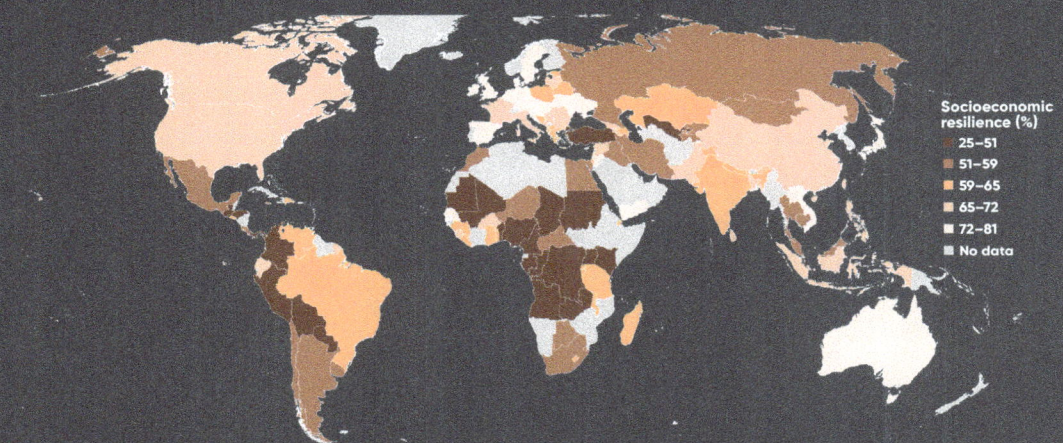

Socioeconomic resilience (%)
- 25–51
- 51–59
- 59–65
- 65–72
- 72–81
- No data

Map 4.3: Risk to well-being combines hazard, exposure, asset vulnerability, and socioeconomic resilience

Risk to well-being as percent of GDP per year, 117 countries

Risk to well-being
(% of GDP per year)
- 0.00–0.30
- 0.30–0.50
- 0.50–0.80
- 0.80–1.50
- 1.50–6.55
- No data

Figure 4.4b shows that, overall, resilience grows with GDP per capita. The fact that rich countries are more resilient than poor countries is not a surprise. Rich countries tend to have lower inequality, better access to finance for the poor, much better social protection, and a greater ability to provide those affected by a disaster with support. Resilience varies across countries of similar wealth because well-being depends on a multitude of factors, including preexisting inequality and safety nets to reduce the instantaneous impacts of a disaster. This finding suggests that all countries, regardless of their geography or income level, can act to reduce risk by increasing resilience.

Figure 4.4: Risk to well-being tends to decrease with income, as a result of lower risk to assets and higher resilience

Risk to assets, socio-economic resilience, and risk to well-being by GDP per capita, 117 countries

Source: World Bank estimates

The country with the lowest socioeconomic resilience in our sample is Guatemala at 25 percent (that is, $1 in asset losses is equivalent to a $4 reduction in national income). This finding stems from the combination of high inequality (the bottom 20 percent receives only 3.8 percent of national income), a large vulnerability differential between the poor and the nonpoor (poor people are almost six times as vulnerable as nonpoor people, one of the largest gaps in the sample), and a relatively low level of social protection and access to finance for the poor and nonpoor.

Figure 4.4

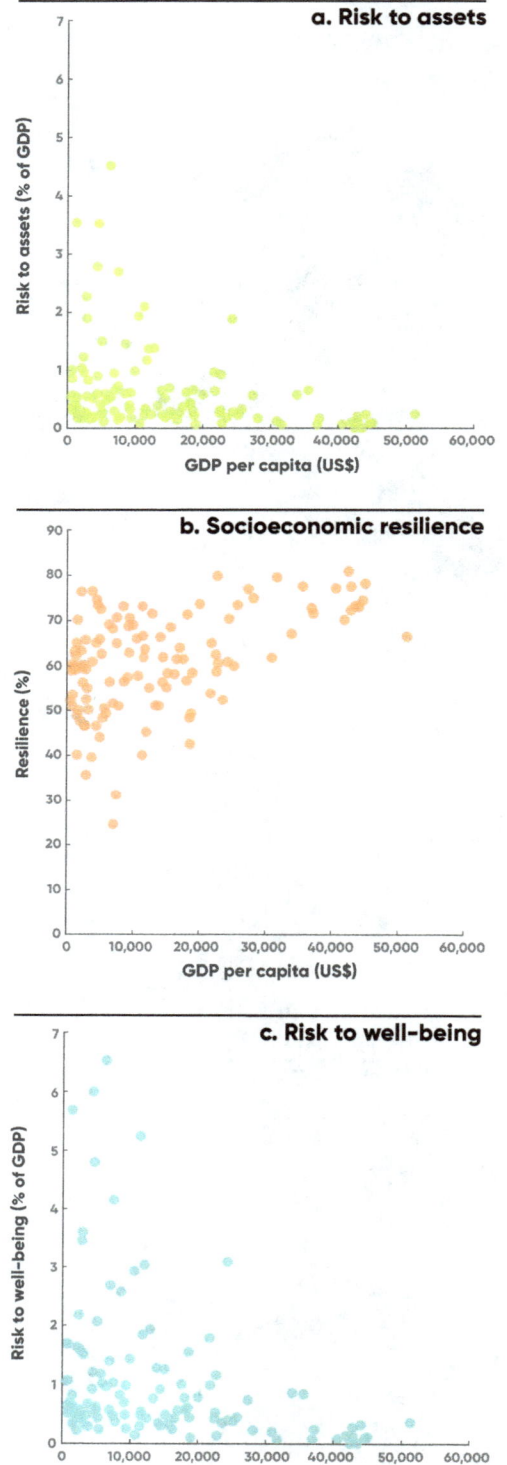

a. Risk to assets

b. Socioeconomic resilience

c. Risk to well-being

The country with the highest socioeconomic resilience is Denmark at 81 percent (that is, well-being losses are only 25 percent larger than asset losses). This high resilience is mostly attributable to relatively low inequality (the income share of the bottom 20 percent is 9.1 percent) and large transfers from social protection, especially for the bottom 20 percent (poor people receive 68 percent of their income from transfers).

A few countries with relatively low income levels also have high resilience. The high levels of resilience of Senegal (76 percent) stem from the distribution of risk across the poor and nonpoor. In Senegal, poor people are less exposed to floods than the nonpoor, and floods are the most important hazard. Also, the buildings are relatively homogeneous, and therefore the vulnerability of the assets of the poor and nonpoor is similar. As a result, poor people—who are less able to cope with asset losses—lose relatively fewer assets than nonpoor people in these countries, reducing the impact of disasters on well-being. However, when comparing the resilience of a country such as Senegal and Germany (both about 76 percent), one must keep in mind the difference in average income. Although $100 in asset losses is equivalent to about $130 in aggregate consumption losses in the two countries, $130 represents different shares of income in the two countries—more than 40 days of average income in Senegal, compared with a little more than a day's income in Germany.

Interestingly, resilience is not correlated with the risk to assets, suggesting that countries did not build their socioeconomic resilience in response to asset risks. The reason is that many drivers of resilience are socioeconomic conditions that are outside the domain of traditional disaster risk management, which focuses on asset losses. No country has ever decided to reduce income inequality because of high exposure to natural hazards, even though inequality is a major driver of socioeconomic resilience.

Reducing poverty increases well-being, but because it increases wealth and the asset stock, it also increases the asset losses from natural disasters. Many studies have looked at the effect of GDP growth on disaster losses, using regression or normalization techniques to separate the effect of growth from other drivers of disaster risk (Barredo 2009; Mendelsohn et al. 2012; Pielke et al. 2008; Simmons, Sutter, and Pielke 2012). They all conclude that losses increase with income, even though it is still debated whether disaster losses increase more slowly than income (and thus whether disaster losses decrease or increase over time when expressed in percentage of GDP).

Our analysis suggests that even if it increases asset losses, poverty reduction also increases global resilience so that well-being losses are reduced. Increasing the wealth of poor people by 10 percent in our model increases global asset losses by $3 billion a year (a 1 percent increase), but increases resilience by 1 percent (0.6 percentage point). The net effect is a $500 million *reduction* in the well-being losses due to disaster. Thus poverty reduction not only increases average well-being, but also reduces the loss of well-being from natural disasters.

Our estimate captures only partially the many dimensions of resilience

Socioeconomic resilience as used here remains an imperfect metric in the sense that it does not include all the dimensions discussed in the resilience field (Barrett and Constas 2014; Engle et al. 2013; Keating et al. 2014; Rose and Krausman 2013). Our framework looks at socioeconomic resilience, but it disregards direct human and welfare effects such as death, injuries, and psychological impacts (see box 4.2); cultural and heritage losses such as the destruction of historical assets); and social and political destabilization and environmental degradation such as when disasters affect industrial facilities and create local pollution. The framework proposed here is for socioeconomic resilience, not for a broader concept of resilience.

We have disregarded the impacts of natural disasters on natural capital, in spite of their importance to the income of poor populations across the world (Angelsen and Dokken 2015) through their effects on soils (through salinization or erosion), fish stocks, and trees, among other things. However, in some places floods have positive impacts on agricultural productivity by supplying nutrients. Including natural capital in the assessment would meet many data-related issues on the local importance of natural capital in income and on the vulnerability of natural capital to floods and other disasters.

Meanwhile, because of data limitations we use income and consumption per household, assuming that resources are well distributed within each household. As a result, we cannot account for the consequences of pre-existing within-household inequality or the impact of differentiated disaster impacts across people, especially for children, the elderly, and, in some cases, women (see chapter 2). Introducing gender inequality and the higher vulnerability of some groups would affect our measure of resilience and well-being losses. Doing so, however, would require intrahousehold data that are much more detailed than those currently available.

As for other factors, the ability of individual firms to cope with a shock and continue to produce in the aftermath of a disaster—the *static resilience* of Rose (2009)—depends on many factors that could be included in the analysis. Various methodologies have been proposed to assess these parameters using input-output or general equilibrium

DISASTERS KILL AND MAIM, ESPECIALLY POOR PEOPLE

Between 2005 and 2014, the database EM-DAT recorded 6,311 disasters that killed 839,342 people.[3] In 2008 and 2010, more than 200,000 people died from disasters, mostly from Cyclone Nargis in Myanmar in 2008 and the earthquake in Haiti in 2010. Also, over the period 2005–14 almost 2 million people were affected by natural disasters, most of them in Asia, followed by Africa. Most of the lives lost were in low-income countries. Between 1980 and 2011, low-income countries experienced 9 percent of recorded disasters but 48 percent of the deaths (Rentschler 2013). And, as already noted, injuries and fatalities have secondary impacts, especially for the other members of a household who may fall into poverty as a result (Krishna 2007).

Fatalities represent only part of the noneconomic impacts of disasters, as sadly illustrated by their psychological consequences. In Nicaragua, a study of adolescents conducted six months after Hurricane Mitch struck the country in 1998 uncovered instances of post-traumatic stress disorder (PTSD), stress, and depression, particularly among those in the most affected communities and those who experienced a death in the household (Goenjian et al. 2001). In Sri Lanka, children between the ages of 8 and 14 in areas affected by the 2004 tsunami had rates of PTSD ranging from 14 to 39 percent within a month of the event (Neuner et al. 2006). These trends can lead to chronic distress and a higher incidence of suicide (Hanigan et al. 2012; Keshavarz et al. 2013). Psychological resilience is influenced by multiple factors, including socioeconomic ones such as income, social support, and education level (see Bonanno et al. 2007), that could be included in the measurement of socioeconomic resilience.

In an important complement to this analysis, Noy (2016) provides a measure of the impact of disasters by calculating the number of life-years lost from them (including mortality, injuries, and other negative impacts on the health of the affected people) and the secondary effect of economic losses. He estimates that over the period 1980–2012 disasters led on average to the loss of 42 million life-years per year, a number close to the global incidence of tuberculosis in 2012. These losses are particularly large in Asia—even considering the share of population living in the region—and in low- and middle-income countries. Including these impacts within our framework is an obvious next step, but it will require additional work.

>>>

BOX 4.3

MULTIPLE INDICATORS FOR NATURAL HAZARDS AND CLIMATE CHANGE RISKS ARE NOW AVAILABLE

In recent years, indicators that measure the vulnerability of countries to natural hazards or climate change have multiplied. Most of these indicators are a weighted or unweighted combination of available indicators measuring different components of risk, resilience, or vulnerability. Examples are the following:

Joint Research Centre, European Commission—InfoRM. InfoRM, released in 2015, measures the risk of humanitarian crisis and disasters and how the conditions that lead to them affect sustainable development. Risk is calculated as the combination of three equally weighted components: (1) hazard and exposure, (2) vulnerability, and (3) lack of coping capacity.

ND-GAIN Index. The ND-Gain score measures a country's preparedness for climate change, including but going beyond natural hazards, and depends on its readiness and vulnerability. Vulnerability is measured by assessing a country's exposure, sensitivity, and capacity to adapt to the negative effects of climate change, looking at six sectors: food, water, health, ecosystem services, human habitat, and infrastructure. Readiness is measured by assessing a country's ability to leverage investments and convert them into adaptation actions, looking at three components: economic readiness, governance readiness, and social readiness.

OECD—Guidelines for Resilience Systems Analysis. The Organisation for Economic Co-operation and Development (OECD) has completed a how-to guide to a Resilience Analysis Tool, which has been piloted in three countries. This tool allows users to design roadmaps for boosting resilience in a system, community, or state. Indicators are based on the status of assets identified for resilience, with the type/status of assets context-specific (OECD 2014).

GIZ—Germany's development agency, GIZ, has assembled a Vulnerability Assessment Sourcebook, which provides guidelines for developing vulnerability indexes and for using this index to measure changes over time (GIZ 2014).

IDB—Disaster Indicators. The Inter-American Development Bank (IDB) has developed several indicators, including the Disaster Deficit Index (DDI), Local Disaster Index (LDI), Prevalent Vulnerability Index (PVI), Risk Management Index (RMI), and Index of Governance and Public Policy for Disaster Risk Management (iGOPP). These indicators provide, in particular, measures of the institutional capacity in disaster risk management.

Zurich Flood Resilience Alliance—Measuring Community Resilience. Zurich Bank, along with the International Institute for Applied Systems Analysis (IIASA), Wharton School of the University of Pennsylvania, the nongovernmental organization Practical Action, and the Red Cross, have joined a project to estimate the resilience of communities in Nepal, Bangladesh, and Peru.

World Development Report 2014: Risk and Opportunity— Indicator of Risk Preparedness. An indicator of risk preparedness was developed in conjunction with the World Bank's World Development Report 2014. The indicator comprises measures of assets and services across four categories: human capital, physical and financial assets, social support, and state support (World Bank 2013).

Center for Global Development—Vulnerability to Climate Change Index. This index provides an accounting of climate change vulnerability by developing a Climate Drivers Index for 233 states. The index quantifies vulnerability to climate change from (1) weather-related disasters, (2) a rise in sea level, and (3) reduced agricultural productivity. This Climate Drivers Index is also combined with data on governance and per capita income to incorporate measures of resilience and with data on project effectiveness within countries. Wheeler (2011) reports on the methodology.

DARA—Climate Vulnerability Monitor. This monitor assesses the impact of climate change in 184 countries. Specifically, it assesses socioeconomic vulnerability, covering four impact areas: (1) habitat change, (2) health impact, (3) industry stress, and (4) environmental disasters.

UN University and University of Bonn—World Risk Index. This index measures the vulnerability of 171 countries to natural disasters. It is composed of four main indicators: (1) exposure to natural hazards; (2) susceptibility, which depends on socioeconomic conditions; (3) coping capacity, which depends on preparedness, governance, and security; and (4) adaptive capacity related to future natural events.

GermanWatch—Global Climate Risk Index. The Global Climate Risk Index, published annually, analyzes to what extent countries have been affected by weather-related losses, including storms, floods, and heat waves. The index is populated with data from Munich Re's NatCatSERVICE and the International Monetary Fund, among other sources.

models (Hallegatte 2014; Rose and Wei 2013; Santos and Haimes 2004) or explicit modeling of supply chains (Battiston et al. 2007; Henriet, Hallegatte, and Tabourier 2012). Furthermore, our framework does not address the ability to "build back better" after a disaster and the possibility of reconstruction that will lead to an improved situation. It also takes the current exposure and vulnerability as a given, without accounting for how behaviors and investments would react to a change in the level of risk (chapter 3).

Other measures of resilience could usefully complement our approach with different methodologies or objectives (for example, some methodologies give more weight to institutional factors; others account for community-level characteristics)—see box 4.3 and a review in Noy and Yonson (2016). The main difference between our approach and other indicators is that we build on a simple model of the impacts of natural disasters on well-being, which provides a way of combining and aggregating the many drivers of resilience. As a result, the most important drivers of resilience will differ country by country (see chapter 7), while other indicators give the same weights to various subindicators in every country. Hallegatte, Bangalore, and Vogt-Schilb (forthcoming) compare our results with a few other available indicators.

Resilience can also be measured at the provincial level: Vietnam

Our approach can be applied on different geographical scales such as at the provincial level. Consider Vietnam, a country in which the natural risks are high and poverty is very heterogeneous. Those geographically targeting public investments in flood management, for example, could usefully consider the level of risk (how often is a province affected by floods?) and the level of socioeconomic vulnerability (where are people most negatively affected by floods?).

One option is to classify each district's poverty headcount rate and flood exposure into three categories (low, medium, and high) and map the results, such as in map 4.4. The results suggest that areas of the Northern Mountains and the Mekong Delta have districts with high poverty and high risk of floods (darkest shade of brown).

Such an analysis is useful, but, because it provides two dimensions without a method for aggregating them, it does not help balance action in places where people are more vulnerable and in places where floods are more frequent or intense.

Map 4.4: Some districts of Vietnam combine high exposure and high poverty

Overlay of poverty and flood exposure at district level, 25-year return period flood with climate change, Vietnam

Source: Bangalore, Smith, and Veldkamp 2016.

To integrate these two dimensions, we calculated the risk to assets and the risk to well-being from floods in the provinces of Vietnam. In calculating the risk to well-being, we accounted for the differences among provinces in household characteristics such as average income, diversification of income sources, and access to social protection.

The results are presented in map 4.5. Panel a shows the risk to assets from floods, panel

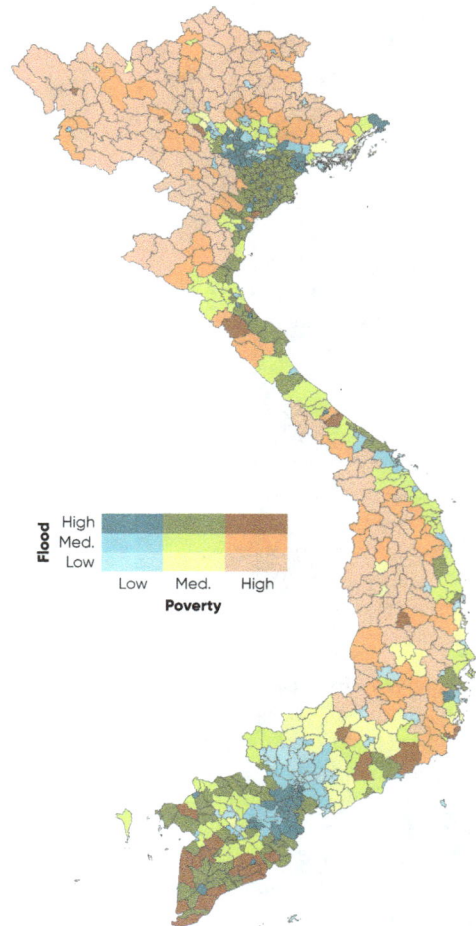

b the socioeconomic resilience, and panel c the resulting risk to well-being. The areas in which risk to well-being is higher match those with high floods and poverty levels in map 4.4. The value of the resilience analysis is that it combines assessment of hazard and social vulnerability in a consistent framework that can then be used to derive policy recommendations. For example, this analysis suggests that the Northern Mountains and the Mekong Delta have similar levels of risk to well-being, but for different reasons. The Northern Mountains have mostly a resilience issue, with high poverty and little ability to cope with shocks, resulting in high well-being losses even from low asset losses, whereas the Mekong Delta (in the south) is a high flood risk area where lack of resilience magnifies the effects on well-being. Box 5.3 in the next chapter shows how the resilience estimates can be used in practice to target investments in disaster risk management.

Map 4.5: Risk to well-being combines physical exposure and vulnerability with socioeconomic characteristics

Risk to assets and well-being (percent of GDP per year) and socioeconomic resilience (percent), Vietnam

*Source: W*orld Bank estimates.

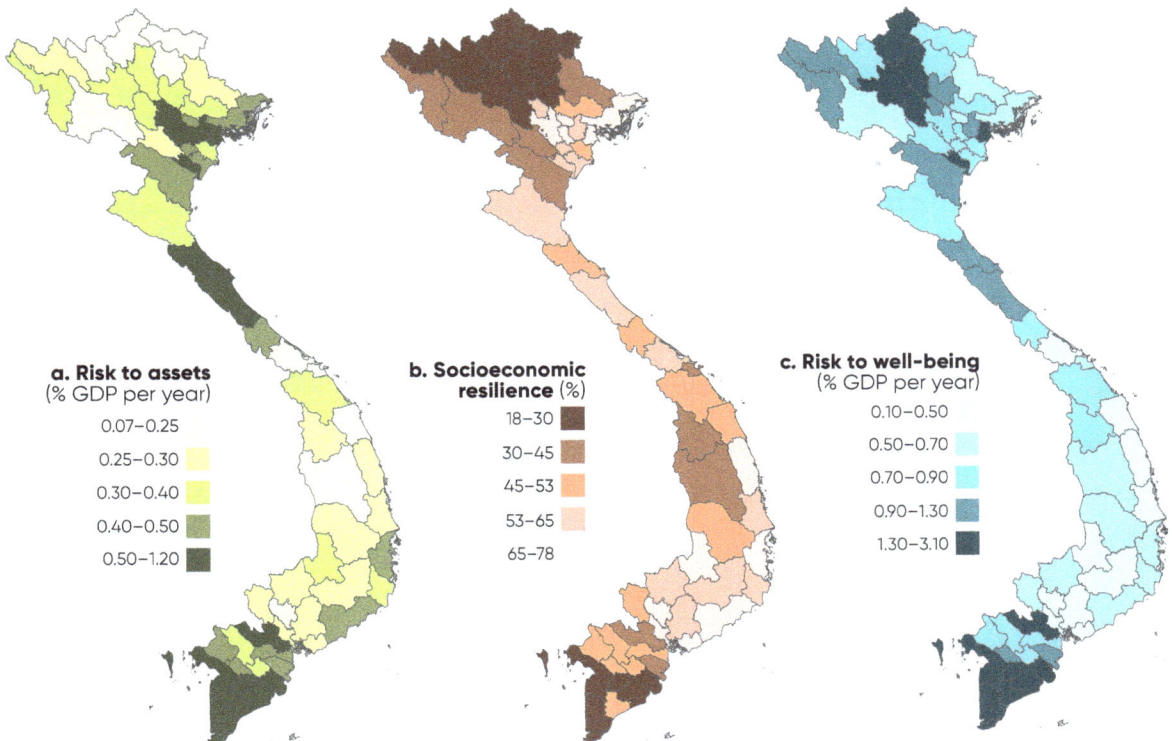

a. Risk to assets
(% GDP per year)

0.07–0.25
0.25–0.30
0.30–0.40
0.40–0.50
0.50–1.20

b. Socioeconomic resilience (%)

18–30
30–45
45–53
53–65
65–78

c. Risk to well-being
(% GDP per year)

0.10–0.50
0.50–0.70
0.70–0.90
0.90–1.30
1.30–3.10

In summary, then, we have proposed a tool to estimate the risk created by natural hazards in countries—or provinces—accounting not only for the hazard, exposure, and vulnerability, but also for the ability of the population to cope with asset losses, which we refer to as socioeconomic resilience. The analysis concludes that disregarding distributional impacts and the specific vulnerability of poor people—for example, by using total asset losses as a metric for disaster impacts— leads to a large underestimation of the importance of natural disasters. Chapter 5 will mobilize this evaluation framework to identify priorities for action in each of the 117 countries in our study. It describes the benefits, in terms of avoided asset and well-being losses, that various measures could generate.

NOTES

1. Sometimes, losses at the national level are not negligible. For example, the island of Grenada lost 200 percent of its gross domestic product, GDP, to Hurricane Ivan in 2004. In these cases, diversification at the national level is less effective at mitigating income losses.

2. Average annual losses are slightly higher than the ones published in the 2015 GAR report because we used revised estimates of the stock of capital. It deviates from observations of annual losses because the model is imperfect, but also because average annual losses include the average losses from low-probability, high-impact events that have not occurred within the last decades and the under-reported losses from high-probability, low-impact events.

3. The International Disasters Database (http://www.emdat.be) is maintained by the Centre pour la Recherche sur l'Epidemiologie des Desastre at the School of Public Health of Catholic University of Louvain.

REFERENCES

Angelsen, A., and T. Dokken. 2015. "Environmental Reliance, Climate Exposure, and Vulnerability: A Cross-Section Analysis of Structural and Stochastic Poverty." Policy Research Working Paper 7474, World Bank, Washington, DC.

Arrow, K. J. 1965. *"The Theory of Risk Aversion." Aspects of the Theory of Risk Bearing.* Helsinki: Yrjo Jahnssonin Saatio. Reprinted in *Essays in the Theory of Risk Bearing.* Chicago: Markham, 1971.

Bangalore, M., A. Smith, and T. Veldkamp. 2016. "Exposure to Floods, Climate Change, and Poverty in Vietnam." Policy Research Working Paper 7765, World Bank, Washington, DC.

Barredo, J. 2009. "Normalised Flood Losses in Europe: 1970–2006." *Natural Hazards and Earth System Sciences* 9: 97–104.

Barrett, C. B., and M. A. Constas. 2014. "Toward a Theory of Resilience for International Development Applications." *Proceedings of the National Academy of Sciences* 111: 14625–30.

Barrett, C. B., T. Reardon, and P. Webb. 2001. "Non-agricultural Income Diversification and Household Livelihood Strategies in Rural Africa: Concepts, Dynamics and Policy Implications." *Food Policy* 26: 315–31.

Battiston, S., D. Delli Gatti, M. Gallegati, B. Greenwald, and J. E. Stiglitz. 2007. "Credit Chains and Bankruptcy Propagation in Production Networks." *Journal of Economic Dynamics and Control* 31: 2061–84.

Bonanno, G. A., S. Galea, A. Bucciarelli, and D. Vlahov. 2007. "What Predicts Psychological Resilience after Disaster? The Role of Demographics, Resources, and Life Stress." *Journal of Consulting and Clinical Psychology* 75 (5): 671.

Cardenas, V., S. Hochrainer, R. Mechler, G. Pflug, and J. Linnerooth-Bayer. 2007. "Sovereign Financial Disaster Risk Management: The Case of Mexico." *Environmental Hazards* 7: 40–53.

Davies, M., C. Béné, A. Arnall, T. Tanner, A. Newsham, and C. Coirolo. 2013. "Promoting Resilient Livelihoods through Adaptive Social Protection: Lessons from 124 Programmes in South Asia." *Development Policy Review* 31: 27–58.

Engle, N. L., A. de Bremond, E. L. Malone, and R. H. Moss. 2013. "Towards a Resilience Indicator Framework for Making Climate-Change Adaptation Decisions." *Mitigation and Adaptation Strategies for Global Change* 19: 1295–1312.

Fleurbaey, M., and P. J. Hammond. 2004. "Interpersonally Comparable Utility." In *Handbook of Utility Theory*, edited by S. Barberà, P. J. Hammond, and C. Seidl, 1179–1285. New York: Springer.

G7 (Group of 7). 2015. "Leaders' Declaration G7 Summit Germany." http://www.international.gc.ca/g8/g7_germany_declaration-g7_allemagne_declaration.aspx?lang=eng.

GIZ. 2014. *The Vulnerability Sourcebook: Concept and Guidelines for Standardised Vulnerability Assessments.* Berlin: GIZ.

Goenjian, A. K., L. Molina, A. M. Steinberg, L. A. Fairbanks, M. L. Alvarez, H. A. Goenjian, and R. S. Pynoos. 2001. "Posttraumatic Stress and Depressive Reactions among Nicaraguan Adolescents after Hurricane Mitch." *American Journal of Psychiatry* 158 (5): 788–94.

Hallegatte, S. 2012. "A Cost Effective Solution to Reduce Disaster Losses in Developing Countries: Hydro-Meteorological Services, Early Warning, and Evacuation." Policy Research Working Paper 6058, World Bank, Washington, DC.

———. 2014. "Modeling the Role of Inventories and Heterogeneity in the Assessment of the Economic Costs of Natural Disasters." *Risk Analysis* 34: 152–67.

Hallegatte, S., M. Bangalore, L. Bonzanigo, M. Fay, T. Kane, U. Narloch, J. Rozenberg et al. 2016. *Shock Waves: Managing the Impacts of Climate Change on Poverty.* Climate Change and Development Series. Washington, DC: World Bank.

Hallegatte, S., M. Bangalore, and A. Vogt-Schilb. 2016. "Assessing Socioeconomic Resilience to Floods in 90 Countries." Policy Research Working Paper 7663, World Bank, Washington, DC.

———. Forthcoming. "Socioeconomic Resilience to Multiple Hazards—An Assessment in 117 Countries." Background paper prepared for this report, World Bank, Washington, DC.

Hallegatte, S., C. Green, R. J. Nicholls, and J. Corfee-Morlot. 2013. "Future Flood Losses in Major Coastal Cities." *Nature Climate Change* 3: 802–6. doi:10.1038/nclimate1979.

Hallegatte, S., and A. Vogt-Schilb. Forthcoming. "Are Losses from Natural Disasters More Than Just Asset Losses? The Role of Capital Aggregation, Sector Interactions, and Investment Behaviors." Background paper prepared for this report, World Bank, Washington, DC.

Hanigan, I. C., C. D. Butler, P. N. Kokic, and M. F. Hutchinson. 2012. "Suicide and Drought in New South Wales, Australia, 1970–2007." *Proceedings of the National Academy of Sciences* 109: 13950–55.

Harberger, A. C. 1978. "On the Use of Distributional Weights in Social Cost-Benefit Analysis." *Journal of Political Economy*, 87–120.

Henriet, F., S. Hallegatte, and L. Tabourier. 2012. "Firm-Network Characteristics and Economic Robustness to Natural Disasters." *Journal of Economic Dynamics and Control* 36: 150–67.

Hochrainer-Stigler, S., R. Mechler, G. Pflug, and K. Williges. 2014. "Funding Public Adaptation to Climate-Related Disasters. Estimates for a Global Fund." *Global Environmental Change* 25: 87–96.

International Labour Organization. 2014. *World Social Protection Report 2014/15: Building Economic Recovery, Inclusive Development and Social Justice.* Washington, DC: Brookings.

Jaiswal, K., D. Wald, and K. Porter. 2010. "A Global Building Inventory for Earthquake Loss Estimation and Risk Management." *Earthquake Spectra* 26 (3): 731–48.

Keating, A., K. Campbell, R. Mechler, E. Michel-Kerjan, J. Mochizuki, K. Howard, J. Bayer et al. 2014. "Operationalizing Resilience against Natural Disaster Risk: Opportunities, Barriers and a Way Forward." Zurich Flood Resilience Alliance.

Keshavarz, H., D. Fitzpatrick-Lewis, D. L. Streiner, R. Maureen, U. Ali, H. S. Shannon, and P. Raina. 2013. "Screening for Depression: A Systematic Review and Meta-analysis." *Canadian Medical Association Open Access Journal* 1: E159–E167.

Kreibich, H., A. H. Thieken, T. Petrow, M. Müller, and B. Merz. 2005. "Flood Loss Reduction of Private Households due to Building Precautionary Measures—Lessons Learned from the Elbe Flood in August 2002." *Natural Hazards and Earth System Sciences* 5: 117–26.

Krishna, A. 2007. "The Stages-of-Progress Methodology and Results from Five Countries." In *Reducing Global Poverty: The Case for Asset Accumulation,* edited by C. Moser, 62–79. Washington, DC: Brookings.

Kunreuther, H. 1996. "Mitigating Disaster Losses through Insurance." *Journal of Risk Uncertainty* 12: 171–87. doi:10.1007/BF00055792.

Le De, L., J. C. Gaillard, and W. Friesen. 2013. "Remittances and Disaster: A Review." *International Journal of Disaster Risk Reduction* 4: 34–43. doi:10.1016/j.ijdrr.2013.03.007.

Mendelsohn, R., K. Emanuel, S. Chonabayashi, and L. Bakkensen. 2012. "The Impact of Climate Change on Global Tropical Cyclone Damage." *Nature Climate Change* 2: 205–09. doi:10.1038/nclimate1357.

Neuner, F., E. Schauer, C. Catani, M. Ruf, and T. Elbert. 2006. "Post-tsunami Stress: A Study of Posttraumatic Stress Disorder in Children Living in Three Severely Affected Regions in Sri Lanka." *Journal of Traumatic Stress* 19: 339–47. doi:10.1002/jts.20121.

Noy, I. 2016. "A Global Comprehensive Measure of the Impact of Natural Hazards and Disasters." *Global Policy* 7 (1): 56–65.

Noy, I., and R. Yonson. 2016. "A Survey of the Theory and Measurement of Economic Vulnerability and Resilience to Natural Hazards." Working Paper Series, School of Economics and Finance, Te Kura Ohaoha Pūtea.

OECD (Organisation for Economic Co-operation and Development). 2014. *Guidelines for Resilience Systems Analysis.* Paris: OECD.

Patankar, A., and A. Patwardhan. 2016. "Estimating the Uninsured Losses due to Extreme Weather Events and Implications for Informal Sector Vulnerability: A Case Study of Mumbai, India." *Natural Hazards.* 80: 285. doi:10.1007/s11069-015-1968-3.

Pielke, R., J. Gratz, C. Landsea, D. Collins, M. Saunders, and R. Musulin. 2008. "Normalized Hurricane Damage in the United States: 1900–2005." *Natural Hazards Review* 9: 29–42. doi:10.1061/(ASCE)1527-6988(2008)9:1(29).

Ranger, N., S. Hallegatte, S. Bhattacharya, M. Bachu, S. Priya, K. Dhore, F. Rafique et al. 2011. "An Assessment of the Potential Impact of Climate Change on Flood Risk in Mumbai." *Climate Change* 104: 139–67.

Rentschler, J. E. 2013. "Why Resilience Matters: The Poverty Impacts of Disasters." Policy Research Working Paper 6699, World Bank, Washington, DC.

Rose, A. 2009. "Economic Resilience to Disasters." CARRI Research Report 8, Community and Regional Resilience Institute.

Rose, A., and E. Krausmann. 2013. "An Economic Framework for the Development of a Resilience Index for Business Recovery." *International Journal of Disaster Risk Reduction* 5:73–83.

Rose, A., and D. Wei. 2013. "Estimating the Economic Consequences of a Port Shutdown: The Special Role of Resilience." *Economic Systems Research* 25: 212–32.

Santos, J. R., and Y. Y. Haimes. 2004. "Modeling the Demand Reduction Input-Output (I-O) Inoperability due to Terrorism of Interconnected Infrastructures." *Risk Analysis* 24: 1437–51.

Siegel, P., and A. de la Fuente. 2010. "Mainstreaming Natural Disaster Risk Management into Social Protection Policies (and Vice Versa) in Latin America and the Caribbean." *Well-Being and Social Policy* 6: 131–59.

Simmons, K. M., D. Sutter, and R. Pielke. 2012. "Normalized Tornado Damage in the United States: 1950–2011." *Environmental Hazards* 1–16.

Skoufias, E. 2003. "Economic Crises and Natural Disasters: Coping Strategies and Policy Implications." *World Developoment, Economic Crises, Natural Disasters, and Poverty* 31: 1087–1102. doi:10.1016/S0305-750X(03)00069-X.

Surminski, S., L. M. Bouwer, and J. Linnerooth-Bayer. 2016. "How Insurance Can Support Climate Resilience." *Nature Climate Change* 6: 333–34. doi:10.1038/nclimate2979.

UNISDR (United Nations Office for Disaster Risk Reduction). 2015. *United Nations Global Assessment Report on Disaster Risk Reduction.* Geneva: UNISDR.

Wheeler, D. 2011. "Quantifying Vulnerability to Climate Change: Implications for Adaptation Assistance." Working Paper (240), Center for Global Development, London.

Winsemius, H., B. Jongman, T. Veldkamp, S. Hallegatte, M. Bangalore, and P. J. Ward. 2015. "Disaster Risk, Climate Change, and Poverty: Assessing the Global Exposure of Poor People to Floods and Droughts." Policy Research Working Paper 7480, World Bank, Washington, DC.

World Bank. 2013. *World Development Report 2014: Risk and Opportunity—Managing Risk for Development.* Washington, DC: World Bank.

5 AVOIDING DISASTERS

> **Well-being losses can be mitigated by reducing asset losses.**

As we have now described, poverty is one of the major drivers of vulnerability to natural disasters (chapter 2), and in turn natural disasters are an obstacle to the reduction of poverty and to development (chapter 3). In chapter 4, we proposed a "resilience tool" to assess the resilience and vulnerability of a population to a natural disaster based on what we know about a household's poverty, localization, asset portfolio, and access to risk management tools. The natural next step, then, is to use this tool to explore how to reduce the burden of disasters on well-being. To this end, this chapter and the ones that follow identify priorities for action, quantify the benefits to be expected from them, and assess in which countries these priorities might prove to be the most efficient.

Considering the simplifications required for a global analysis, the priorities identified here are not a definitive answer to what needs to be done. What we do offer is a starting point for engagement with decision and policy makers, a guide to the design of more in-depth country- or local-level analyses, and an integrated framework to discuss interventions in very different domains. But making the final decision on any given intervention would require more in-depth analysis than what is proposed here.

Identification of the promising policy options can guide the development of a consistent policy package to reduce welfare losses from natural disasters. Such a package would bring together tools that are usually designed by very different actors and agencies that do not always coordinate their decisions on things such as land-use plans, building norms, social protection, and early warning systems. Risk management is about creating a consistent policy package using these different tools, ensuring that they complement each other and create synergies. Designing a cost-effective package requires investigating how these tools interact. The efficiency of social protection depends on the asset vulnerability of poor people; the cost of insurance depends on the protection provided by hard infrastructure such as dikes and drainage systems; and postdisaster support is more important when land-use plans cannot be enforced.

This chapter begins by looking at measures to cut back on asset losses—that is, reducing exposure or asset vulnerability. Its main conclusion is that there is a very large potential to reduce the asset losses due to disasters—from investments in infrastructure and enactment of building regulations to ecosystem conservation and early warning systems. But there is a trade-off between monetary and well-being gains: while actions targeting richer people would prevent larger losses of asset and deliver larger monetary benefits, protecting poor people would deliver higher benefits in terms of well-being. Our analysis provides an evaluation tool to ensure that investments in disaster risk management are not only directed toward the highest value assets (and toward the wealthiest regions and individuals), but also protect the poor and vulnerable and maximize the well-being gains that can be obtained with a given budget.

Several policies can reduce exposure to disasters

The option most often discussed to reduce losses from natural disasters is to ensure that people do not live where they could be affected by disasters such as floods or landslides. Of course, this option is different for different hazards with different spatial scales. For hurricane winds, drought, and earthquakes, the large spatial scale of the events makes it difficult to avoid any development in areas at risk. For cities or regions located along fault lines or hurricane-prone coastlines, development in at-risk areas is simply unavoidable. But there are small-scale differences in soil characteristics that make some areas especially at risk of landslides and earthquakes, and development can be prevented there. Furthermore, flood and landslide risks are highly heterogeneous and concentrated, and it is possible to develop any city or region while avoiding building in areas with high levels of these risks. In those cases, the questions are which areas have acceptable levels of risk, and what kinds of regulations and policies will ensure that development does not occur outside these areas?

Land-use and urbanization plans need to be risk-sensitive. Land-use regulations can help by ensuring that new development occurs in places that are safe or can be easily and cheaply protected. They can also avoid unchecked urban development that leaves too little porous green space, which further increases runoff and flood risk (Lall and Deichmann 2012).

Implementing risk-based land-use plans remains challenging, however. Countries need strong institutions that can ensure that land-use plans are actually enforced. In most of the world today, risk-sensitive land-use plans face strong political economy obstacles and are only rarely enforced (World Bank 2013). One of the main obstacles is the asymmetry between the costs and benefits of risk-sensitive land-use planning. The costs of flood zoning are immediate, visible, and concentrated in the form of reduced land values for landowners and higher housing costs for tenants (Viguie and Hallegatte 2012). By contrast, the benefits are avoided losses—which nobody can see—some time in the future and for unknown people. In such a context, the opponents of flood zoning are usually vocal and well organized, whereas the beneficiaries are absent, making such policies difficult to pass and enforce (Trebilcock 2014).

One answer to these political economy issues is to frame flood zoning in a more positive way: instead of just prohibiting new development in flood zones through regulations, government and local authorities can steer development toward the safest areas through provision of infrastructure and other services. And instead of producing the usual maps of flood-prone areas, analysts could overlay maps of safe areas with maps of high-potential underdeveloped zones, which should be priorities for future investments.

Doing so would not be easy. Countries often lack the data needed to identify places that are too risky to develop or those in which development is possible provided that buildings and infrastructure are built according to strict rules. Unfortunately, access to risk information still varies greatly and is quite limited in low-income environments. To address this issue, the World Bank and the Global Facility for Disaster Reduction and Recovery (GFDRR) is investing in risk information. The GFDRR's Open Data for Resilience Initiative supports the creation of GeoNode, a web-based open source platform that makes it easier to develop, share, manage, and publish geospatial data (http://www.geonode.org). More recently, the ThinkHazard! tool was released; it allows professionals and the public to access easy-to-understand information about the various hazards in their country, province, or city (see box 5.1). Such initiatives can make a difference locally by making risk information freely available not only to professionals but also to the public.

Countries also need to remember that land-use regulations can have unintended consequences, particularly for poor people. Restrictive flood zoning policies can increase housing costs, making it more difficult for rural poor people to move to cities and enjoy the opportunities of an urban life such as better-paying jobs and better health care and education. Furthermore, if poor people have already settled in an area just declared uninhabitable by a zoning policy, these households may have to be resettled, with high costs for both the resettled households and the government, as evidenced in the Mekong Delta of Vietnam (Bangalore, Smith, and Veldkamp 2016). Restrictive policies can also worsen risks. In Mumbai, because of strict regulations, buildings have been held to between a fifth and a tenth of the number of floors allowed in other major cities (Lall and Deichmann 2012). The resulting low-rise topography contributes to land scarcity, higher housing prices, and slum formation, including in flood zones.

More and better infrastructure can protect people, poor and nonpoor.
Poor people suffer from frequent disasters because they lack the type of protective infrastructure that is common in wealthier countries. As described in chapter 2, lower protection levels are one of the main reasons flood risks are higher in relative terms in poor countries than in rich ones. And the difference is even more obvious within countries, or within cities. For example, poor households are often exposed to recurrent floods because of lack of infrastructure, or its poor condition, especially

BOX 5.1
THINKHAZARD!: RAISING AWARENESS OF RISK LEVELS

Assessing potential disaster and climate risks is critical for development experts, project developers, planners, officials, and other decision makers. But determining those risks can be a highly technical and time-consuming process.

To make this understanding of risk more accessible and increase the resilience of projects around the world, the Global Facility for Disaster Reduction and Recovery's Innovation Lab has collaborated with partners from across academia, the private sector and with multilateral institutions to develop ThinkHazard! This new online tool provides a level of hazard—down to the district level—across eight types of natural hazards for 196 countries.

ThinkHazard! is a free open source tool that puts information in the public domain that was previously proprietary or only for expert use. It not only helps users better understand relevant climate and disaster risks, but also provides recommendations and resources to help address those risks. The open data platform means new data can be contributed by the global community, improving the tool over time.

The tool is accessible at **ThinkHazard.org**.

drainage systems. Solving this problem requires investing more, investing better, and investing for the poor.

Investing more. Governments in both developed and developing countries already struggle to finance infrastructure. Millions of people in developing countries still lack access to safe water, improved sanitation, electricity, and transport. Even beyond climate concerns, developing countries need substantially more infrastructure to grow and address poverty, inequality, and unemployment. Few data exist on how much is being spent on infrastructure, but the World Bank estimates that at least $1 trillion a year would be needed in developing countries to close the infrastructure gap, with about $100 billion for Africa alone.

And protection infrastructure can be expensive. In the Netherlands, the estimated cost of the fifth Delta Program, which is aimed at improving national flood safety and the fresh water supply, is €20 billion. The investment cost of the new protection system against floods in New Orleans—a city with less than 1 million inhabitants—is about $15 billion. Multibillion dollar projects are also under consideration in many other coastal cities. Such protection systems are so costly in part because they must meet very rigorous design and construction standards and undergo perfect maintenance. Defense failure can lead to losses that would be much larger than what would occur in the absence of protection (Hallegatte 2012b).

The problem is that infrastructure does not attract enough capital, especially in developing countries: long-term, largely illiquid investments are not perceived as attractive destinations for global capital, and many countries are simply too poor to generate domestically the needed pool of savings. Many others lack local capital markets that are sufficiently developed to transform local liquidity into the patient capital needed for longer-term investments. Furthermore, public spending is limited by a low tax base—10–20 percent of the gross domestic product (GDP) in many countries—and low debt ceilings.

For resilience investment, the challenge of attracting private capital is increased by the nature of the benefits, largely in the form of avoided losses that are difficult to monetize and transform into a financial flow.

Recommendations typically include leveraging private resources to make the most of available capital, which involves well-known steps such as improving the investment climate (making sure regulations are clear and predictable and the rule of law and property rights are enforced), developing local capital markets, and providing a pipeline of "bankable" projects (Fay et al. 2015). Official development assistance (ODA) can play a catalytic role in mobilizing additional resources, but it is constrained by donors' fiscal constraints and remains limited relative to overall needs.

Investing better. New and additional investments will reduce the long-term vulnerability of the population only if new infrastructure is designed to resist natural hazards, absorb climate change, and remain efficient in spite of changes in climatic and environmental conditions. But doing so is made difficult by the lack of data and the deep uncertainty about the likelihood of extremely unlikely events, as well as the effect of climate change on hazard distribution and frequency.

Fortunately, new methodologies have been developed to support long-term decision making in the presence of such deep uncertainty. These approaches seek to identify robust decisions—that is, those that satisfy decision makers' multiple objectives in many plausible futures and over multiple time frames (Bonzanigo and Kalra 2014; Kalra et al. 2014; Lempert et al. 2013). They help evaluate the trade-offs among the different options (using different measures of success such as economic return, number of people benefiting, and whether poor or nonpoor people are the main beneficiaries) and identify policies that reduce the vulnerability of future investments.

Often, these methodologies favor soft and flexible options over hard ones, including monitoring systems to ensure risks are systematically assessed throughout the life of a project so that solutions can be adjusted over time. They also encourage decision makers to look beyond within-sector interventions and combine prevention and reactive actions within a consistent strategy. The World Bank is piloting projects following these methodologies. They include water supply in Lima, flood risk management in Ho Chi Minh City and Colombo, hydropower investment in Nepal, and road network resilience in Peru and Nepal (see box 5.2).

Investing for the poor. When investing in risk management, decision makers have to concentrate their action where it is the most economically efficient to ensure that scarce resources generate as many benefits as possible, but also where people are the most vulnerable to ensure that benefits in terms of well-being are maximized. Consider the use of a budget to build flood protection. Facing a set of possible projects—say, dikes in multiple regions—decision makers need methodologies to select the "best" projects—that is, the projects that will deliver the most benefits. If this budget is allocated based on a cost-benefit analysis that considers only the monetary benefits, the analysis will compare the cost of possible dikes with the flood losses each dike can avoid. Projects would then be selected based on their rate of

BOX 5.2
DEEP UNCERTAINTY CAN BE MANAGED TO DESIGN MORE ROBUST INFRASTRUCTURE

LIMA, PERU. The World Bank recently helped SEDAPAL, the water utility serving Lima, Peru, ensure long-term water reliability by drawing on methods for decision making under deep uncertainty. Through extensive iteration and collaboration with SEDAPAL, the Bank used the Decision Making Under Deep Uncertainty (DMU) methodology to define an investment strategy that is robust, ensuring water reliability across as wide a range of future conditions as possible (including extreme water scarcity), while also being economically efficient. Upon completion, the study was able to help SEDAPAL realize that not all projects included in its master plan were necessary to achieve water reliability, and that it could save 25 percent (over $600 million) in investment costs. Indeed, the study revealed that SEDAPAL can start with identified no-regret investments, which the city needs no matter what the future will bring, and postpone lower-priority investments. Then as more information on feasibility, climate, and demand becomes available, SEDAPAL can adapt its strategy by following a pre-established contingency plan. The study also highlighted the need to focus future efforts on demand side management, pricing, and soft infrastructure—a refocusing that is difficult to achieve in traditional utility companies—and helped SEDAPAL gain the support of regulatory and budget agencies because of its careful analysis of alternatives.

NEPAL. The World Bank also supported evaluation of the trade-offs between robustness and reliability of hydropower investments in the Upper Arun, Nepal. Hydropower development also faces a number of uncertainties, including climate change, high sediment loads, and environmental, social, and financial risks. Investments in hydropower development must compromise between robustness to a changing and uncertain future and providing the country with sufficient energy all year long. Energy agencies often struggle to reconcile these two dimensions in their planning efforts. The World Bank supported the Nepal Energy Agency by stress testing the robustness of five different designs for a run of the river hydropower investment. It then ranked them in terms of trade-offs between dry season production and robustness. The analysis revealed that the 1,000-megawatt design was a potentially better choice than the original 335-megawatt design. The better performance during the dry season would help reduce the chances of load shedding, a particular concern of the government.

Source: Laura Bonzanigo.

return (the amount of avoided losses per $1 of construction cost). This approach, however, is likely to drive investments toward rich areas and regions, where high asset values and densities ensure that one dike can avoid large asset losses. The poorer regions are unlikely to benefit from these resources, even though floods may have a disproportional impact on well-being in these regions.

If, on the other hand, projects are selected based only on the impact of floods on the most vulnerable people, investments may take place in places where asset values and densities—and potentially population densities—are so low that the available budget will protect few people. Such an approach will also lead to protecting areas that may be better abandoned considering their low value and high level of risk.

These two extreme solutions—focusing only on economic returns or only on vulnerability—are both inappropriate. What is needed is a tool that would balance the need for economic efficiency and the imperative to protect the most vulnerable.[1]

The resilience model proposed in the previous chapter can serve as a tool for looking at this issue. Because it considers not only the loss of assets but also the consequences for consumption and well-being, it acts as a tool for an economic analysis that combines the need to invest in efficient projects and the imperative to protect the poorest. It does so by measuring the well-being effect of asset losses, accounting for preexisting inequality and income, income diversification, and coping capacity (through financial inclusion and access to social protection), so that $1 in avoided losses is valued more if it protects highly vulnerable people. If a new dike can reduce expected asset losses by $1 million a year in an area with a 50 percent resilience, then well-being benefits can be estimated as equivalent to $2 million in additional consumption. Box 5.3 illustrates how this tool could be used to target investments within a country.

It is important to protect the ecosystems that protect people

Ecosystems play an important role in protecting livelihoods against risks. Trees on steep slopes protect rural villages from landslides when heavy rains fall, and mangroves protect coastal livelihoods during storm surges (Badola and Hussain 2005; Das and Vincent 2009). Forest cover helps reduce the occurrence of drought (Bagley et al. 2013; Davidson et al. 2012). Protecting ecosystems can therefore contribute to reducing the exposure to natural disasters.

In Sri Lanka, Colombo's urban wetlands are a critical component of the city's long-term development and urban resilience. In addition to offering multiple economic

ESTIMATES OF SUBNATIONAL SOCIOECONOMIC RESILIENCE CAN BE USED TO TARGET INVESTMENTS

Those making decisions on where to invest scarce resources in disaster risk management might consider using a resilience indicator to scale a project's benefits expressed in terms of avoided asset losses.

For example, two projects in Vietnam are able to protect population and assets and reduce disaster-related asset losses, but they are competing for resources. The traditional approach would call for estimating the cost of each project, and its benefits, and selecting the project with the highest benefit-cost ratio (or the largest net present value). But as already discussed, doing so would probably lead to investments only in the richest areas of the country. An assessment of resilience can help rebalance investment toward the most vulnerable.

To simplify, let us assume that the two projects have the same cost, $5 million, and would reduce asset losses by $1 million a year. But the two projects are located in two different provinces: Binh Dinh province, which has an estimated resilience of 69 percent, and Kien Giang province, in the Mekong Delta, which has estimated resilience of 29 percent (chapter 4). The difference stems mostly from the difference in average income in the provinces, combined with differences in social protection coverage.

Because the risk to well-being is the ratio of the risk to assets to resilience, the well-being gains—expressed in an equivalent increase in annual consumption—from one project is also the ratio of the avoided asset losses to resilience. If the two projects would avoid asset losses amounting to $1 million a year, their well-being benefits are valued at $1.4 million a year in Binh Dinh ($1 million divided by 69 percent) and at $3.4 million a year in Kien Giang ($1 million divided by 29 percent). Because of the lower resilience in Kien Giang, a project delivering the same asset benefit would create much more well-being.

This well-being estimate can then be compared with the cost of the project. Instead of picking the project with the higher monetary benefit-cost ratio, one can select the project with the higher well-being gain to cost ratio.

and environmental benefits, including improved water quality and treatment capacity, biodiversity, and lower urban temperatures, the wetlands supplement standard flood mitigation instruments, such as canals and pumping stations, because of their natural water retention capacity.

In 2015 a flood risk assessment was conducted in Colombo, taking into account the deep uncertainty around the city's current hydrological conditions and vulnerabilities in order to compare the economic consequences of floods with and without Colombo's wetlands—a comparison that uses the methodology to manage uncertainty described in box 5.2. While it is impossible to predict with certainty future flood risks in the city, the study reveals that the well-being consequences of floods could exceed 1 percent of Colombo's GDP every year (which the authorities consider an intolerable level of risk) only in scenarios in which all wetlands disappear (figure 5.1).

Figure 5.1: **If wetlands disappear in Colombo, some scenarios lead to unacceptable losses, exceeding 1 percent of Colombo's GDP**

Comparison of expected annual losses (as percent of city's GDP) from floods today and in the future, assuming all wetlands have disappeared, Colombo, Sri Lanka

Source: Rozenberg et al. 2015.

Note: The figure shows the expected annual losses from floods in Colombo, based on 2013 exposure data. The cost is expressed as a percentage of Colombo's GDP. Hydrological conditions and vulnerabilities are uncertain because of lack of data, and therefore many scenarios were run combining assumptions on runoff, boundary conditions, and vulnerability of assets. Blue crosses represent different scenarios for current expected annual losses. Orange crosses represent different scenarios for expected annual losses if all wetlands disappeared. The tolerable loss threshold was defined as 1 percent of GDP.

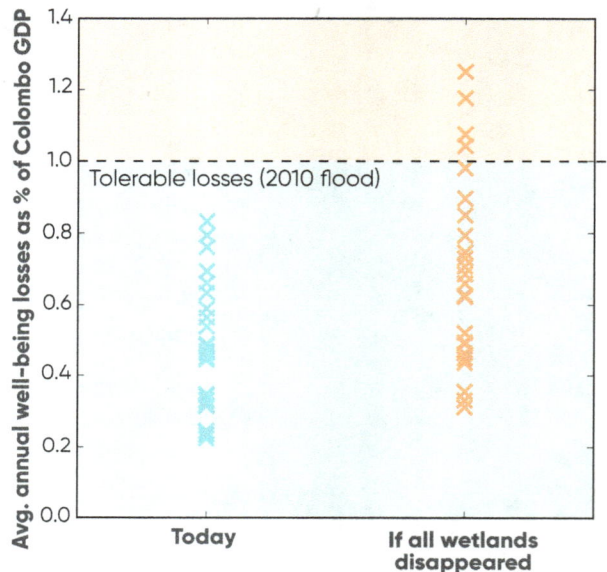

Expected annual losses (based on 2013 data)

The well-being benefits of developing the land were found to be smaller than the well-being costs of losing the wetlands in most scenarios for two reasons. First, the macroeconomic benefits from land development would be offset by higher flood losses every year. Second, middle- and high-income people benefit from land development, while poor people in Colombo suffer the most from wetland loss, exacerbating well-being costs.

Reducing exposure can offer large economic benefits

To assess the potential benefits of better land-use plans or from investments in infrastructure or ecosystems that protect the population against hazards, we consider two policy experiments, assuming that similar policies are implemented globally:

» In the first experiment, we assume a 5 percent reduction in the fraction of the population exposed to natural hazards, achieved by reducing the exposure of poor people (among the bottom 20 percent). If the entire world did so, asset losses would be reduced by about $7 billion a year (2 percent of today's asset losses), but the gain in well-being would be much larger, equivalent to a $40 billion increase in global income (a reduction by 8 percent of today's loss of well-being).

» In the second experiment, we assume the same 5 percent reduction in the fraction of the population exposed to natural hazards, but this time achieved by reducing the exposure of the nonpoor only (among the top 80 percent). In that case, because the nonpoor have so much more in assets than the poor, the avoided asset losses would be much larger than when policies target poor people: they would reach $19 billion. But the well-being gains would be smaller: they would be equivalent to a $22 billion increase in global income.

These results highlight the trade-off between monetary gains (expressed in avoided asset losses) and gains in well-being (looking at the equivalent increase in consumption). Concentrating efforts on poor people instead of the rest of the population would generate less than half of the monetary benefits, but almost twice as much in well-being gains.

It is unlikely that such gains could be realized in all countries. So where would these policies be particularly attractive? In figure 5.2, we identify the 15 countries in which reducing the exposure of poor people is most efficient to reduce the risk to well-being in absolute and in relative terms. For comparison, figure 5.3 shows the 15 countries in which it is most efficient to reduce the exposure of nonpoor people.

Panel a of figure 5.2 shows the avoided asset losses and the avoided well-being losses arising from the reduction in exposure, expressed in millions of U.S. dollars per year. When looking at the absolute numbers, one sees large economies (China, India, and the United States are in the top 10) as well as countries subject to very high risk (such as the Philippines, Colombia, and Bangladesh).

Panel b of figure 5.2 shows the same results but expressed in relative terms, as a share of the current average annual asset and well-being losses. The ranking in relative terms highlights countries in which reducing exposure is an efficient way to reduce local risk.

The impact of reducing the exposure of poor people depends on whether they are particularly vulnerable in their country—for example, reducing the exposure of the poor is more efficient in countries in which the poor live in very fragile buildings, are not well covered by social protection, and do not have access to finance. In these countries (such as Mali, Niger, or Guatemala), resilience is low. In Mali or Niger, for example, reducing the exposure of the population by 5 percent can reduce asset losses by more than 10 percent and well-being losses by 25 percent, if the action targets poor people.

The concentration of risk on poor people in these countries makes it very efficient to concentrate efforts on protecting them. Unfortunately, these countries are often also those in which reducing exposure is extremely difficult because of lack of land tenure or of institutional weakness that makes plans difficult to enforce in practice.

Figure 5.2: Large well-being losses can be avoided by reducing the exposure of poor people

Avoided asset losses and gains in well-being in absolute and relative terms from 5 percent reduction in exposure, poor people only

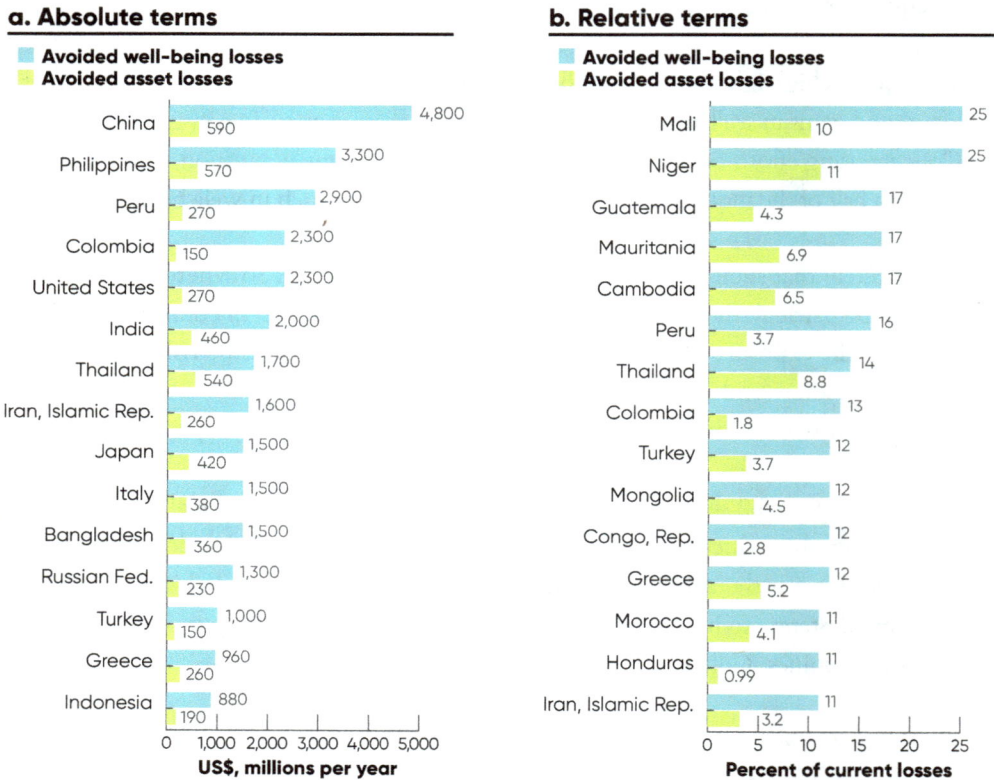

a. Absolute terms

- Avoided well-being losses
- Avoided asset losses

Country	Avoided well-being losses	Avoided asset losses
China	4,800	590
Philippines	3,300	570
Peru	2,900	270
Colombia	2,300	150
United States	2,300	270
India	2,000	460
Thailand	1,700	540
Iran, Islamic Rep.	1,600	260
Japan	1,500	420
Italy	1,500	380
Bangladesh	1,500	360
Russian Fed.	1,300	230
Turkey	1,000	150
Greece	960	260
Indonesia	880	190

US$, millions per year
(axis: 0, 1,000, 2,000, 3,000, 4,000, 5,000)

b. Relative terms

- Avoided well-being losses
- Avoided asset losses

Country	Avoided well-being losses	Avoided asset losses
Mali	25	10
Niger	25	11
Guatemala	17	4.3
Mauritania	17	6.9
Cambodia	17	6.5
Peru	16	3.7
Thailand	14	8.8
Colombia	13	1.8
Turkey	12	3.7
Mongolia	12	4.5
Congo, Rep.	12	2.8
Greece	12	5.2
Morocco	11	4.1
Honduras	11	0.99
Iran, Islamic Rep.	11	3.2

Percent of current losses
(axis: 0, 5, 10, 15, 20, 25)

Source: World Bank estimates.

Note: Figure shows the avoided asset losses and avoided well-being losses from a 5 percent reduction in exposure, achieved by reducing the exposure of poor people only—in absolute terms in panel a (millions of U.S. dollars per year, purchasing power parity–adjusted) and in relative terms in panel b (percentage of current average asset and well-being losses).

Figure 5.2 can also be interpreted the other way around. It reveals the cost in well-being if the exposure of poor people increases. The countries in panel b of the figure are those in which the disaster-related cost of uncontrolled urbanization is the largest in well-being terms. Because they are often undergoing rapid urbanization, these countries are likely to experience large increases in risk to well-being in the next decades. They represent, without a doubt, the priorities for action on exposure, even if it is extremely challenging.

Figure 5.3: A reduction in exposure of the nonpoor rather than the poor would reduce asset losses more but well-being losses less

Avoided asset losses and gains in well-being in absolute and relative terms from 5 percent reduction in exposure, nonpoor only

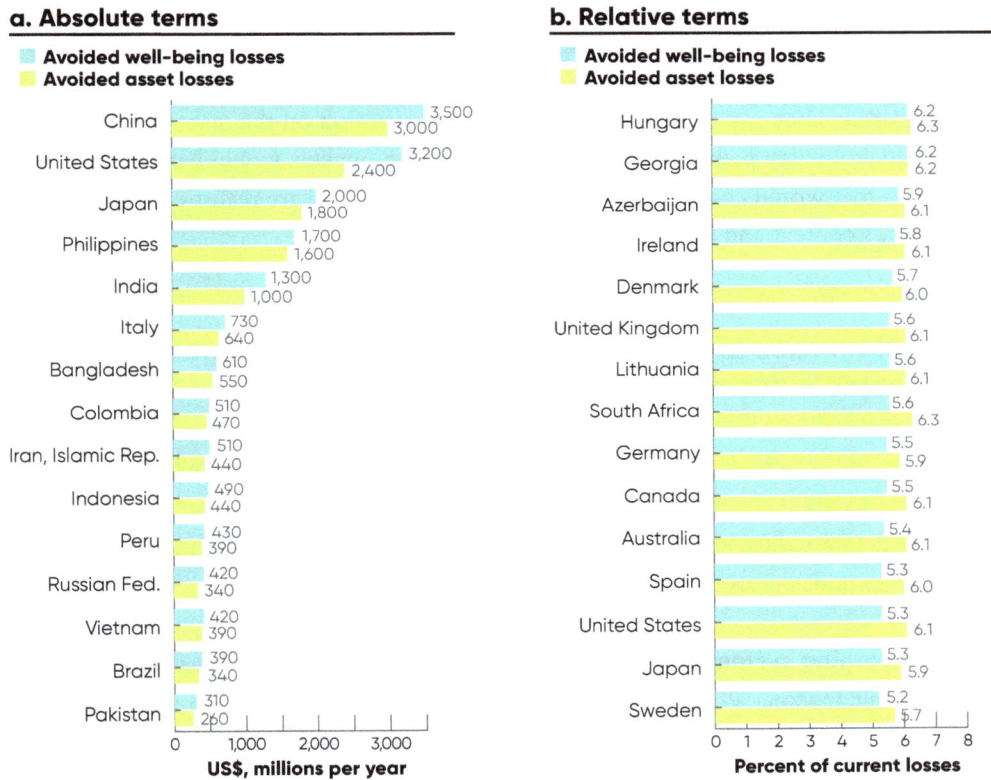

a. Absolute terms

☐ **Avoided well-being losses**
☐ **Avoided asset losses**

Country	Avoided well-being losses	Avoided asset losses
China	3,500	3,000
United States	3,200	2,400
Japan	2,000	1,800
Philippines	1,700	1,600
India	1,300	1,000
Italy	730	640
Bangladesh	610	550
Colombia	510	470
Iran, Islamic Rep.	510	440
Indonesia	490	440
Peru	430	390
Russian Fed.	420	340
Vietnam	420	390
Brazil	390	340
Pakistan	310	260

US$, millions per year

b. Relative terms

☐ **Avoided well-being losses**
☐ **Avoided asset losses**

Country	Avoided well-being losses	Avoided asset losses
Hungary	6.2	6.3
Georgia	6.2	6.2
Azerbaijan	5.9	6.1
Ireland	5.8	6.1
Denmark	5.7	6.0
United Kingdom	5.6	6.1
Lithuania	5.6	6.1
South Africa	5.6	6.3
Germany	5.5	5.9
Canada	5.5	6.1
Australia	5.4	6.1
Spain	5.3	6.0
United States	5.3	6.1
Japan	5.3	5.9
Sweden	5.2	5.7

Percent of current losses

Source: World Bank estimates.

Note: Figure shows the avoided asset losses and avoided well-being losses from a 5 percent reduction in exposure, achieved by reducing the exposure of nonpoor only—in absolute terms in panel a (millions of U.S. dollars per year, purchasing power parity–adjusted) and in relative terms in panel b (percentage of current average asset and well-being losses).

Of course, decisions on projects or policies to reduce exposure cannot be based only on benefits; costs also need to be taken into account. However, depending on the approach taken to reduce exposure, costs will differ in nature and in magnitude.

Large infrastructure such as dike systems and pumping stations involves high up-front investment costs and regular maintenance expenditures. The cost of ecosystem conservation more often takes the form of opportunity costs—for example, those incurred when urban wetlands are not developed. For softer approaches such as land-use planning, there is no large investment cost, but enforcing the plans requires the right institutions such as a cadaster, land-use regulations, and resources and willingness to enforce the plan. These institutions can be difficult (and costly) to put in place, especially in countries with low institutional capacity. Moreover, the impact of land-use plans on land and housing prices needs to be considered: when they increase scarcity and are not supplemented with the appropriate social policies, they can contribute to housing affordability issues, especially for the poor (Viguie and Hallegatte 2012).

The estimates provided here are thus only half of the equation that must be considered. They can be used to engage in a conversation on the instruments available to policy makers to reduce exposure. Policy makers would be searching for options that would cost less than the estimated benefits and are realistic given their country's context and capacity.

Opportunities are also on hand to reduce the vulnerability of people's assets to natural disasters

Only so much can be done to reduce people's exposure to natural hazards. Such measures need to be supplemented with other actions to reduce losses when a disaster actually occurs. They include early warning systems to save lives and preparedness measures that reduce losses, building norms to reduce damage to dwellings and other buildings, and actions related to food production and food security.

Early warning systems and disaster preparedness can save lives and reduce economic losses. Weather forecasts enable the anticipation of and preparation for extreme events. The value of preparedness was illustrated when Cyclone Phailin, with wind speeds of 200 kilometers an hour, made landfall in the state of Odisha, India, in the evening of October 12, 2013. The storm that hit the same coastline 14 years earlier, Cyclone 05B in 1999, caused massive devastation, killing more than 10,000 people and destroying housing and public infrastructure in coastal Odisha. This time, however, the story unfolded differently. After 72 hours, the official death toll was 38 persons, less than 0.4 percent of the death toll from the 1999 cyclone. Close to a million people were evacuated to cyclone shelters, safe houses, and inland locations in Odisha (about 850,000) and in Andhra Pradesh (about 150,000). This success was made possible by years of effort by the Odisha State Disaster

Management Authority (OSDMA) and the government of Odisha, which planned, constructed disaster risk mitigation infrastructure, set up evacuation protocols, identified potential safe buildings for housing communities, and, most important, worked with communities and local organizations to set up volunteer teams and local champions who knew what needed to be done when the time came to act.

Preparing a house before a hurricane (by shuttering windows, for example) can reduce damage by up to 50 percent (Williams 2002). As for floods, studies show that before the Elbe and Danube floods in Europe in 2002, 31 percent of the population in flooded areas implemented preventive measures (Kreibich et al. 2005; Thieken et al. 2007). These measures included moving goods to the second floor of buildings, moving vehicles outside the flood zone, protecting important documents and valuables, disconnecting electricity and gas supplies and unplugging electric appliances, and installing water pumps. Timing of the warning was critical: the businesses that protected their equipment or inventories were those that received the warning early enough. One study estimates that a warning issued 48 hours before a flood enables the overall damage to be reduced by more than 50 percent (Carsell, Pingel, and Ford 2004).

In simulations made for this report, we evaluated the benefits of providing universal access to early warning systems globally, assuming that state-of-the-art warnings can reduce asset losses from storms, floods, and tsunamis by up to 20 percent on average. We learned that asset losses would be reduced by about $13 billion a year, and the well-being gains would be equivalent to an increase in income of $22 billion. Even though this assessment considers only the asset losses (and not the human lives that could be saved), it is much larger than previous assessments (Hallegatte 2012a).

These benefits could be compared with the cost of providing such a service globally. Although no solid estimate exists, a back-of-the-envelope calculation is about $1 billion a year (Hallegatte 2012a), confirming that investing in an early warning system makes economic sense, even without considering its main benefit—the lives that can be saved (Rogers and Tsirkunov 2013).

In which countries would an improvement in early warning systems provide the most benefits? Figure 5.4 shows the top 15 countries in which universal access to an early warning system would most reduce the risk to well-being. In relative terms (panel b), the countries listed are those in which early warning systems are currently not available, according to self-reporting from the Hyogo Framework for Action (HFA). For all of these countries, assuming full access means that asset losses would be reduced by 20 percent, and the gains in well-being would be similar in magnitude. Of course, countries that did not contribute to the HFA system may have better access to early warning than what is assumed here—for example, Ireland. As for any other measures, moving to implementation requires country-level studies that use the information that is available at the country level but is absent from the global databases we use here.

Figure 5.4: Early warning would decrease asset losses and provide large gains in well-being

Effects on asset losses and well-being in absolute and relative terms of an early warning system for natural disasters

a. Absolute terms

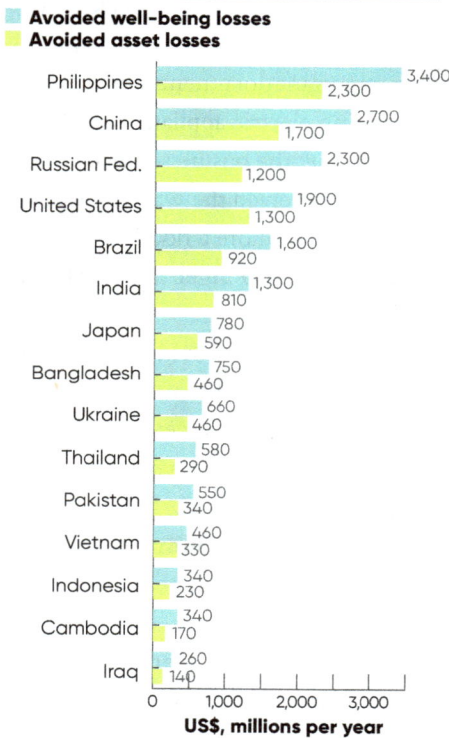

- Avoided well-being losses
- Avoided asset losses

Country	Avoided well-being losses	Avoided asset losses
Philippines	3,400	2,300
China	2,700	1,700
Russian Fed.	2,300	1,200
United States	1,900	1,300
Brazil	1,600	920
India	1,300	810
Japan	780	590
Bangladesh	750	460
Ukraine	660	460
Thailand	580	290
Pakistan	550	340
Vietnam	460	330
Indonesia	340	230
Cambodia	340	170
Iraq	260	140

US$, millions per year

b. Relative terms

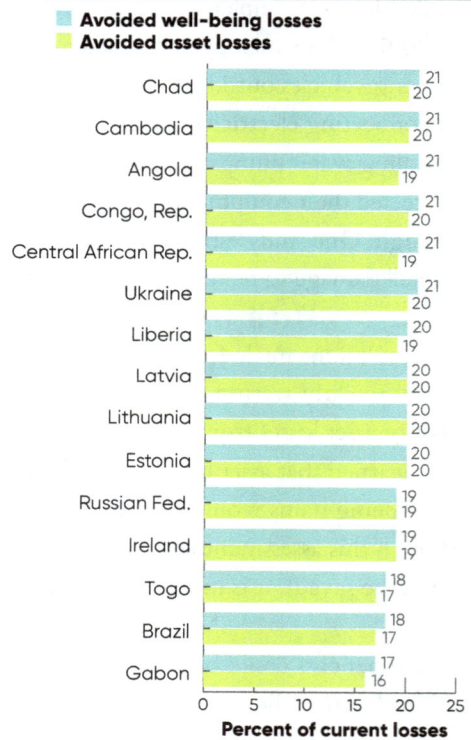

- Avoided well-being losses
- Avoided asset losses

Country	Avoided well-being losses	Avoided asset losses
Chad	21	20
Cambodia	21	20
Angola	21	19
Congo, Rep.	21	20
Central African Rep.	21	19
Ukraine	21	20
Liberia	20	19
Latvia	20	20
Lithuania	20	20
Estonia	20	20
Russian Fed.	19	19
Ireland	19	19
Togo	18	17
Brazil	18	17
Gabon	17	16

Percent of current losses

Source: World Bank estimates.

Note: Figure shows the avoided asset losses and gains in well-being from assuming universal access to early warning systems—in absolute terms in panel a (millions of U.S. dollars per year, purchasing power parity–adjusted) and in relative terms in panel b (percentage of current average asset and well-being losses).

In spite of their large benefits, early warning and evacuation systems are still underdeveloped. In the subdistrict of Shyamnagar in Bangladesh, only 15 percent of nonpoor people and 6 percent of poor people attend cyclone preparedness training (Akter and Mallick 2013). In the Lamjung district of Nepal, the penetration of early warning in flood and landslide-prone communities is lower than 1 percent (Gentle et al. 2014). These shortfalls highlight the challenges and the opportunities associated with building hydrometeorological institutions and systems that could produce actionable warnings (Rogers and Tsirkunov 2013).

Building norms and stronger infrastructure are critical

One reason poor people lose a larger share of their assets and income is that they live in buildings with low resistance to natural hazards. In Latin America, a 1993 inventory found that 37 percent of its housing stock provided inadequate protection against disaster and illness (Fay 2005). Since then, rising trends in urbanization, settlements in risky areas, and the low quality of those settlements have likely increased this share (Lall and Deichmann 2012).

Many factors influence building vulnerability. One factor is the lack of clear and effectively enforced land and property rights, which discourages poor households from making more robust and durable—but also costlier—investments in their homes. Facing the permanent risk of eviction, they are unlikely to invest in the physical resilience of their homes, such as retrofitting to strengthen homes against disasters (Rentschler 2013). In Buenos Aires, fear of eviction, along with low levels of household income, is the main reason for underinvestment in housing infrastructure, according to a survey of two informal settlements without tenure security (van Gelder 2010). By contrast, in Tanzania households with home ownership (and especially those holding some form of documentation) invest significantly more in their dwelling (Rentschler 2013).

Another factor is the quality of construction and the role of building regulations. The world will see the construction of 1 billion new dwelling units by 2050 (GFDRR 2016a). However, this growth may lead to a rapid increase in risk. With current practices, the expected number of buildings sustaining heavy damage or collapsing from a large earthquake in Kathmandu, Nepal, nearly doubles every 10 years (GFDRR 2016b). And yet this growth creates an opportunity for inexpensive reductions in risk through appropriate building regulations. Appropriately designed new construction can be rendered disaster-resistant for a small fraction, 5–10 percent, of the cost of construction. However, retrofit of existing vulnerable structures may require a major expenditure, in the range of 10–50 percent of building value.

Priority 3 of the post-2015 Sendai Framework for Disaster Risk Reduction calls for a coordinated effort around rehabilitation of building codes and standards. It acknowledges the need for a localized and calibrated approach, with a focus on vulnerable settlements, irrespective of the broader income category of the country.

The GFDRR (2016a) has identified three core components of any building code regulatory regime: (1) a legal and administrative framework at the national level; (2) a building code development and maintenance process; and (3) a set of implementation mechanisms at the local level. In 2016 the GFDRR proposed a Building Regulation for Resilience Program to answer to these challenges (see box 5.4).

Building quality is more than housing quality; public buildings and infrastructure are also particularly important. Studies show that most of the deaths after earthquakes occur in countries where public sector corruption is widespread, where building norms are not enforced, and where public buildings are often not built according to design standards (Ambraseys and Bilham 2011; Escaleras, Anbarci, and Register 2007). The same is likely true for climate-related disasters such as floods and storms, although data are not available.

The Global Program for Safer Schools, created by the World Bank and the GFDRR, aims at making school facilities and the communities they serve more resilient to natural hazards, with a strong focus on the enforcement of building norms. Engagements have started in 11 countries across five regions (Armenia, El Salvador, Indonesia, Jamaica, Mozambique, Nepal, Peru, Turkey, Samoa, Tonga, and Vanuatu). For example, the program supports a safety diagnostic of schools in Lima, Peru, and provides technical assistance in Mozambique to optimize the delivery of resilient schools at the local level, targeting both government and community construction. In Peru, the nationwide risk assessment for the education sector led to the development of a National Plan and a Seismic Retrofitting Program for School Infrastructure. In its first phase, implementation will begin with 373 schools and benefit 278,000 students, with a target of 12,000 safer schools over the next few years.

Similar actions exist in other sectors. For example, the World Health Organization, the International Strategy for Disaster Reduction, and the World Bank partnered in 2008 in the "Safe Hospitals" initiative to help health facilities withstand natural shocks.

To measure the benefits of higher building resistance to natural hazards, we explore, using our global resilience model, the effects of reducing asset vulnerability. As we did earlier for exposure, we look here at two scenarios:

» In the first scenario, we reduce by 30 percent the asset vulnerability of 5 percent of the population from within the top 80 percent. This scenario would reduce asset losses by $6 billion a year, and it would generate annual well-being benefits of $7 billion.

» In the second scenario, we reduce by 30 percent the asset vulnerability of 5 percent of the population from within the bottom 20 percent. As earlier for exposure, focusing on the poorest generates smaller benefits in terms of asset losses ($2 billion versus $6 billion), but much larger benefits in terms of well-being ($14 billion versus $7 billion).

Figure 5.5 shows the 15 countries in which reducing the vulnerability of poor people's assets would be the most efficient action to reduce risks. In absolute terms, again the large countries predominate, especially those with high levels of risk. And in relative terms, the countries with low resilience, where avoiding asset losses is highly desirable, predominate. Comparing the same action focusing on the nonpoor (not shown here) reveals again that acting on the vulnerability of poor people is less efficient in monetary terms (in Peru, avoided asset losses of $79 million a year versus $120 million a year), but more efficient in well-being terms (in Peru, $960 million a year versus $120 million a year).

Figure 5.5: Reducing the asset vulnerability of poor people would avoid large well-being losses

Effects on asset losses and well-being of 30 percent reduction in asset vulnerability of 5 percent of the population, poor people

a. Absolute terms

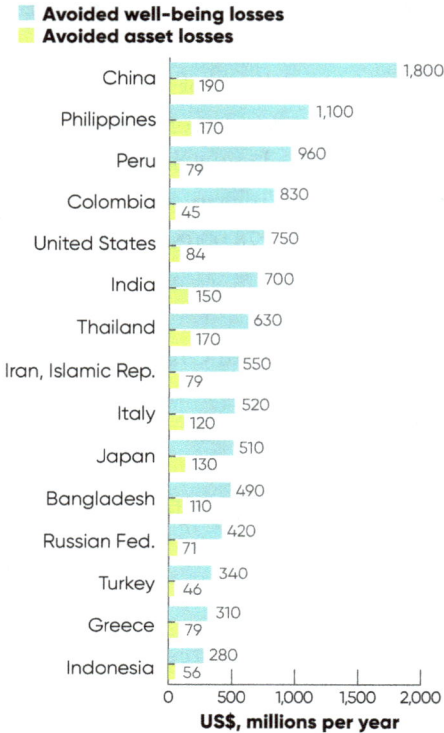

- ▨ Avoided well-being losses
- ▨ Avoided asset losses

Country	Well-being	Asset
China	1,800	190
Philippines	1,100	170
Peru	960	79
Colombia	830	45
United States	750	84
India	700	150
Thailand	630	170
Iran, Islamic Rep.	550	79
Italy	520	120
Japan	510	130
Bangladesh	490	110
Russian Fed.	420	71
Turkey	340	46
Greece	310	79
Indonesia	280	56

US$, millions per year

b. Relative terms

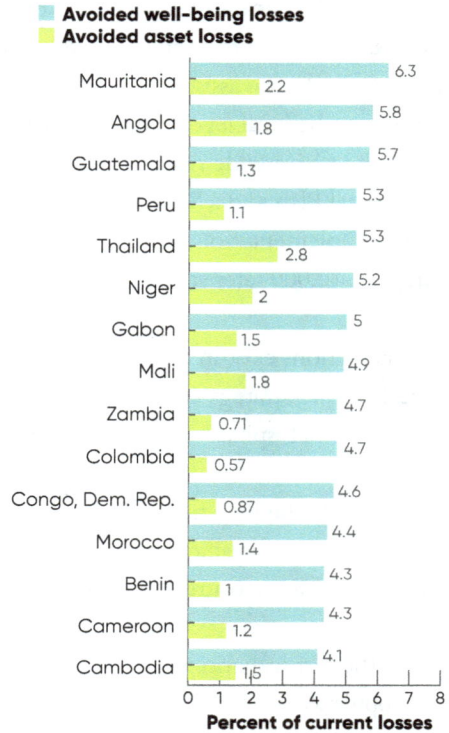

- ▨ Avoided well-being losses
- ▨ Avoided asset losses

Country	Well-being	Asset
Mauritania	6.3	2.2
Angola	5.8	1.8
Guatemala	5.7	1.3
Peru	5.3	1.1
Thailand	5.3	2.8
Niger	5.2	2
Gabon	5	1.5
Mali	4.9	1.8
Zambia	4.7	0.71
Colombia	4.7	0.57
Congo, Dem. Rep.	4.6	0.87
Morocco	4.4	1.4
Benin	4.3	1
Cameroon	4.3	1.2
Cambodia	4.1	1.5

Percent of current losses

Source: World Bank estimates.

Note: Figure shows the avoided asset losses and gains in well-being from a 30 percent reduction in the asset vulnerability of 5 percent of the population, taken among poor people—in absolute terms in panel a (millions of U.S. dollars per year, purchasing power parity–adjusted) and in relative terms in panel b (percentage of current average asset and well-being losses).

Climate-smart agriculture, access to markets, and efficient transport contribute to food security

Although it is not included in the current version of our resilience model, natural disasters regularly send food prices soaring, disproportionately harming poor people. In 2010 flooding in Pakistan inundated more than 7,700 square miles of land and sent wheat prices up by 50 percent. In 2013 the onslaught of Typhoon Haiyan in the Philippines caused rice production losses of some 260,000 tons. And drought has even larger effects on food security: in Lesotho, the recent drought placed more than 500,000 people, about 25 percent of the population, at risk of food insecurity in early

2016, with poor households experiencing a 44 percent decline in their food and cash income (MDAT 2016). Here, we review some evidence on this important channel through which disasters can affect well-being, see the *Shock Waves* report by Hallegatte et al. (2016) for more detail (but this channel will require further work, the goal being to include it in our quantified assessment).

Climate-smart agricultural practices can increase productivity and make agricultural production more resilient and populations less food-insecure. In the countries most exposed to climate variability and change, disaster preparedness and resilient and diverse farming systems go hand in hand (World Bank 2011). For example, Vietnam is improving its water resource management so that its cropping and aquaculture regimes are better adapted to rising flood risk and salinity levels.

Better technologies are needed to tackle future food security challenges (FAO, IFAD, and WFP 2014). These might include improvements in crop varieties, smarter use of inputs, methods to strengthen crop resistance to pests and diseases, and reduction of postharvest losses (Beddington 2010; Tilman et al. 2011). Improved crops and better use of water and soil can increase both farmers' incomes and their resilience to climate shocks (Cervigni and Morris 2015). One key way to make agricultural systems more climate-resilient is to develop and adopt higher-yielding and more climate-resistant crop varieties and livestock breeds (Tester and Langridge 2010). In a randomized control trial in Orissa, India, a recent study showed the benefits of using a new flood-resistant variety of rice, which offers a 45 percent yield gain relative to the current most popular variety (de Janvry 2015).

Disseminating improved technologies and making them accessible to poor farmers will be critical to realizing the gains from such technologies. However, adoption of new technological packages is often slow and limited. For example, in Africa fertilizer application remains low because of high transport costs and poor distribution systems (Gilbert 2012). Furthermore, cultural barriers, lack of information and education, and implementation costs have to be overcome. Agricultural extension services can help make better use of new technologies.

Meanwhile, more resilient food production should be complemented with well-functioning markets and better access to markets, which will help countries and people cope with production shocks. Rural road development offers strong potential to lower transport costs and spur market activity. Indeed, a productivity shock at the local level can lead to much greater price fluctuations if local markets are isolated. For example, a recent study of the statistical effect of road quality and distance from urban consumption centers on maize price volatility in Burkina Faso found that volatility is greatest in remote markets, suggesting that enhancing road infrastructure would strengthen the links between rural markets and major consumption centers, thereby also stabilizing maize prices in the region (Moctar, D'Hôtel Elodie, and Tristan 2015).

Food stocks can help reduce price volatility and food insecurity. However, they can be costly and difficult to manage. In the case of a large importing region—the Middle East and North Africa—one study has shown that a strategic storage policy at the regional level could smooth global prices, but it is much more costly than a social protection policy such as food stamps or cash transfers that dampens the effects of price increases on consumers (Larson et al. 2013).

This chapter has highlighted the many options that can be explored to reduce the risk to assets by protecting the population or making assets more resistant, and it has identified countries in which these options are particularly promising. It has also highlighted the need to account for people's socioeconomic vulnerability and resilience in targeting disaster risk management investments and to ensure that these investments also protect poor people, even if they are so poor that avoided asset losses remain limited. However, no matter how many efforts are made to prevent disasters or reduce the damages they pose for assets, risk cannot be reduced to zero, and additional measures are needed to make populations better able to cope with the losses that cannot be avoided. This is the topic of the next chapter.

NOTES

1. If we could use redistribution through transfers to manage equity concerns ex post, then we could separate efficiency and equity considerations and select projects based on their efficiency only. For instance, risk management projects could maximize avoided asset losses and then, if investments benefit rich people disproportionately, make them compensate the poorer, less protected people. Because such ex post redistribution rarely happens in practice, however, project selection needs to consider both efficiency and equity.

REFERENCES

Akter, S., and B. Mallick. 2013. "The Poverty–Vulnerability–Resilience Nexus: Evidence from Bangladesh." *Ecological Economics* 96: 114–24. doi:10.1016/j.ecolecon.2013.10.008.

Ambraseys, N., and R. Bilham. 2011. "Corruption Kills." *Nature* 469: 153–55. doi:10.1038/469153a.

Badola, R., and S. A. Hussain. 2005. "Valuing Ecosystem Functions: An Empirical Study on the Storm Protection Function of Bhitarkanika Mangrove Ecosystem, India." *Environmental Conservancy* 32: 85–92.

Bagley, J. E., A. R. Desai, K. J. Harding, P. K. Snyder, and J. A. Foley. 2013. "Drought and Deforestation: Has Land Cover Change Influenced Recent Precipitation Extremes in the Amazon?" *Journal of Climatology* 27: 345–61. doi:10.1175/JCLI-D-12-00369.1.

Bangalore, M., A. Smith, and T. Veldkamp. 2016. "Exposure to Floods, Climate Change, and Poverty in Vietnam." Policy Research Working Paper 7765, World Bank, Washington, DC.

Beddington, J. 2010. "Food Security: Contributions from Science to a New and Greener Revolution." *Philosophical Transactions of the Royal Society B: Biological Science* 365: 61–71.

Bonzanigo, L., and N. Kalra. 2014. "Making Informed Investment Decisions in an Uncertain World: A Short Demonstration." Policy Research Working Paper 6765, World Bank, Washington, DC.

Carsell, K. M., N. D. Pingel, and D. T. Ford. 2004. "Quantifying the Benefit of a Flood Warning System." *Natural Hazards Review* 5: 131–40.

Cervigni, R., and M. Morris. 2015. *Enhancing Resilience in African Drylands: Toward a Shared Development Agenda.* Washington, DC: World Bank.

Das, S., and J. R. Vincent. 2009. "Mangroves Protected Villages and Reduced Death Toll during Indian Super Cyclone." *Proceedings of the National Academy of Sciences* 106: 7357–60.

Davidson, E. A., A. C. de Araújo, P. Artaxo, J. K. Balch, I. F.Brown, M. M. Bustamante, M. T. Coe et al. 2012. "The Amazon Basin in Transition." *Nature* 481: 321–28. doi:10.1038/nature10717.

de Janvry, A. 2015. "Quantifying through Ex Post Assessments the Micro-level Impacts of Sovereign Disaster Risk Financing and Insurance Programs." Policy Research Working Paper 7356, World Bank, Washington, DC.

Escaleras, M., N. Anbarci, and C. A. Register. 2007. "Public Sector Corruption and Major Earthquakes: A Potentially Deadly Interaction. *Public Choice* 132: 209–30.

FAO (Food and Agriculture Organization), IFAD (International Fund for Agricultural Development), and WFP (World Food Programme). 2014. *The State of Food Insecurity in the World 2014. Strengthening the Enabling Environment for Food Security and Nutrition.* Rome: FAO.

Fay, M. 2005. "The Urban Poor in Latin America." Directions in Development—General, World Bank, Washington, DC.

Fay, M., S. Hallegatte, A. Vogt-Schilb, J. Rozenberg, U. Narloch, and T. Kerr. 2015. *Decarbonizing Development : Three Steps to a Zero-Carbon Future.* Washington, DC: World Bank.

Gentle, P., R. Thwaites, D. Race, and K. Alexander. 2014. "Differential Impacts of Climate Change on Communities in the Middle Hills Region of Nepal." *Natural Hazards* 74: 815–36. doi:10.1007/s11069-014-1218-0.

GFDRR (Global Facility for Disaster Reduction and Recovery). 2016a. "Building Regulation for Resilience." Washington, DC. _____. 2016b. "The Making of a Riskier Future: How Our Decisions Are Shaping Future Disaster Risk." World Bank, Washington, DC.

Gilbert, N. 2012. "African Agriculture: Dirt Poor." *Nature* 483: 525–27. doi:10.1038/483525a.

Hallegatte, S. 2012a. "A Cost Effective Solution to Reduce Disaster Losses in Developing Countries: Hydro-Meteorological Services, Early Warning, and Evacuation." Policy Research Working Paper 6058, World Bank, Washington, DC.

_____. 2012b. "An Exploration of the Link between Development, Economic Growth, and Natural Risk." Policy Research Working Paper 6216, World Bank, Washington, DC.

Hallegatte, S., M. Bangalore, L. Bonzanigo, M. Fay, T. Kane, U. Narloch, J. Rozenberg et al. 2016. *Shock Waves: Managing the Impacts of Climate Change on Poverty.* Climate Change and Development Series. Washington, DC: World Bank.

Kalra, N., S. Hallegatte, R. Lempert, C. Brown, A. Fozzard, S. Gill, and A. Shah. 2014. "Agreeing on Robust Decisions: New Processes for Decision Making under Deep Uncertainty." Policy Research Working Paper 6906, World Bank, Washington, DC.

Kreibich, H., A. H. Thieken, T. Petrow, M. Müller, and B. Merz. 2005. "Flood Loss Reduction of Private

Households due to Building Precautionary Measures—Lessons Learned from the Elbe Flood in August 2002." *Natural Hazards and Earth System Sciences* 5: 117–26.

Lall, S. V., and U. Deichmann. 2012. "Density and Disasters: Economics of Urban Hazard Risk." *World Bank Research Observer* 27: 74–105.

Larson, D. F., J. Lampietti, C. Gouel, C. Cafiero, and J. Roberts. 2013. "Food Security and Storage in the Middle East and North Africa." *World Bank Economic Review* 28 (1).

Lempert, R. J., S. W. Popper, D. G. Groves, N. Kalra, J. R. Fischbach, S. C. Bankes, B. P. Bryant et al. 2013. "Making Good Decisions without Predictions." Rand Corporation Research Brief 9701.

MDAT (Multi-Agency Drought Assessment Team). 2016. "Lesotho: Rapid Drought Impact Assessment Report." Lesotho.

Moctar, N., M. D'Hôtel Elodie, and L. C. Tristan. 2015. "Maize Price Volatility: Does Market Remoteness Matter?" Policy Research Working Paper 7202, World Bank, Washington, DC.

Rentschler, J. E. 2013. "Why Resilience Matters—The Poverty Impacts of Disasters." Policy Research Working Paper 6699, World Bank, Washington, DC.

Rogers, D. P., and V. V. Tsirkunov. 2013. *Weather and Climate Resilience: Effective Preparedness through National Meteorological and Hydrological Services.* Washington, DC: World Bank.

Rozenberg, J., M. Simpson, L. Bonzanigo, M. Bangalore, and L. Prasanga. 2015. "Wetlands Conservation and Management: A New Model for Urban Resilience in Colombo." World Bank, Washington, DC.

Tester, M., and P. Langridge. 2010. "Breeding Technologies to Increase Crop Production in a Changing World." *Science* 327: 818–22.

Thieken, A. H., H. Kreibich, M. Müller, and B. Merz. 2007. "Coping with Floods: Preparedness, Response and Recovery of Flood-Affected Residents in Germany in 2002." *Hydrological Sciences Journal* 52: 1016–37.

Tilman, D., C. Balzer, J. Hill, and B. L. Befort. 2011. "Global Food Demand and the Sustainable Intensification of Agriculture." *Proceedings of the National Academy of Sciences* 108: 20260–64.

Trebilcock, M. J. 2014. *Dealing with Losers: The Political Economy of Policy Transitions.* Oxford: Oxford University Press.

van Gelder, J.-L. 2010. "Tenure Security and Housing Improvement in Buenos Aires." *Land Lines* 33(1):126-146.

Viguie, V., and S. Hallegatte. 2012. "Trade-offs and Synergies in Urban Climate Policies." *Nature Climate Change.* doi:10.1038/nclimate1434.

Williams, B. A. 2002. "Fran, Floyd and Mitigation Policy." Berry A. Williams and Associates, Inc., Collinsville, IL.

World Bank. 2011. *Climate-Smart Agriculture: Increased Productivity and Food Security, Enhanced Resilience and Reduced Carbon Emissions for Sustainable Development—Opportunities and Challenges for a Converging Agenda: Country Examples.* Washington, DC: World Bank.

_____. 2013. *World Development Report 2014: Risk and Opportunity—Managing Risk for Development.* Washington, DC: World Bank.

6 MANAGING THE UNAVOIDABLE

>> **Risk can be reduced by improving resilience.**

N o matter how much countries try to reduce people's exposure to natural hazards or to make their assets more resistant to hazards such as earthquakes and floods, natural risk cannot be reduced to zero. Disasters will continue to inflict damage, and so it is critical to supplement actions on exposure and vulnerability with improvements in the ability of people to cope with the shocks that cannot be avoided.

Such action requires in turn a holistic and flexible risk management strategy with a range of policy instruments appropriate for different disasters and affected populations (figure 6.1). Revenue diversification and basic social protection, where it exists, can help households at all income levels cope with small shocks. Remittances make people less vulnerable to income shocks. And financial inclusion helps poor people save in forms less vulnerable to natural hazards than in-kind savings like livestock and housing, and diversifies risk.

But when a shock is larger, these instruments will not be sufficient, and additional tools will be needed. For relatively wealthier households, savings will help, and market insurance can provide them with efficient protection for larger losses. However, for the poorest households savings is often not an option, and high transaction costs and affordability issues make access to private insurance challenging.

Figure 6.1: Poorer and richer households have different needs and can be supported with different instruments

Risk finance strategy for households and governments

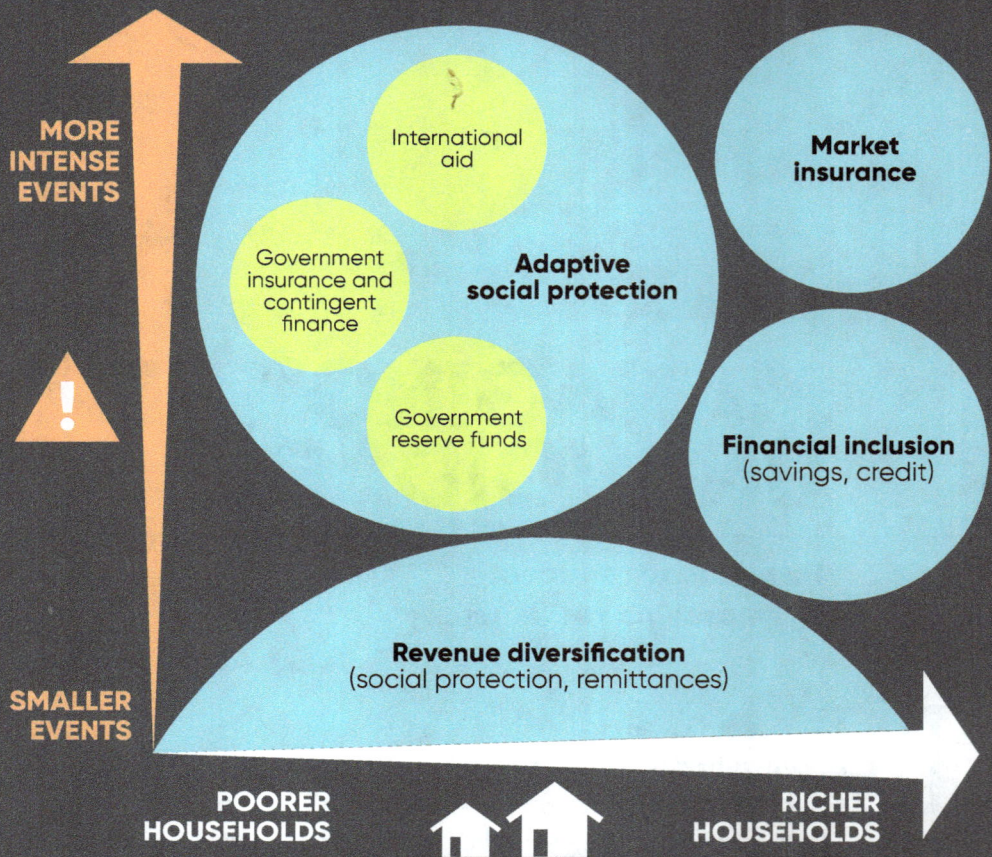

MORE INTENSE EVENTS

International aid

Government insurance and contingent finance

Adaptive social protection

Government reserve funds

Market insurance

Financial inclusion (savings, credit)

Revenue diversification (social protection, remittances)

SMALLER EVENTS

POORER HOUSEHOLDS

RICHER HOUSEHOLDS

Source: Hallegatte et al. 2016.
Note: In blue, instrument targeting households; in green, instruments for governments or local authorities.

For the poorest households—and to cover the largest shocks—well-targeted and easily scalable social safety nets are needed. These systems should be designed to maintain incentives to invest in long-term adaptation to economic and environmental changes. Such an adaptive social protection system does, however, create a liability for a government, which may need to rely on financial instruments such as reserve funds (for small-scale events), contingent finance, or reinsurance products.

This chapter assesses some of these options to make households more resilient and therefore better able to absorb asset losses without suffering a large loss in well-being. Its main finding is that building resilience is good economics and an important addition to the disaster risk management interventions discussed in the previous chapter. Indeed, the package of resilience-building policies highlighted in this chapter could generate an increase in well-being equivalent to a $100 billion increase in global consumption, if implemented globally. This chapter also reveals that interventions that promote poverty reduction and development, such as financial inclusion and social protection, are very efficient at building resilience, but that the resilience gains could be enhanced if natural risks are taken into account in the design of these development policies—for example, by making social protection adaptive and responsive to natural disasters.

Better financial inclusion increases resilience and reduces the impacts of disasters on well-being

Financial inclusion has multiple benefits in terms of resilience. First, better financial inclusion—especially savings products—helps households diversify their portfolio of assets and make their wealth less vulnerable to natural disasters. Second, financial instruments—especially credit—help with the recovery and reconstruction after a disaster, making it possible to rebuild faster and to rebuild better.

A more diversified portfolio means less vulnerability. People use financial instruments, notably their savings, to smooth consumption and limit the effects of income shocks (Kinnan and Townsend 2012; Morduch 1995). However, most households—and almost all poor households—have no or little savings in financial form. And poor people often lack access to formal financial instruments, because of the cost of bank accounts, the long distance and time involved in accessing a financial agent, or the lack of documentation and mistrust in banks (World Bank 2013).

To illustrate the benefits of better financial inclusion (or savings in general) for disaster risk reduction, we estimate the change it makes in risk to assets and to well-being, assuming universal access to financial institutions and that 10 percent at least of their wealth is in the form of financial assets. In this scenario, part of household assets are in financial form and are therefore better diversified. Financial inclusion does not reduce asset losses because it does not affect directly the quantity or vulnerability of physical assets, but the better diversification does reduce the impact on well-being, equivalent to an increase in consumption of $14 billion in the 117 studied countries.

The 15 countries in which financial inclusion would do the most to reduce losses in well-being are identified in figure 6.2. Countries in which the benefits are largest are those in which very few people currently have savings in financial institutions and in which the risks are large. In Gabon, for example, less than 2 percent of the poor, and less than 15 percent of the nonpoor, have savings at a financial institution. In such countries, the savings instruments that are appropriate for low-income people—with easy and free withdrawal, for example (see Banerjee and Duflo 2012)—could contribute greatly to building resilience. In Gabon, improved financial inclusion alone could reduce disaster impacts on well-being by 6.5 percent.

Figure 6.2: Financial inclusion can reduce welfare losses through better risk diversification

Effects on asset and well-being losses of 100 percent of population having savings in a financial institution

a. Absolute terms

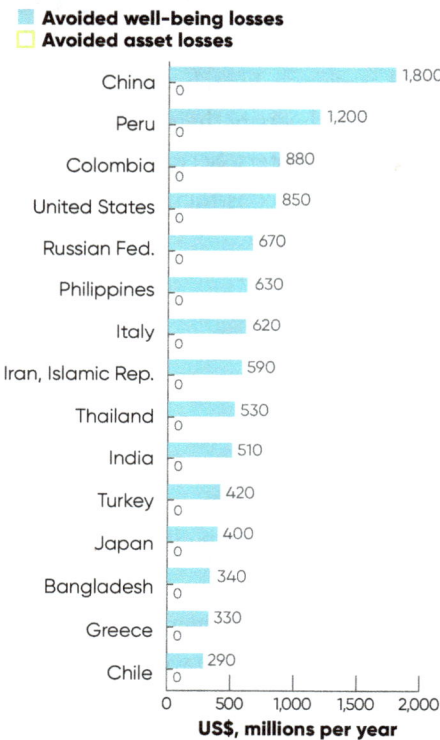

- Avoided well-being losses
- Avoided asset losses

Country	US$, millions per year
China	1,800 / 0
Peru	1,200 / 0
Colombia	880 / 0
United States	850 / 0
Russian Fed.	670 / 0
Philippines	630 / 0
Italy	620 / 0
Iran, Islamic Rep.	590 / 0
Thailand	530 / 0
India	510 / 0
Turkey	420 / 0
Japan	400 / 0
Bangladesh	340 / 0
Greece	330 / 0
Chile	290 / 0

b. Relative terms

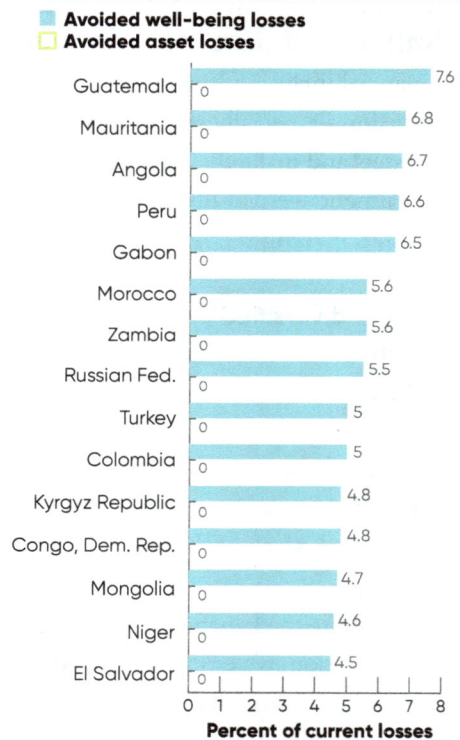

- Avoided well-being losses
- Avoided asset losses

Country	Percent of current losses
Guatemala	7.6 / 0
Mauritania	6.8 / 0
Angola	6.7 / 0
Peru	6.6 / 0
Gabon	6.5 / 0
Morocco	5.6 / 0
Zambia	5.6 / 0
Russian Fed.	5.5 / 0
Turkey	5 / 0
Colombia	5 / 0
Kyrgyz Republic	4.8 / 0
Congo, Dem. Rep.	4.8 / 0
Mongolia	4.7 / 0
Niger	4.6 / 0
El Salvador	4.5 / 0

Source: World Bank estimates.

Note: Figure shows the avoided asset losses and gains in well-being from assuming that 100 percent of population has savings at a financial institution—in absolute terms in panel a (millions of U.S. dollars per year, purchasing power parity–adjusted) and in relative terms in panel b (percentage of current average asset and well-being losses).

Even if we cannot take it into account at this stage in our quantification, financial inclusion also enables people and firms to reduce risk in the first place. For example, access to credit makes it possible for households to finance investments in flood prevention—investments that often have very short payback periods. Without access to credit, these measures may be unaffordable, thereby forcing households to pay much more in constant repairs than they would in loan repayment.

Progress in expanding access to financial institutions has been rapid, and new technologies offer further opportunities to enhance financial inclusion at low cost. Over the last decade, an alternative method of extending banking services has developed: mobile money. Most adults in the world today—poor people included—have access to mobile phones. In fact, the United Nations estimates that out of 7.3 billion people, 6 billion have access to these devices. Mobile money accounts, by providing more convenient and affordable financial services, offer promise for reaching the unbanked adults traditionally excluded from the formal financial system such as women, poor people, young people, and those living in rural areas (Demirgüç-Kunt et al. 2015). Thus the expansion of mobile money has the potential to improve financial inclusion and to make the savings and assets portfolio of poor people less vulnerable to natural disasters.

Diversification can also be supported through other instruments such as by helping rural households enter into nonagricultural occupations. For example, according to Macours, Premand, and Vakis (2012), combining a cash transfer with other diversification interventions—such as vocational training or a productive investment grant—helps households diversify their income sources and become more resilient to drought. They even find that vocational training provides households with a "potential diversification," in the sense that even if households do not diversify their income before a shock, they can decide to engage in nonfarm activities after a shock. These results are supported by the results from the Bangladesh Rural Advancement Committee (BRAC), which suggest that combining cash grants or the transfer of free productive assets with productive interventions (from training to coaching and access to saving account) has a positive impact not only on income but also on many other indicators correlated with resilience—for example, those related to food security (Banerjee et al. 2015).

Our estimates provide useful input for discussions by countries and others on whether to invest in financial inclusion. But making actual decisions on financial inclusion requires more information, especially on the cost of various measures and the other benefits—that is, those not linked to disaster resilience. Development considerations are sufficient to justify investments in financial inclusion (World Bank 2014), and resilience considerations only make the case stronger.

Financial instruments also facilitate and accelerate recovery and reconstruction

Lack of access to finance after a shock also is a significant obstacle to recovery and reconstruction, slowing down the return to normalcy and prompting people and firms to rebuild as fast as possible at the expense of quality (Benson and Clay 2004; Hallegatte and Dumas 2009). As described in a background paper for this report (Hallegatte and Vogt-Schilb, forthcoming), the length of the reconstruction phase has a direct influence on total consumption losses: the longer it takes to rebuild, the larger are the total consumption losses. Figure 6.3 plots the ratio between total consumption losses and asset losses as a function of the duration of the reconstruction period in a simple idealized model. If reconstruction is instantaneous, then consumption losses are equal to asset losses (they correspond to the consumption that has to be sacrificed to pay for reconstruction). However, consumption losses increase as the reconstruction period becomes longer and longer.

This result translates into a reduction in global losses in well-being from disasters when reconstruction is accelerated. For example, if policies allow reducing the duration of reconstruction by one-third globally, then the average global loss of well-being from disasters decreases, leading to a gain equivalent to a $32 billion increase in annual consumption—a 6 percent reduction in the global well-being losses from disasters. Figure 6.4 shows the countries in which accelerated reconstruction would deliver the larger gains, with the United States and China the most important in absolute terms and Sudan and Nigeria the first two in relative terms.

Figure 6.3: As reconstruction duration increases, consumption losses become larger than asset losses

Scaling factor in simple economic model between total discounted consumption losses and asset losses as a function of total reconstruction duration

Source: Hallegatte and Vogt-Schilb forthcoming.

Note: ΔC = discounted consumption losses; ΔK = total asset losses.

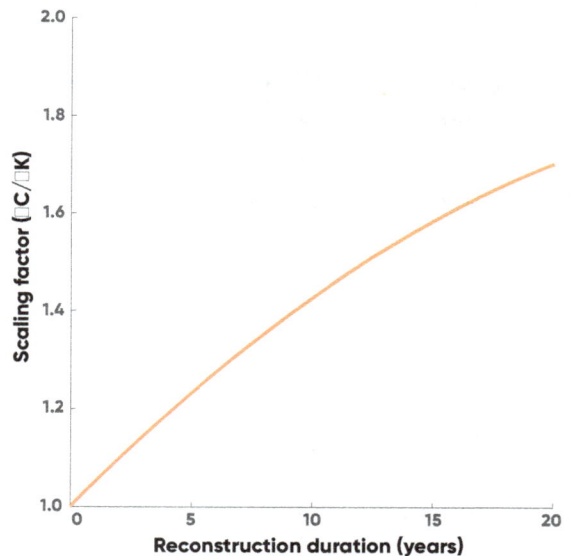

Figure 6.4: Accelerating reconstruction would reduce well-being losses from natural disasters

Effects on asset and well-being losses of reducing reconstruction duration by one-third

a. Absolute terms

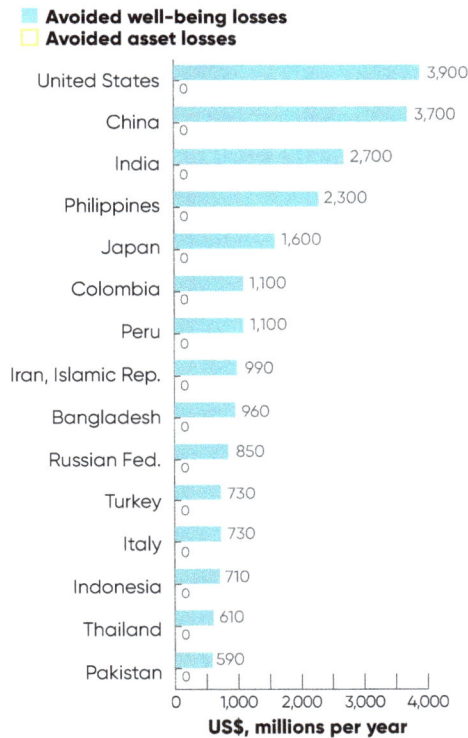

■ Avoided well-being losses
□ Avoided asset losses

Country	US$, millions per year
United States	3,900
China	3,700
India	2,700
Philippines	2,300
Japan	1,600
Colombia	1,100
Peru	1,100
Iran, Islamic Rep.	990
Bangladesh	960
Russian Fed.	850
Turkey	730
Italy	730
Indonesia	710
Thailand	610
Pakistan	590

US$, millions per year

b. Relative terms

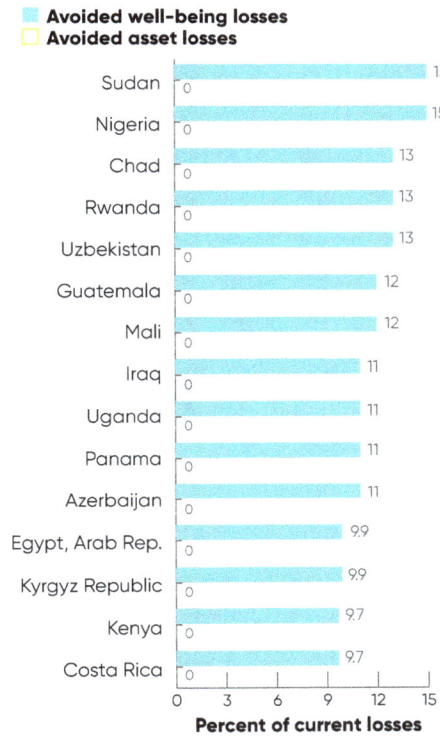

■ Avoided well-being losses
□ Avoided asset losses

Country	Percent of current losses
Sudan	15
Nigeria	15
Chad	13
Rwanda	13
Uzbekistan	13
Guatemala	12
Mali	12
Iraq	11
Uganda	11
Panama	11
Azerbaijan	11
Egypt, Arab Rep.	9.9
Kyrgyz Republic	9.9
Kenya	9.7
Costa Rica	9.7

Percent of current losses

Source: World Bank estimates.

Note: Figure shows the avoided asset losses and gains in well-being from reducing the reconstruction duration by one-third—in absolute terms in panel a (millions of U.S. dollars per year, purchasing power parity–adjusted) and in relative terms in panel b (percentage of current average asset and well-being losses).

Financial instruments can also facilitate the reconstruction of public infrastructure. The benefits of the reconstruction funds made available to local authorities in Mexico have been documented by de Janvry, del Valle, and Sadoulet (2016). They find that access to disaster funding boosts local economic activity by between 2 and 4 percent in the year following a disaster, including a large and sustained 76 percent increase in the growth of local construction employment, and that the positive impact can persist for as long as a year and a half after a disaster.

But governments and local authorities often struggle to finance reconstruction. Budget contingencies usually represent about 2–5 percent of government expenditures (such as in Vietnam, Indonesia, and Colombia), and such contingencies must contend with all shocks, not just natural hazards. As reported by Ghesquiere and Mahul (2010), Vietnam has been hit several times by cyclones in November, when the contingency budget had already been fully exhausted. Many governments, especially small states such as small islands, cannot afford sufficient reserves to respond to major events.

Financial resources help to build back better and offset part of the cost of a disaster. Old and low-quality construction is generally more vulnerable to damage than more recent capital. When a disaster hits, the destruction of low-quality assets may allow the possibility of "building back better," thereby improving the situation postdisaster. For example, an earthquake may destroy old, low-quality buildings, making it possible to rebuild under improved building norms. After the Victoria bushfires in Australia in 2009, measures to build back better, including land-use planning and structural design improvements, were successfully implemented (Mannakkara, Wilkinson, and Potangaroa 2014). Meanwhile, in Mexico innovative financing arrangements have been initiated under its Natural Disasters Fund (FONDEN) to incentivize investment, build back better, and relocate housing to lower-risk areas (Hoflinger et al. 2012).

Building back better (and quicker) depends not only on financial resources but also on the ability to plan and implement the reconstruction process efficiently. The reconstruction process in Haiti after the 2010 earthquake has revealed that building back better may be difficult in practice because of lack of technical expertise and other issues such as lack of raw materials in the disaster location (Kijewski-Correa and Taflanidis 2011).

Insurance can play a key role

There are limits to what savings and access to borrowing can achieve. For example, borrowing can create a debt trap from which poor households have trouble escaping. Risks created by indebtedness are illustrated by what happened after Cyclone Nargis hit Myanmar in 2008. Farmers, laborers, and fishermen increased their borrowing in response to the shock, creating repayment issues when agriculture and fisheries productivity declined as a result of the storm. According to the World Bank (2015a), 20–50 percent of farmers in villages with poor farming conditions had to pawn assets or to rent out or sell their land because of excess debt, and many creditors seized borrowers' collateral, particularly land.

For large shocks, insurance products can provide protection at a lower cost than savings or borrowing. A study of the Christchurch earthquake in New Zealand in 2011 shows that insurance helps firms bounce back, and even rebound, after a shock (Poontirakul et al. 2016). Over the medium term, a firm with business interruption insurance has a significantly higher likelihood (by some 15 percentage points) of enhanced productivity and improved performance after a disaster.

However, insurance markets are complex, and behaviors often deviate from what theory suggests, making it challenging to provide the appropriate insurance products for poor households or small firms in developing countries, which are often exposed to many risks.

Private insurance is part of the solution package. In the developed world, and increasingly in developing countries, the private sector has demonstrated its effectiveness as a mechanism for the financial protection of individuals, businesses, and government assets.[1] The 2014 publication *Financial Protection against Disasters: An Operational Framework for Disaster Risk Financing and Insurance* (UNISDR 2014) highlights four key areas in which the private sector can contribute to the disaster risk financing and insurance agenda: (1) providing risk capital; (2) providing technical expertise; (3) driving innovation through competition and a push to access new markets/market segments; and (4) participating in public-private partnerships in insurance programs—for example, in the delivery of payouts to beneficiaries as well as in the education of consumers.

Examples of developing country governments using the private sector to transfer excess risk include risk-pooling schemes in the Pacific, Caribbean, and Africa; sovereign risk transfer for individual countries such as Malawi, Uruguay, and Mexico; and a number of new schemes in the pipeline for developing countries that are likely to come to fruition in the next 24 months. The value of access to this global pool of risk capital was demonstrated after the 2010 earthquake in Chile, where an estimated 95 percent of the $8 billion in insured losses was passed out of the domestic market and onto international reinsurers, protecting domestic carriers.[2]

Domestic insurance markets have also proven to be an effective channel for developing the resilience of disaster-exposed households and businesses. The Turkish Catastrophe Insurance Pool (TCIP) and the Mongolian Livestock Insurance Pool are good examples of public-private partnerships. In both of these cases, the domestic insurance market provides the mechanism through which governments are able to reach households and businesses with insurance products to realize their policy goals of expanding the financial resilience of the population to disasters. Both partnerships have substantially increased insurance penetration at the local level.

When insurance providers price the risk correctly, the price itself indicates the risk level, which can help people and firms make better-informed decisions about risk taking and risk mitigation investments. For example, a potential buyer may decide not to buy a home because of the high cost of insuring it against floods, even if information on flood risk is not easily available. And a homeowner could decide to invest in risk mitigation if the reduction in risk translates into an immediate and visible reduction in the annual insurance premium instead of a potential reduction in losses if a flood occurs. In such a context, insurance can create powerful incentives for people to manage their risk better and reduce losses.

Developing insurance markets is, however, challenging, particularly in low-income environments. Where insurance is not compulsory, the pick-up rates remain low. Even in the United States and Italy, high-income countries in which insurance against floods or earthquakes is subsidized, less than 30 percent of homeowners are covered (Insurance Bureau of Canada 2015). And a successful scheme such as the Mongolian Livestock Insurance Pool, which covers more than 10,000 herders and was initiated in 2005, still has a relatively low pick-up rate (less than 15 percent of the herders in the covered areas). There are many reasons why pick-up rates are so low, including affordability issues and behavioral biases (Kunreuther, Pauly, and McMorrow 2013). In developing countries, affordability issues, magnified by large transaction costs, are particularly problematic, but weak institutions and lack of trust also play a key role. And insurance requires the availability of robust data so the insurer can assess risks ex ante—something that is often lacking in developing countries (Rogers and Tsirkunov 2013).

Index-based insurance addresses some of the limits of indemnity insurance.

Index-based insurance refers to products in which insurance payments are not based on observed losses. Instead, they are based on when a physical variable—such as a rainfall deficit, wind speed, or area-based yields—or another index exceeds a predetermined threshold (regardless of the existence of losses). For example, a farmer will receive a predefined insurance payment if rainfall falls below a minimum threshold over a one-month period. Index-based insurance schemes have major advantages over the traditional contracts: (1) transaction costs are reduced because losses do not need to be measured; (2) individuals are still encouraged to take preventive measures because the payout does not depend on the losses or the actions taken to reduce risks (in other words, there is no moral hazard attached to index-based insurance); and (3) the payment decision is simple and objective, making it easier to enforce contracts.

The first weather insurance product in India, and indeed in the developing world, was a rainfall insurance contract underwritten and designed in 2003 by ICICI-Lombard General Insurance Company for groundnut and castor farmers (Clarke et al. 2012). This pilot spurred rainfall insurance product offerings from other insurers, leading to a high rate of growth in the number of farmers insured between 2003 and 2007. As a result, the government of India launched a pilot of the Weather-Based Crop Insurance Scheme in 2007, and it became a largely compulsory, publicly subsidized program that insured more than 10 million farmers for a range of crops. (Following a recent review, it has been replaced by a new scheme, the Pradhan Mantri Fasal Bima Yojana.)

Although the private sector plays a key role in the design of new products, experience has shown that the public sector is needed to reach the critical mass required to sustainably scale up such initiatives, thereby encouraging innovation by private companies. Similar innovations have also supported sovereign risk transfer via parametric products for developing country governments. Examples are the catastrophe bonds issued by the government of Mexico for earthquake and hurricane risk, the Caribbean Catastrophe Risk Insurance Facility established in 2007, the Pacific Catastrophe Risk Insurance Pilot begun in 2013, and the African Risk Capacity facility launched in 2014.

One problem, however, is that index-based insurance suffers from "basis risk"— that is, the difference between the payment received by contract holders and the actual losses they suffer. If the index is well correlated with actual losses, contract holders will receive an adequate insurance payment when (and only when) they have losses. But, in practice, the correlation between losses and payout can be low because of wide variations in the impacts of natural hazards and the limitations of hydrometeorological observation systems. As a result, contract holders may receive a payment in the absence of losses, or receive nothing even in the presence of large losses, which would be catastrophic for those close to the subsistence level. Therefore, when exploring index based insurance products, it is very important to: (i) invest in high quality indices which look to minimize basis risk, and; (ii) ensure the contract holder understands fully the limitations of the index.

Despite its advantages, the pick-up of index-based insurance is low. Of the several reasons offered (Brown, Zelenska, and Mobarak 2013; Cole et al. 2012, 2013), one is that basis risk plays a key role because the low correlation between losses and payout undercuts the product's benefits (Karlan et al. 2012; Mobarak and Rosenzweig 2013). Another is that index insurance typically covers only one type of risk, whereas producers may be exposed to many (such as a price risk or supply chain risk). Other reasons include a general distrust of the insurance policy, limited financial literacy, and insufficient understanding of the product. The decision to purchase an insurance contract may hinge on whether the individual has had prior experience with it, especially with having received a payout (Karlan et al. 2012).

Some of these obstacles can be removed by improving technology and policy design, as well as adopting best practices—for example, modernizing observation systems and improving index designs may reduce the basis risk and strengthen index-based instruments (Barnett, Barrett, and Skees 2008; Rogers and Tsirkunov 2013). However, overall, the evidence suggests that the pick-up of index-based insurance requires large subsidies and, as with indemnity insurance, subsidies can make the schemes unsustainable (Brown, Zelenska, and Mobarak 2013; Cole et al. 2012, 2013).

Universal health coverage contributes to resilience to natural disasters.

Disaster risk insurance is not the only type of insurance that can boost resilience; another type critical to managing natural risks is health insurance. Indeed, natural disasters cause injuries and disabilities, and health shocks tend to push households into poverty, particularly where people have to borrow, often at high interest rates, to access care (Krishna 2006). The World Health Organization (WHO) estimates that about 100 million people fall into poverty each year just to pay for health care (WHO 2013). A big problem is that financial risk protection varies widely, with people in low-income countries having to bear very high and variable shares of out-of-pocket health expenditures.

Thus better health care coverage and lower out-of-pocket expenses would be efficient ways to reduce the health impacts of natural disasters and reduce poverty, especially by helping the poor to manage catastrophic health expenditures (Jamison et al. 2013). Providing health coverage is possible at all income levels, but context and implementation challenges will determine the optimal path for countries. Rwanda invested in a universal health coverage system following the 1994 genocide, and today over 80 percent of its population is insured. This achievement has contributed to more than doubling life expectancy.

Employment-based social insurance is limited to the formal sector. But strategic policies that promote equitable and pro-poor financing mechanisms can accelerate the process toward universal health coverage. In Thailand, the government has expanded coverage to the informal sector with a minimal charge of $0.70 per health care consultation, drawing on general tax revenues. In parts of Africa and Asia, an efficient tool is community-financed coverage schemes that pool expenditure risks at lower levels. Strong community solidarity and administrative capacity are important for these interventions (O'Donnell 2007).

Of course, insurance coverage is not enough. Often, treatable illnesses are not addressed because of lack of health care services. In rural areas, transportation may not be available to transfer the ill to clinics. Meanwhile, many rural clinics do not have adequate equipment or trained health personnel and require payment up front. Today, the share of births attended by skilled health staff is close to 100 percent for countries with GDP per capita of more than $20,000, but varies widely below this level, suggesting progress is possible at low-income levels. If skilled health staff are not available—for births and to treat injuries and diseases—people's health, income, and well-being are more likely to suffer permanent consequences. Improving health care systems (staff training, vaccination programs, information campaigns, access to rapid diagnostic kits, and drugs for treatment) is therefore essential. If significant investments are made over the next 20 years, it is possible to raise the level of health care in low-income countries to that of the best middle-income countries today (Jamison et al. 2013).

Wider access to disaster risk insurance would increase resilience significantly.
More insurance would massively increase resilience, even without risk transfers to international markets. However, providing everybody with access to market insurance is challenging. For one thing, the size of the annual payout would be extremely large. Covering 25 percent of all asset losses would require payout and premium averaging of $82 billion a year, possibly creating capacity and solvency issues, especially for large-scale disasters. For another, as discussed earlier, insurance involves high transaction costs and so is difficult to implement in a low-income environment. Meanwhile, these challenges are magnified when weak institutions and legal systems threaten the value of contracts and trust in commercial relationships (World Bank 2013).

Here, we consider a policy that would offer market insurance, and we assume that coverage reaches 25 percent of the population, but only among people in the top 80 percent. We therefore assume that the bottom 20 percent will not use market insurance because of institutional and affordability issues. (Note that, as discussed shortly, expanding insurance for the nonpoor can benefit poor people because a government can then focus its support on them.) For those who buy insurance, we assume that 50 percent of their asset losses are covered, and that they pay the actuarially fair premium. Globally, this policy would increase resilience by 1.3 percentage points, to 65 percent, and would produce well-being gains of $10 billion a year. These benefits would be entirely generated by the smoothing and diversification effect of insurance—well-being increases when irregular and large individual losses are replaced by predictable and small insurance premium payments—because our model does not capture the impact of insurance on saving and investment behaviors (chapter 3).

Poor people can be protected by social protection systems

The instruments described up to now—savings, borrowing, and insurance—have their limits, and these limits are particularly strong for the poorest households. Social protection can therefore play a key role, based either on traditional social protection instruments such as cash transfers or work programs or on dedicated instruments such as adaptive social protection (for example, in Ethiopia during the 2015 drought) or ad hoc government or international transfers (for example, in Pakistan after the 2010 floods).

Transfers increase diversification and reduce risk. The impact of asset losses on income depends on the sources of income. People's income will be reduced less by a local disaster if a fraction of it is from transfers such as social protection payments from the government or remittances from family members who migrated to cities or foreign countries. As already discussed in chapter 2, however, many poor people are not covered by social protection schemes, and remittances often go to the better-off.

Much can be done, however, to improve this situation. Many countries now have social protection programs, and access to contributory schemes has improved. Moreover, at least one social safety net program is in place in each country. The number of countries with conditional cash transfers has increased dramatically, from 27 in 2008 to 64 in 2014, and the number of countries with public works programs grew from 62 in 2011 to 94 in 2014 (World Bank 2015b). Even if these programs are not designed to protect people against natural disasters—and even if they cannot be adjusted or scaled up in response to a shock—they increase the fraction of income from transfers, especially for the poor, and thereby increase their resilience to localized shocks. In Bangladesh, the Chars Livelihood Programme protected 95 percent of recipients from losing their assets after the 2012 floods (Kenward, Cordier, and Islam 2012). And in Mexico, beneficiaries of Prospera, the national cash transfer program (previously known as Oportunitades or Progresa), are less likely to withdraw their children from school after a shock (de Janvry et al. 2006; Fiszbein, Schady, and Ferreira 2009; Gertler 2004).

Public transfers are sometimes in kind—for example, through waived fees for education and health services. People are also dependent on other public services such as transportation, water, or sanitation. The provision of such services makes people more resilient provided that the services remain available in postdisaster situations. The continuity of public services, or the ability to restore them rapidly, is therefore an important consideration in any assessment of people's vulnerability and resilience. Our analysis, based on the ASPIRE database, captures part of those in-kind transfers.

Meanwhile, further action could support the positive impacts of remittances on resilience. Globally, the burden of remittance transfer costs stood at 7.7 percent of overall transfers in 2014. Those costs tend to be the highest in Sub-Saharan Africa, where they average 11.5 percent (Ratha et al. 2015), reflecting in part the limited competition among service providers. The United Nations Open Working Group on Sustainable Development has proposed reducing remittance costs to 3 percent, which would translate into savings of over $20 billion annually for migrants. Commonly available technologies such as instant money transfers through mobile phones could play a key role in streamlining processes and reducing transaction costs.

Figure 6.5: Larger transfers from social protection to poor people would reduce the impacts of disasters on well-being without affecting asset losses

Effects on asset losses and well-being when bottom 20 percent receive at least 33 percent of their income from social protection

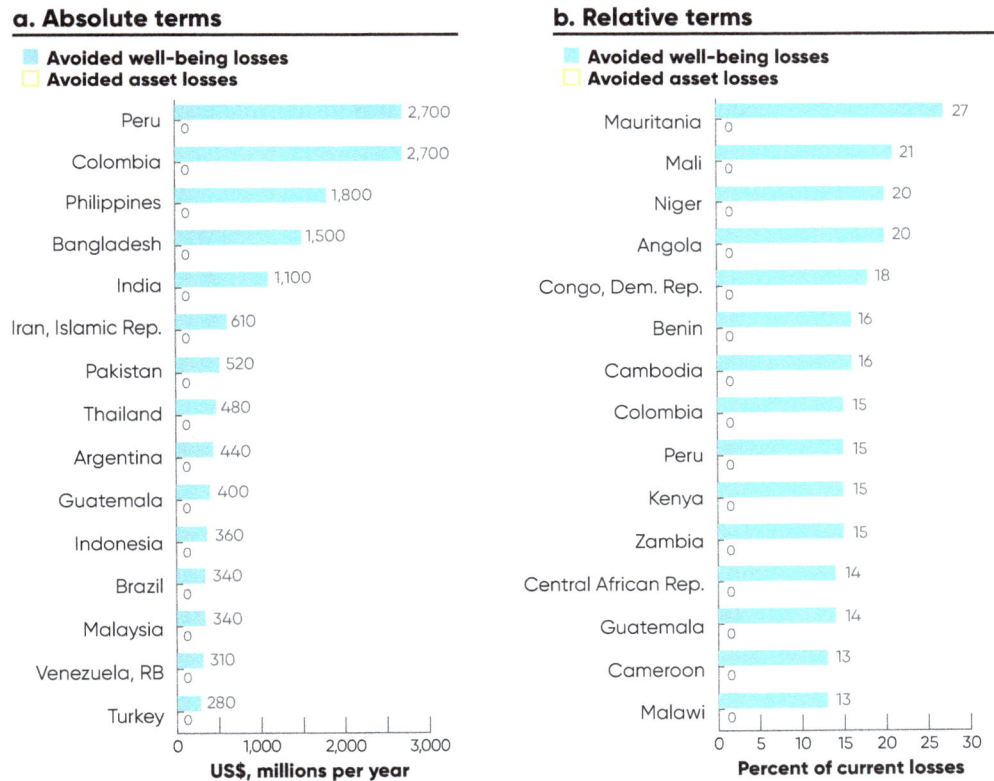

a. Absolute terms

- Avoided well-being losses
- Avoided asset losses

Country	US$, millions per year
Peru	2,700 / 0
Colombia	2,700 / 0
Philippines	1,800 / 0
Bangladesh	1,500 / 0
India	1,100 / 0
Iran, Islamic Rep.	610 / 0
Pakistan	520 / 0
Thailand	480 / 0
Argentina	440 / 0
Guatemala	400 / 0
Indonesia	360 / 0
Brazil	340 / 0
Malaysia	340 / 0
Venezuela, RB	310 / 0
Turkey	280 / 0

b. Relative terms

- Avoided well-being losses
- Avoided asset losses

Country	Percent of current losses
Mauritania	27 / 0
Mali	21 / 0
Niger	20 / 0
Angola	20 / 0
Congo, Dem. Rep.	18 / 0
Benin	16 / 0
Cambodia	16 / 0
Colombia	15 / 0
Peru	15 / 0
Kenya	15 / 0
Zambia	15 / 0
Central African Rep.	14 / 0
Guatemala	14 / 0
Cameroon	13 / 0
Malawi	13 / 0

Source: World Bank estimates.

Note: Figure shows the avoided asset losses and gains in well-being from assuming that the bottom 20 percent receives at least 33 percent of their income from social protection—in absolute terms in panel a (millions of U.S. dollars per year, purchasing power parity–adjusted) and in relative terms in panel b (percentage of current average asset and well-being losses).

Even if income is unchanged, we find that if at least 33 percent of the income of people in the bottom 20 percent in all countries was from transfers, either social transfers or remittances, the effect of increased income diversification alone would increase resilience by 2.1 percentage points globally, and global losses of well-being would fall by $17 billion a year (a 3 percent decrease). Figure 6.5 shows the 15 countries in which the benefits would be larger, in both absolute and relative terms. In many countries, the benefits would exceed $200 million a year, and they would reduce well-being losses by more than 10 percent, especially in Sub-Saharan Africa. Of course, the resilience benefits from such a policy are only a small part of the benefits that need to be taken into account in the decision on (and the design of) a social protection scheme. Developing social protection brings benefits that go beyond increased resilience and include economic benefits even in the absence of shocks. Thus resilience gains necessarily underestimate the desirability of social protection.

Adaptive and scalable social protection acts as insurance for the poor.
According to a growing body of evidence, social insurance and social safety nets can support poor people affected by disasters or environmental and economic shocks even more efficiently if they can react quickly to shocks.

White and Porter (2016) measured the impact of drought on the consumption of farmers in rural Ethiopia in 2005 and 2011 and found the visible effects of a change in a drought metric. A 10 percent loss in crops from a drought led to a 2 percent reduction in consumption, but people covered by the Productive Safety Net Programme (PSNP)—an innovative adaptive safety net program—reduced their consumption by only 1.5 percent, suggesting that a quarter of the impact is avoided on average by the adaptive safety net.

Although designing effective social protection can be a challenge, recent experience from social protection systems globally offers encouraging and valuable lessons. It suggests that countries at all income levels can set up systems that increase resilience to natural hazards. But to do so, they have to ensure that the systems are rapidly scalable in case of crisis and feature targeting mechanisms flexible enough to adjust quickly to new situations. Three key approaches stand out: (1) increasing the amount transferred by an existing program to its beneficiaries or relaxing rules and conditionality so that the transfers increase; (2) extending the coverage of an existing program to include new beneficiaries; and (3) introducing extraordinary payments or creating an entirely new program (Bastagli 2014). These options are described in more detail in chapter 5 of *Shock Waves* using case studies on Ethiopia, Pakistan, and the Philippines (Hallegatte et al. 2016), and in the sections that follow.

Increasing the amount or value of transfer. This approach works best when the beneficiaries of existing social protection programs are those most affected by the crisis, when the shock primarily affects the poorest, and when there is already at least one large-scale social protection program in place with efficient delivery systems for a disaster response. An example of such a program with built-in mechanisms for rapid scale-up in response to a shock is Mexico's Temporary Employment Public Works Program (PET). Similarly, after Typhoon Yolanda hit the Philippines in 2013, external actors such as the World Food Programme and the United Nations Children's Fund (UNICEF) used the existing Pantawid Pamilyang Pilipino Program (4Ps) conditional cash transfer program to deliver their support to affected 4Ps beneficiaries, thereby increasing the value of the transfer. For some shocks, such as changes in food prices, indexing of social transfers on observed prices (such as for food) is a way to automatically adjust the amount of transfers to a changing situation without a discretionary decision. In Malawi, for example, two schemes—the Food and Cash Transfers and Dowa Emergency Cash Transfers—adjust the transfers before each monthly disbursement based on observed prices (Sabates-Wheeler and Devereux 2010).

It is also possible to increase transfers by relaxing program rules and conditionality. Disasters may make existing program rules impractical or inappropriate—for example, if a disaster destroys schools in a region, attendance is no longer an applicable condition for disbursing conditional cash transfers. In Colombia, the cash transfer scheme Familias en Acción suspended conditionality temporarily in 2008 to accommodate the shortfalls in service provision as a result of damaged infrastructure. In the Philippines, all conditionality linked to the 4Ps cash transfers was relaxed in response to Typhoon Yolanda, allowing the government to quickly release a total of 550.5 million pesos ($12.5 million) between November 2013 and February 2014 in temporarily unconditional transfers.

Expanding the coverage. In severe shocks and those with heterogeneous impacts (such as a flood), even relatively well-off households may lose enough to be pushed into poverty—possibly becoming poorer than existing beneficiaries. Any program seeking to provide adequate support to such at-risk households must be expanded to include the people affected by the shock. In 2008 the Mexican government expanded the coverage of the national Oportunidades cash transfer scheme by 1 million recipients to mitigate the food and fuel crisis. Ultimately, the total number of Mexicans assisted by the program reached 5 million households or one in four families (Demeke, Pangrazio, and Maetz 2009). In Ethiopia, the Productive Safety Net Programme incorporates innovative features to scale up automatically and enroll additional beneficiaries when there is poor rainfall.

In 2015 the Hunger Safety Net Programme (HSNP) in Kenya delivered support to more than 100,000 additional households in response to drought. Thanks to the use of satellite data and clear thresholds, the preregistration of all households in the covered counties, and the provision of bank accounts to all potential beneficiaries, transfers could proceed two weeks after the decision to scale up was made. In October 2015, the scheme was used for a special transfer to 200,000 households in anticipation of the drought expected from El Niño. Thus the program moved from a reactive scheme to a forecast-based instrument that provides support before a shock occurs to enable households to prepare for it.

Creating a new program. In the absence of an appropriate program that can be used or extended to respond to a crisis, it is possible to introduce new programs or initiatives. And this additional support can be provided in kind or in cash, depending on the context (box 6.1). In Chile, the government paid a one-time bonus (40,000 pesos or about $66) in March 2009 to 1.7 million poor families to cope with the effects of the ongoing financial crisis. A similar measure was introduced in March 2010 following a major earthquake. At other times, new, durable programs have been introduced. The 1990 Honduran Programa de Asignación Familiar and the 2001 Colombian cash transfer scheme Familias en Acción were launched during recessions and macroeconomic adjustment periods, and they were later transformed into permanent programs as part of the national safety net system. In Guatemala, the food and fuel crisis in 2008 prompted the introduction of a new program, Mi Familia Progresa.

But the challenge is larger when responding to a disaster or a crisis with immediate and urgent needs. Creating and rolling out a new program takes time, which is why countries with existing scalable programs are more resilient and better prepared to respond to crises and disasters.

Adaptive social protection needs to balance timeliness with targeting accuracy.
To extend support to new beneficiaries—whether through an existing or a new program—a country must be able to identify them rapidly. A challenge is to strike a balance between providing rapid support when needed and targeting precisely those in most need. Case studies suggest that the cost of a drought to households can increase from $0 to about $50 per household if support is delayed by four months, and to about $1,300 if support is delayed by six to nine months (Clarke and Hill 2013). This rapid increase is due to the irreversible impacts of drought on children and distress sales of assets (especially livestock).

Postdisaster responses can have multiple stages, with the initial (survival-related) support delivered quickly, even at the expense of targeting and accuracy, and reconstruction support provided later with more effort to target support appropriately.

IN CHOOSING BETWEEN IN-KIND AND CASH SUPPORT, THE CONTEXT SHOULD DECIDE

Food is often distributed after disasters, severe economic crises, or conflicts, even if the distribution may distort local markets and reduce local production. During the food, fuel, and financial crisis of 2007–08, Benin, Burkina Faso, Mali, and Niger introduced emergency food distribution and used cereal banks to sell food at reduced prices. Evidence suggests that, on average, food and cash transfers are equally good at providing food security (World Bank 2016). Specific differences among cash and in-kind transfers are not very significant and depend on which indicator is used to measure food security (such as calorie availability and dietary diversity). Although the effectiveness of cash and in-kind transfers is similar, cash transfers seem to be more efficient to deliver than in-kind modalities, suggesting on average they might be more cost-effective (del Ninno, Coll-Black, and Fallavier 2016). This finding stems from the fact that money is often easier to transport than food because it can be dematerialized and does not come with expiration dates and temperature requirements. On the other hand, cash can have its own limitations, especially in the absence of functioning markets or when the food supply is depleted.

Source: World Bank 2016.

In Pakistan after the 2010 floods, the government implemented the Citizen's Damage Compensation Program (CDCP), a rapid response cash grant program that included two phases to better balance the urgency of postdisaster support and the need to carefully target the larger transfers supporting reconstruction.

In the aftermath of a crisis or a disaster, it can be difficult to identify those affected and at risk of being pushed into poverty. Of the several approaches to targeting beneficiaries, all face challenges. Disaster consequences are often heterogeneous, making geographic or demographic targeting approaches problematic (Alderman and Haque 2006; Grosh et al. 2008). Registries containing socioeconomic information and precise location are seldom available. The usual targeting methods (such as proxy means testing) are based on slowly changing household characteristics (such as assets) and are slow and expensive to implement—that is, they cannot capture sudden changes in income and consumption. And affected populations are often displaced in camps or with family or friends and thus are hard to reach.

Because these approaches always have inclusion and exclusion errors, grievance appeal mechanisms are critical. In Pakistan, the grievance redress system in the second phase of the CDCP cut exclusion errors from an initial 61 percent to 32 percent.

Options to manage this challenge include the development—before a crisis occurs—of large and flexible social registries that include both potential and existing beneficiaries, the use of self-targeting methods, and the use of subsidies.

Social registries. These registries are crucial because they facilitate quickly identifying households that are vulnerable to being pushed into poverty by a disaster. Such registries should include demographic, socioeconomic, and location information on households that could potentially be supported by a social program.

In Brazil, the Cadastro Unico registry includes households with a per capita income of less than half the national minimum wage—a threshold that is higher than the income eligibility threshold of existing social programs. As a result, the registry includes households that are not currently beneficiaries of social protection but are considered to be vulnerable to economic shocks or disasters. Moreover, individuals can register at any time based on self-reported income, thereby reducing transaction costs (Bastagli 2009). Such a design ensures that the Bolsa Familia cash transfer program can be rapidly adjusted when shocks occur, thereby acting as an insurance facility for vulnerable households. In Kenya, all households from the four counties covered by the HSNP are preregistered, and they have been provided with bank accounts to ensure quick delivery of cash transfers after an emergency or a crisis.

Large social registries make it possible to introduce dynamic targeting in which potential beneficiaries are segmented—before a disaster or a crisis—into multiple categories based on their income, assets, location, or occupation (such as farmer or fisherman). The categories then receive varying levels of support, depending on the situation. For example, potential beneficiaries can be ranked, starting from the poorest, and the number of people provided with support (how far a government goes down the list) can depend on the situation—for example, more people would have to receive support during a drought. The level of support in each category can even be based on an objective rule or a weather index (such as using cumulative rainfall or a trigger based on wind speed).

When social registries are not available, an alternative is to combine *geographical targeting* (to concentrate resources on the most affected municipalities or communities) and *community targeting* (to use local knowledge to concentrate resources on the most affected households). Pakistan adopted this approach in the first phase of the CDCP after the 2010 floods, when timeliness was a priority and there were no reliable data on the distribution of losses. The second phase—less urgent but with larger transfers—placed a stronger emphasis on targeting, using housing damages as a proxy for livelihood losses.

Self-targeting through work programs. This approach, which does not require much institutional capacity, can be carried out using work programs. These programs provide jobs and income by putting in place public projects (such as road construction, maintenance, irrigation infrastructure, reforestation, soil conservation) or, especially in postdisaster situations, reconstruction tasks. Such programs usually offer a below-market wage, and people join only if alternative income sources are lacking (Cazes, Verick, and Heuer 2009). In Côte d'Ivoire, the Highly Labour Intensive Works Program was created to support and rehabilitate 35,000 former combatants through road building and reconstruction work. The key drawback is that work programs fail to reach those who face constraints that prevent them from working (such as disabilities, sickness, and exclusion) and who are often the poorest.

The use of work programs as a social protection measure in postdisaster situations depends on being able to readily identify cost-effective and socially beneficial projects before a crisis strikes. In practice, however, extreme natural events, such as storms or floods, are typically associated with obvious and significant labor needs. Rebuilding public infrastructure and clearing rubble are examples of needs that can be met by work programs, which can benefit affected poor and vulnerable people (even those with low skills), as well as the wider community.

Subsidies. This approach is used widely to help poor people, especially in the absence of other social protection programs, and not least because subsidies can be simple and quick to implement. The Egyptian food subsidy program was expanded in 2008 to include 15 million additional beneficiaries (Jones et al. 2009), thereby avoiding an increase in the poverty rate because of increases in food prices. Indonesia used a system of generalized subsidies as a safety net during the 1997 financial crisis.

That said, subsidies have many drawbacks. For one thing, they can lead to waste and corruption. For example, analyses of India's Public Food Distribution Program, which provides subsidized food and fuel, uncovered a number of operational challenges, including underprovided entitlements as a result of "leakages" of food through the supply chain, diverted commodities, underweighted food, overcharged beneficiaries, closed shops, and food falsely being declared out of stock (Drèze and Khera 2015; Government of India 2011; World Bank 2011).

Subsidies are often difficult to end when a crisis is over. And they are an expensive and inefficient tool for supporting poor people because often a large portion of the funds goes to those who do not need the funds the most. Fossil fuel subsidies, for example, are typically implemented and publicly justified by the rationale of helping poor people gain access to energy and energy services. However, even though low energy prices do reduce poverty by reducing the cost of energy services, they do so in an extremely inefficient way because energy is overwhelmingly consumed by the wealthier (Fay et al. 2015).

Postdisaster support is good economics, even when imperfect

Difficulty in targeting does not threaten the value of postdisaster transfers. To explore this issue, we calculated, using our resilience model, the benefit-cost ratio of transferring $1 to each individual affected by a disaster. We included targeting errors, assuming that 33 percent of the affected individuals are "missed" by the support and that the same number of people are wrongly compensated. (The 33 percent is close to the performance of the second phase of Pakistan's Citizen's Damage Compensation Program, which had a 30–32 percent exclusion error.) The benefit-cost ratio represents the average benefit in well-being that is generated by the $1 distributed.

Figure 6.6: Postdisaster transfers are good economics even if some transfers miss their targets

Benefit-cost ratio of postdisaster support as function of GDP per capita, 117 countries

Source: World Bank estimates.

Note: Figure shows the benefit-cost ratios of postdisaster support under two assumptions regarding targeting. Each country is represented by two dots, assuming either perfect or imperfect targeting.

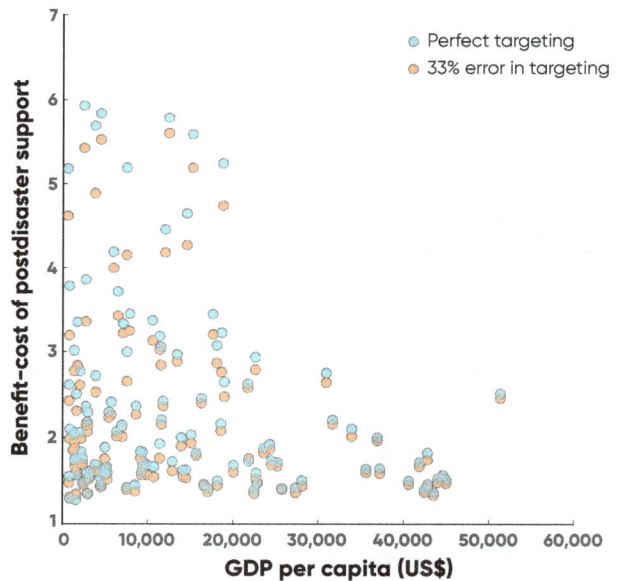

The analysis suggests that these transfers are a good economic choice, even with targeting errors (figure 6.6): the benefit-cost ratio is higher than 1.3 in all countries, and its average value across countries is 2.2 (weighting countries by their population). In many countries, the ratio exceeds 3 or 4 (table 6.1). No trend with income is obvious (postdisaster support makes sense in poor and rich countries), but countries with the highest benefit-cost ratios have income per capita of less than $25,000 a year (in purchasing parity power–adjusted U.S. dollars).

Table 6.1: In many countries, postdisaster support is a very good investment

Fourteen countries with highest benefit-cost ratios of postdisaster transfers (assuming a 33 percent targeting error)

Source: World Bank estimates.

Country	Benefit-Cost Ratio	Country	Benefit-Cost Ratio
South Africa	5.6	Brazil	4.3
Honduras	5.5	Colombia	4.2
Lesotho	5.4	Angola	4.2
Botswana	5.2	Bolivia	4.0
Zambia	4.9	Swaziland	3.4
Panama	4.7	Kenya	3.4
Central African Republic	4.6	Paraguay	3.2

In general, postdisaster transfers are most desirable where the exposed population is the poorest and where poor people have a high vulnerability (such as because of building quality or low income diversification). South Africa and Honduras are examples of such countries. In some countries, the benefit-cost ratio is relatively low—such as in the Slovak Republic —because the better-off people are more exposed. There, postdisaster transfers are going to the better-off (whose income after the shock is still larger than the predisaster income of poor people). Overall, targeting errors have only a limited impact on the benefit-cost ratio (figure 6.6).

If raising the resources needed for the transfers has a cost—for example, if the collection and distribution of $1 leads to $0.25 in losses for the economy—then the benefit-cost ratio is reduced by the same amount. (Note that these losses are different from poor targeting: instead of being received by the wrong person, this $0.25 is assumed to disappear through, for example, administrative costs or because higher tax collection reduces economic activity.) Here, for example, if the cost of $1 in public resources is more than $1.40, then the benefit-cost ratio of postdisaster transfers in the Slovak Republic becomes lower than 1. Estimates of the cost of public resources vary from a few cents to more than $2 per $1 of raised revenue, with most estimates in the range of $0.10–0.60 on the dollar (Massiani and Picco 2013). Overall, however, the cost of transferring resources through the existing social protection infrastructure is lower than through a humanitarian response (del Ninno, Coll-Black, and Fallavier 2016).

A question related to targeting is how much money to disburse. Many countries give the same amount to all people affected. In view of how difficult and costly it is to measure individual losses after a disaster (even though recent technologies have made loss assessment quicker and easier), a uniform transfer to those affected is a useful simplification of the targeting mechanism.

In India, postdisaster support often takes the form of an ad hoc financial transfer, such as the 5,000 rupees (Rs) given to victims of the 2005 floods in Mumbai. In Pakistan, after the 2010 floods eligible households also received uniform amounts from the federal government's Citizen's Damage Compensation Program. In the first phase, eligible households were given a one-off cash grant in the amount of Rs 20,000 (about $213), based on the funds available to cope with the urgent needs of a very large flood-affected target population. In the second phase, the size of the grant to eligible households was doubled to Rs 40,000 (about $426).

Other countries allocate support in proportion to the losses. Such a distribution rule mimics insurance. In Vietnam, for example, the postdisaster support system is based on an estimate of damage per household. The Emergency Assistance Program is the main social assistance response to a disaster. Introduced in 2007, the program provides cash and rice to disaster-affected households, as a function of their losses. Compensation for destruction of or serious damage to housing or relocation following landslides or floods is 5 million dong ($235) per household. Similarly, agricultural losses are compensated in a proportional manner (see box 6.2). Richer households who lose more in absolute terms are therefore likely to receive more compensation.

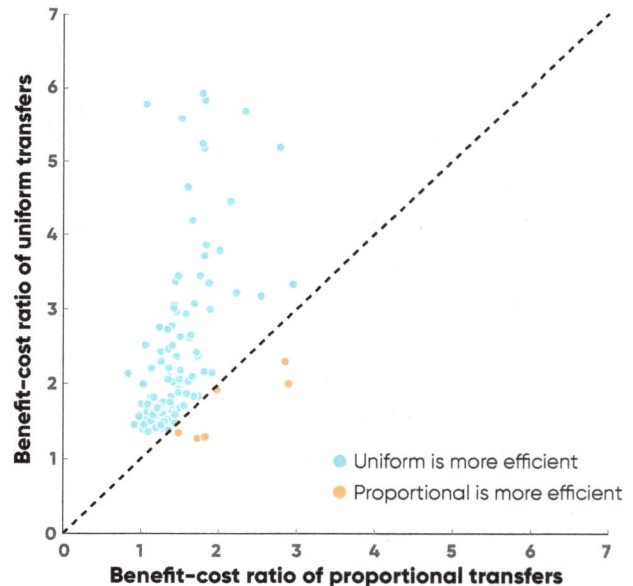

Figure 6.7: Uniform transfers are usually more efficient than proportional transfers

Difference in benefit-cost ratio of uniform versus proportional postdisaster support

Source: World Bank estimates.

Note: Figure shows the benefit-cost ratios of postdisaster support, assuming perfect targeting, and under two assumptions about the amount disbursed. Each dot represents a country.

Figure 6.7 compares the efficiency of uniform transfers and transfers proportional to losses. We looked at the benefit-cost ratio of giving $1 to each person affected and the benefit-cost ratio of spending the same amount of money, but distributing it in proportion to losses. Figure 6.7 reveals that in most countries the benefits of the uniform transfer are greater. Because rich people usually lose more in absolute terms, a proportional scheme tends to transfer more resources to rich people than to poor people and can be regressive

BOX 6.2

POSTDISASTER SUPPORT FOR FARMERS IN VIETNAM IS PROPORTIONAL TO LOSSES

SUPPORT FOR CROPS

» **Plain rice cultivation area, damaged ...**
More than 70 percent: D 1 million (about $48) per hectare
30–70 percent: D 500,000 ($24) per hectare

» **Hybrid rice acreage, damaged ...**
More than 70 percent: D 1.5 million ($70) per hectare
30–70 percent: D 750,000 ($35) per hectare

» **Corn/vegetable acreage, damaged ...**
More than 70 percent: D 1 million ($48) per hectare
30–70 percent: D 500,000 ($24) per hectare

» **Industrial crops/fruit trees and perennials, damaged ...**
More than 70 percent: D 2 million ($94) per hectare
30–70 percent: D 1 million ($48) per hectare

SUPPORT FOR LOST LIVESTOCK

» **Bird—**D 7,000–15,000 ($0.30–0.70) per animal

» **Pig—**D 500,000 ($24) per hatchling

» **Bovine, equine—**D 2 million ($94) per animal breed

» **Deer, sheep, goats—**D 1 million ($48) per hatchling

SUPPORT FOR AQUACULTURE, SEAFOOD LOSSES

» **Area, damaged ...**
More than 70 percent: D 3–5 million ($144–240) per hectare
30–70 percent: D 1 –3 million ($48–144) per hectare

» **Cages, damaged ...**
More than 70 percent: D 3–5 million ($144–240)
per 100 cubic meter cages
30–70 percent: D 1 –3 million ($48–144)
per 100 cubic meter cages

Source: Decision No.: 187/2010/TT-BTC (2009) Circular Provisions on the Mechanism, Policy Support Plant Breeding, Livestock, Aquatic Production to Recover the Losses due to Natural Disasters, Disease.

(see Hallegatte, Bangalore, and Vogt-Schilb, forthcoming, for details). And because the resources available for postdisaster support are usually small compared with the total losses, a proportional scheme leads to a situation in which compensation represents a very small share of individual losses, reducing the usefulness of the compensation.

Adaptive and scalable social protection requires appropriate financing mechanisms

Just how costly is social protection? Certainly, the cost of providing coverage to vulnerable people affected by natural hazards changes from year to year. A recent study found that in the Horn of Africa and Sahel regions—assuming that vulnerable people can be protected against the worst effects of drought with an annual social protection package of $300 per capita (the typical size of such support systems in the region)—1 percent of the region's GDP would be sufficient to cover this population, although more is needed in some countries. In fact, the total cost of providing this protection to disaster victims in Africa during the period 2010–13 was lower than what was spent on humanitarian relief measures (del Ninno, Coll-Black, and Fallavier 2016).

However, adaptive social protection means that social expenditures become more variable from one year to the next. Managing this volatility can be a challenge for governments that often face reduced tax revenues following a disaster (Noy and Nualsri 2011; Ouattara and Strobl 2013). Fortunately, various instruments have been developed and implemented to cover these liabilities created by natural hazards and other environmental risks (Cardenas et al. 2007; Ghesquiere and Mahul 2010; Hochrainer-Stigler et al. 2014; Mahul and Ghesquiere 2007). The optimal choice of instruments is country-specific and depends not only on costs but also on the many other co-benefits these instruments can provide in terms of timeliness and transparency, as well as facilitation of postdisaster planning (see box 6.3).

Reserve funds. In the Philippines, the National Disaster Risk Reduction and Management Fund finances a range of disaster-related expenditures, but it is not able to disburse rapidly in response to a crisis. For that reason, the government created the Quick Response Fund, which focuses on an emergency response. In Mexico, FONDEN was created as a budgetary tool to rapidly allocate federal funds for the rehabilitation of public infrastructure affected by disasters.

However, reserve funds have limited capacities and cannot be designed to cope with the rarer and more extreme events. In the Philippines, Typhoon Yolanda raised questions about the adequacy of the Quick Response Fund volume and the process

BOX 6.3
FINANCIAL INSTRUMENTS CAN ACT AS FACILITATORS OF DISASTER RISK MANAGEMENT

All the financial instruments discussed here can be used to do more than simply provide a government with resources after a disaster. They can serve as an opportunity to create contingency and emergency plans that will facilitate the provision of support to the affected population, the continuity of public services, or the implementation of the reconstruction process (Clarke and Dercon 2016). The choice and design of these instruments should therefore also take into account their co-benefits, including timeliness, predictability, and transparency (Clarke et al. 2016).

In Uganda, the design of a disaster risk financing instrument to make a safety net program scalable has helped link social protection with disaster risk management. This linkage also allows the inclusion of disaster risk in the design of public works activities to ensure that they contribute to risk mitigation. In India, the government invested in higher-quality crop data to support the creation of a national agriculture insurance program, and these data are a valuable asset beyond insurance uses, including for disaster planning, preparation, and response. And in Mexico, FONDEN has created incentives for states to become more proactive in arranging insurance protection and thus increase the speed at which they can respond and recover.

The World Bank's development policy loan with a Catastrophe Deferred Drawdown Option (Cat-DDOs) is a contingent credit line that aims not only to provide immediate liquidity to countries affected by a disaster, but also to function as a mechanism to incentivize proactive actions toward risk reduction. To be eligible for a Cat-DDO, governments are required to develop an ex ante capacity to manage natural risks. In this way, the CAT-DDO is the first instrument to link immediate disaster response funding with proactive engagement in risk reduction.

These financial instruments can also incentivize, facilitate, and support risk reduction by making the cost of the disaster risk liability more visible, which helps to overcome the political economy obstacles to risk reduction investments.

to replenish it if it is emptied by a major event (or a series of smaller disasters). Thus additional instruments have been developed to protect public finances.

Insurance and catastrophe bonds. The contingency fund FONDEN in Mexico leverages private sector financing as part of a strategy that combines risk retention and risk transfers. In 2006 FONDEN issued a $160 million catastrophe bond to transfer Mexico's earthquake risk to the international capital markets—the first parametric catastrophe bond issued by a national government. Even though they are costly, these financial schemes are able to disburse funds rapidly—indeed, more rapidly than would be possible with public budgets. And by predefining payout rules for allocating postdisaster support, formal insurance and financial products can reduce political economy biases (Clarke et al. 2016).

Regional risk-sharing facilities. The Caribbean Catastrophe Risk Insurance Facility (CCRIF) currently pools disaster risk across 16 countries. It was the world's first regional catastrophe insurance facility, using parametric insurance to provide participating governments with quick, short-term liquidity for financing responses and early recovery from major earthquakes or hurricanes. The Pacific Catastrophe Risk Assessment and Financing Initiative (PCRAFI) and African Risk Capacity are other, more recent examples of donor-supported regional mechanisms that offer quick-disbursing, index-based coverage against tropical cyclones and earthquakes. In response to Cyclone Pam in March 2015, PCRAFI rapidly provided Vanuatu with $1.9 million to support immediate postdisaster needs. This payout was limited compared with the total losses and reconstruction needs—estimated at $184 million—but it was still eight times the size of the annual emergency relief fund held by the government and seven times more than the annual insurance premium (which is largely subsidized by international donors).

Contingent credit. In 2007 the World Bank introduced Catastrophe Deferred Drawdown Options (Cat-DDOs), a new financing instrument that allows countries eligible to borrow from the International Bank for Reconstruction and Development (IBRD) to access budget support in the immediate aftermath of a disaster. A contingency loan can be rapidly disbursed if a state of emergency is declared, and thus it can help governments finance the upscaling of social protection. Other institutions such as the Inter-American Development Bank and the Japan International Cooperation Agency have since introduced similar instruments. Countries not eligible for IBRD loans are using other instruments in innovative ways to finance disaster response. For instance, the Government of Uganda is using US$10 million of their International Development Association (IDA) allocation as a contingent line of credit to finance the scale up of their safety net, the Northern Uganda Social Action Fund.

Cat-DDOs have proven to be an effective instrument for implementing disaster risk management strategies and supporting postdisaster responses. However, experience has shown that, facing a finite financing envelope, governments tend to favor cash in hand over contingency instruments. As a result—and despite strong interest from client countries—the uptake of Cat-DDOs has been limited. One option to improve access to contingent finance and build the resilience of developing countries would be to remove the trade-off between cash in hand and contingent finance by separating the budget allocated to contingency instruments from the budget allocated to traditional lending.

International aid. When a country exceeds its capacity to cope with a disaster, international aid and humanitarian emergency measures can be critical. Foreign aid includes essential in-kind support (including emergency equipment such as water treatment stations, reconstruction material, equipment and machinery, and relief goods such as food, blankets, and clothes), as well as financial aid for social protection and reconstruction costs.

In the past, however, increases in foreign aid in response to a disaster have been small, averaging only a small percentage of the total economic losses stemming from a disaster (Becerra, Cavallo, and Noy 2013). Generally, studies have found that increases in financial aid are larger for more severe disasters and for particularly poor countries with limited disaster management capacities. This finding suggests that these resources are relatively well targeted and not politically biased (Becerra, Cavallo, and Noy 2013). Nonetheless, increases in foreign aid in response to disasters remain sensitive to media coverage, are hardly predictable, and can be slow to arrive—all of which make it ever more difficult to prepare contingency plans based on available resources. Foreign aid should thus be regarded as a resource of last resort.

To improve the timeliness, transparency, and predictability of postdisaster or crisis international aid, and to provide additional financing, a special Crisis Response Window (CRW) was created in 2011 as part of the International Development Association, the World Bank Group's fund for the poorest countries. Its primary objective is to (1) provide poor countries with extra resources in a timely manner; (2) help them respond to severe economic crises, price shocks, and major natural disasters; and (3) return to their long-term development paths. In Malawi, the CRW provided $40 million in postdisaster support after the large floods that affected the country in January 2015.

Combining adaptive social protection and financial instruments in a consistent policy package would deliver large benefits. What are the potential benefits of these options? Using our resilience model, we estimate them by assessing the effects of a policy package inspired by the previous sections. Such a package would be introduced in all countries and would include:

» Financial instruments (reserve fund, contingent finance or risk–sharing instrument, or insurance product) so that the government has access to enough liquidity and resources for the postdisaster response.

» A preparation and contingency plan so that the budget can be reallocated to the disaster victims in a timely fashion. This plan would include a budgetary process (to transfer additional resources to the social protection programs), registries, and delivery mechanisms to ensure that the resources are distributed to the victims, with the objective of providing all victims with a uniform cash transfer that is calibrated to cover 80 percent of the losses suffered by the bottom 20 percent.

Compared with a scenario in which there is no policy package, the average resilience rises to 65 percent, an increase of 1.6 percentage points over the current situation. This would represent a gain in well-being of $13 billion. Figure 6.8 shows the 15 countries where such a package would deliver the largest benefits in both absolute and relative terms.

This simple exercise illustrates the potential of public finance protection (such as insuring government) or contingent finance instruments (such as Cat-DDOs) to increase countries' resilience. For all countries to provide postdisaster support, an average of $23 billion in postdisaster support would have to be financed annually. (For this $23 billion additional cost, the additional support would deliver $36 billion in benefits, and thus $13 billion in net benefits.)

This analysis also reveals the complementarity between interventions that facilitate access to financial resources in the aftermath of disasters and interventions that improve preparedness (such as registries and automatic scaling–up mechanisms). It is not very useful to provide a government with liquidity if it cannot deliver support to the affected population, and even the best delivery mechanism cannot improve well-being in the absence of financial resources. Combined, these interventions produce much larger benefits than the sum of the two performed independently.

Our analysis points as well to the complementarity between the development of market insurance for the middle class and adaptive social protection that targets poor people:

» Market insurance is difficult to provide to poor people because of its transaction costs, institutional and legal requirements, and affordability issues. But even if it covers only the nonpoor, market insurance can generate large resilience gains. And it reduces the financial pressure on the government, with fewer needs to support the middle class after a disaster.

» Adaptive social protection cannot easily protect the nonpoor because of the limits in available resources and more pressing priorities. But it can be very efficient in helping poor people cope with and recover from disasters.

Figure 6.8: A package to make social safety nets scalable includes financial instruments and delivery mechanisms and makes people more resilient

Effects on asset losses and well-being of a package to improve postdisaster support

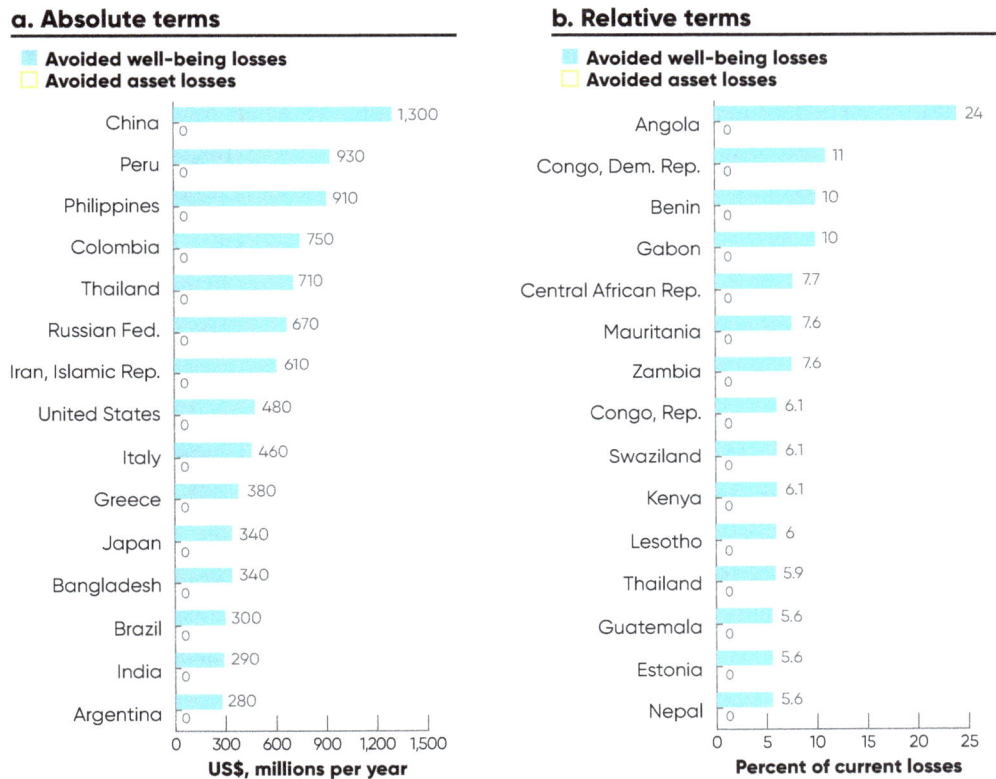

a. Absolute terms

■ Avoided well-being losses
□ Avoided asset losses

Country	US$, millions per year
China	1,300
Peru	930
Philippines	910
Colombia	750
Thailand	710
Russian Fed.	670
Iran, Islamic Rep.	610
United States	480
Italy	460
Greece	380
Japan	340
Bangladesh	340
Brazil	300
India	290
Argentina	280

b. Relative terms

■ Avoided well-being losses
□ Avoided asset losses

Country	Percent of current losses
Angola	24
Congo, Dem. Rep.	11
Benin	10
Gabon	10
Central African Rep.	7.7
Mauritania	7.6
Zambia	7.6
Congo, Rep.	6.1
Swaziland	6.1
Kenya	6.1
Lesotho	6
Thailand	5.9
Guatemala	5.6
Estonia	5.6
Nepal	5.6

Source: World Bank estimates.

Note: Figure shows the avoided asset losses and gains in well-being from the implementation of a package that includes financial instruments to ensure that the government has access to resources after a disaster and a delivery mechanism to provide support to the affected population. Gains are in absolute terms in the first panel (millions of U.S. dollars per year, purchasing power parity–adjusted) and in relative terms in the second panel (percentage of current average asset and well-being losses).

A way forward is therefore to combine the two measures: (1) develop market insurance to protect the middle class and ensure that governments can use their resources to help the poor after disasters, and (2) create adaptive social protection systems to protect the poor, who cannot access or afford market insurance.

The solution: Combining disaster risk reduction and a global resilience package to reduce the impact of disasters on well-being

What shape will a global resilience package take? Table 6.2 summarizes all of the policy options explored in chapters 5 and 6 and breaks them down into two packages. The first package—aimed at reducing asset losses—includes exposure and asset vulnerability reduction and early warning and corresponds to the traditional disaster risk management measures. The second package is geared toward increasing resilience by accelerating recovery and reconstruction and helping households smooth the consequences of a shock by means of financial inclusion, insurance, and adaptive social protection.

Looking at the potential benefits of these packages at the global level reveals that the benefits from each package are not equal to the sum of the benefit of each policy because policies interact, sometimes positively and sometimes negatively. For example, we already flagged that financial instruments and scalable social safety nets are important complements. At the same time, a strong social protection system slightly reduces the benefits of financial inclusion, because the protection system offers people alternative ways of smoothing the impact of a disaster.

Taken together, the five measures in the asset loss package (reducing the exposure and asset vulnerability of poor and nonpoor people and ensuring universal access to early warnings) would reduce average global asset losses by $44 billion a year, a 14 percent decrease. The gain in well-being would be equivalent to a $97 billion increase in annual consumption.

The resilience package—the set of policies that increases the ability of a population to cope with *asset losses* without reducing the asset losses themselves—has the potential to reduce the *well-being losses* from a disaster by generating the equivalent of an $78 billion gain in consumption, which translates into an 11 percentage point increase in global resilience, reaching 74 percent. Adding universal access to early warning would increase the well-being benefits to $96 billion and push resilience to 75 percent.

The overall benefit of such a global resilience package is equivalent to the benefits from the asset losses package. It would also be equivalent to reducing global exposure to natural hazards by almost 20 percent, a very ambitious and difficult objective for land-use planning and infrastructure development. It would also be more efficient than reducing the vulnerability of assets by 20 percent through better construction and building norms. Considering the well-known difficulty in enforcing land-use plans, resettling people, and enforcing building norms and standards, such a resilience package deserves careful investigation at the country level to see how it could complement actions on exposure and asset vulnerability.

And, of course, such a package of policies would deliver benefits that extend beyond the avoided losses discussed here. First, as discussed in chapter 3, disaster risk reduction can generate growth and benefits by promoting investment. Evaluations of the World Food Programme's R4 Rural Resilience Initiative and Mexico's CADENA program have shown that insurance is helping farmers increase their investments in productive assets, boosting their productivity (Madajewicz, Tsegay, and Norton 2013; de Janvry, Ritchie, and Sadoulet 2016). Changes in people's investment and saving behaviors can make risk reduction investment more profitable than avoided losses suggest.

And these policies would also generate benefits that are not related to disasters and natural risks: financial inclusion, access to health and nonhealth insurance, and stronger social protection protect people against all sort of shocks, facilitate investment and innovation, and promote development and poverty reduction.

This chapter has introduced a resilience package and has discussed the impact of each of its components on a global scale. In the next chapter, we show how this package can be adapted to the local context in each country and how to prioritize the several policy options.

Table 6.2: Disaster risk management should combine multiple actions and could deliver large benefits

Policy packages and their policy actions, with estimates of their global effects on asset and well-being losses

Policy action	Example of policies	Description in the analysis	Avoided global asset losses	Avoided global well-being losses
POLICY PACKAGE: REDUCE ASSET LOSSES				
Reduce exposure of the poor	Upgrade slums with improved drainage; initiate resettlement programs away from at-risk areas; undertake ecosystem conservation and management	Reduces total exposure by 5 percent through reduction in poor people's exposure	$7 billion	$40 billion
Reduce exposure of the nonpoor	Adopt land-use and urbanization plans; influence future urban developments; undertake ecosystem conservation and management	Reduces total exposure by 5 percent through reduction in nonpoor people's exposure	$19 billion	$22 billion
Reduce the vulnerability of poor people's assets	Provide land titles to enhance investment in housing; improve infrastructure that serves the poor	Reduces by 30 percent the asset vulnerability of some poor people, representing 5 percent of the population	$2 billion	$14 billion
Reduce the vulnerability of nonpoor people's assets	Change construction and building norms; improve general infrastructure	Reduces by 30 percent the asset vulnerability of some nonpoor people, representing 5 percent of the population	$6 billion	$7 billion
Provide universal access to early warning systems	Invest in hydrometeorological observation systems and weather forecasting capacity; ensure capacity to issue and communicate early warning and for people to react	Assumes full access to early warning for storms, surges, floods, and tsunamis (not earthquakes); early warning reduces asset losses by 20 percent	$13 billion	$22 billion
POLICY PACKAGE: INCREASE RESILIENCE				
Favor savings in financial forms	Develop banking sector and favor mobile banking; support development of savings instruments that fit the needs of the poor	Assumes that everybody has a fraction of his or her wealth in the form of financial savings	0	$14 billion
Accelerate reconstruction	Develop access to borrowing and insurance for people, firms, and local authorities to facilitate recovery and reconstruction; ensure the government has the liquidity to fund reconstruction; increase openness for workers, materials, and equipment to facilitate reconstruction; streamline administrative processes (such as for building permits)	Allows reconstruction to be completed 33 percent faster	0	$32 billion

Increase income diversification (social protection and remittances)	Create new cash transfers; ensure that contributory social protection schemes are available to poor people; reduce the cost of remittances	Increases the share of income of the bottom 20 percent from transfers to at least 33 percent	0	$17 billion
Make social safety nets more scalable	Create social registries that are be able to add beneficiaries; implement a budgetary process to increase social expenditures after a disaster; create the right delivery mechanism; develop indicators and procedures for the automatic scale-up of social safety nets	Relaxes one of the two constraints on postdisaster support—the one linked to preparedness and mechanisms	0	$5 billion
Develop contingent finance and reserve funds	Create reserve funds with utilization rules; prepare access to contingency credit lines (such as Cat-DDOs); create regional risk pools (such as CCRIF); transfer part of the risk to global reinsurance or global capital markets (such as FONDEN bonds)	Relaxes one of the two constraints on postdisaster support—the one linked to access to liquidity	0	$5 billion
Improve capacity to deliver postdisaster support	Combine the two previous sets of actions	Relaxes the two constraints on postdisaster support	0	$13 billion
Improve access to insurance for firms and households	Create insurance markets and ensure their sustainability	Assumes that 50 percent of the losses of 25 percent of the nonpoor are shared in each country (without international sharing)	0	$10 billion

Note: Cat-DDO = Catastrophe Deferred Drawdown Option; CCRIF = Caribbean Catastrophe Risk Insurance Facility. The benefits of each policy is assessed using the resilience model as presented in chapter 4, assuming that the policy is implemented in all 117 countries. The costs of implementation depend on the solution used for implementation, such as reducing exposure to floods by means of a land-use plan or flood management infrastructure, and are country-specific.

NOTES

1. This section, contributed by the World Bank–GFDRR Disaster Risk Financing and Insurance Program, was drafted by Emily While based on the 2014 *Global Assessment Report* publication *Financial Protection against Disasters, An Operational Framework for Disaster Risk Financing and Insurance* (UNISDR 2014).

2. According to the Munich Re NatCat Service.

REFERENCES

Alderman, H., and T. Haque. 2006. "Countercyclical Safety Nets for the Poor and Vulnerable." *Food Policy* 31: 372–83.

Banerjee, A., and E. Duflo. 2012. *Poor Economics: A Radical Rethinking of the Way to Fight Global Poverty.* Reprinted. New York: Public Affairs.

Banerjee, A., E. Duflo, N. Goldberg, D. Karlan, R. Osei, W. Parienté, J. Shapiro et al. 2015. "A Multifaceted Program Causes Lasting Progress for the Very Poor: Evidence from Six Countries." *Science* 348 (6236).

Barnett, B. J., C. B. Barrett, and J. R. Skees. 2008. "Poverty Traps and Index-Based Risk Transfer Products." *World Development,* special section: "The Volatility of Overseas Aid." 36: 1766–85. doi:10.1016/j.worlddev.2007.10.016.

Bastagli, F. 2009. "From Social Safety Net to Social Policy? The Role of Conditional Cash Transfers in Welfare State Development in Latin America." Working Paper, International Policy Centre for Inclusive Growth, Brasilia, Brazil.

———. 2014. *Responding to a Crisis—The Design and Delivery of Social Protection.* London: Overseas Development Institute.

Becerra, O., E. Cavallo, and I. Noy. 2013. "Where Is the Money? Post-Disaster Foreign Aid Flows." *Environment and Development Economics* 1–26.

Benson, C., and E. Clay. 2004. *Understanding the Economic and Financial Impacts of Natural Disasters, Disaster Risk Management.* Washington, DC: World Bank.

Brown, J., T. Zelesnka, and A. Mobarak. 2013. "Barriers to Adoption of Products and Technologies That Aid Risk Management in Developing Countries." World Development Report Background Papers, World Bank, Washington, DC.

Cardenas, V., S. Hochrainer, R. Mechler, G. Pflug, and J. Linnerooth-Bayer. 2007. "Sovereign Financial Disaster Risk Management: The Case of Mexico." *Environmental Hazards* 7: 40–53.

Cazes, S., S. Verick, and C. Heuer. 2009. "Labour Market Policies in Times of Crisis." Employment Working Paper No. 35, International Labour Office, Geneva.

Clarke, D., O. Mahul, R. Poulter, and T. Ling Teh. 2016. "Evaluating Sovereign Disaster Risk Finance Strategies: A Framework." Policy Research Working Paper 7721, World Bank, Washington, DC.

Clarke, D., O. Mahul, K. Rao, and N. Verma. 2012. "Weather Based Crop Insurance in India." Policy Research Working Paper 5985, World Bank, Washington, DC.

Clarke, D. J., and R. V. Hill. 2013. "Cost-Benefit Analysis of the African Risk Capacity Facility." Discussion Paper 01292, International Food Policy Research Institute, Washington, DC.

Clarke, D. J., and S. Dercon. 2016. *Dull Disasters? How Planning Ahead Will Make a Difference.* Oxford: Oxford University Press.

Cole, S., G. Bastian, S. Vyas, C. Wendel, and D. Stein. 2012. "The Effectiveness of Index-Based Micro-Insurance in Helping Smallholders Manage Weather-Related Risks." EPPI-Center, Social Science Research Unit, Institute of Education, University of London.

Cole, S., X. Gine, J. Tobacman, P. Topalova, R. Townsend, and J. Vickery. 2013. "Barriers to Household Risk Management: Evidence from India." *American Economic Journal: Applied Economics* 5: 104–35. doi:10.1257/app.5.1.104.

de Janvry, A., F. Finan, E. Sadoulet, and R. Vakis. 2006. "Can Conditional Cash Transfer Programs Serve as Safety Nets in Keeping Children at School and from Working When Exposed to Shocks?" *Journal of Development Economics* 79: 349–73.

de Janvry, Alain, Alejandro del Valle, and Elisabeth Sadoulet. 2016. "Insuring Growth: The Impact of Disaster Funds on Economic Reconstruction in Mexico." Policy Research Working Paper 7714, World Bank, Washington, DC.

del Ninno, Carlo, Sarah Coll-Black, and Pierre Fallavier. 2016. *Social Protection Programs for Africa's Drylands: Social Protection Programs.* Washington, DC: World Bank.

Demeke, M., G. Pangrazio, and M. Maetz. 2009. "Country Responses to the Food Security Crisis: Nature and Preliminary Implications of the Policies Pursued." Food and Agriculture Organization, Rome.

Demirgüç-Kunt, A., L. Klapper, D. Singer, and P. Van Oudheusden. 2015. "The Global Findex Database 2014: Measuring Financial Inclusion around the World." World Bank, Washington, DC.

Drèze, J., and R. Khera. 2015. "Understanding Leakages in the Public Distribution System." *Economic and Political Weekly* 50: 39.

Fay, M., S. Hallegatte, A. Vogt-Schilb, J. Rozenberg, U. Narloch, and T. Kerr. 2015. *Decarbonizing Development: Three Steps to a Zero-Carbon Future.* Washington, DC: World Bank.

Fiszbein, A., N. R. Schady, and F. H. Ferreira. 2009. "Conditional Cash Transfers: Reducing Present and Future Poverty." World Bank, Washington, DC.

Gertler, P. 2004. "Do Conditional Cash Transfers Improve Child Health? Evidence from PROGRESA's Control Randomized Experiment." *American Economic Review* 336–41.

Ghesquiere, F., and O. Mahul. 2010. *Financial Protection of the State against Natural Disasters: A Primer.* Washington, DC: World Bank.

Government of India. 2011. *Report of the Working Group on Urban Poverty, Slums and Service Delivery System.* Delhi.

Grosh, M. E., C. del Ninno, E. Tesliuc, and A. Ouerghi. 2008. *For Protection and Promotion: The Design and Implementation of Effective Safety Nets.* Washington, DC: World Bank.

Hallegatte, S., M. Bangalore, L. Bonzanigo, M. Fay, T. Kane, U. Narloch, J. Rozenberg et al. 2016. *Shock Waves: Managing the Impacts of Climate Change on Poverty.* Climate Change and Development Series. Washington, DC: World Bank.

Hallegatte, S., and P. Dumas. 2009. "Can Natural Disasters Have Positive Consequences? Investigating the Role of Embodied Technical Change." *Ecological Economics* 68: 777–86.

Hallegatte, S., and A. Vogt-Schilb. Forthcoming. "Are Losses from Natural Disasters More Than Just Asset Losses? The Role of Capital Aggregation, Sector Interactions, and Investment Behaviors." Background paper prepared for this report, World Bank, Washington, DC.

Hallegatte, S., M. Bangalore, and A. Vogt-Schilb. Forthcoming. "Socioeconomic Resilience to Multiple Hazards—An Assessment in 117 Countries." Background paper prepared for this report, World Bank, Washington, DC.

Hochrainer-Stigler, S., R. Mechler, G. Pflug, and K. Williges. 2014. "Funding Public Adaptation to Climate-Related Disasters: Estimates for a Global Fund." *Global Environmental Change* 25: 87–96.

Hoflinger, R., O. Mahul, F. Ghesquiere, and S. Perez. 2012. *FONDEN: Mexico's Natural Disaster Fund—A Review.* Washington, DC: World Bank.

Insurance Bureau of Canada. 2015. "The Financial Management of Flood Risk. An International Review: Lessons Learnt from Flood Management Programs in G8 Countries." Toronto.

Jamison, D. T., L. H. Summers, G. Alleyne, K. J. Arrow, S. Berkley, A. Binagwaho, F. Bustreo et al. 2013. "Global Health 2035: A World Converging within a Generation." *The Lancet* 382: 1898–955. doi:10.1016/S0140-6736(13)62105-4.

Jones, N., C. Harper, S. Pantuliano, S. Pavanello, K. Kyunghoon, S. Mitra, and K. Chalcraft. 2009. *Impact of the Economic Crisis and Food and Fuel Price Volatility on Children and Women in the MENA Region.* London and New York: Overseas Development Institute and UNICEF.

Karlan, D., R. D. Osei, I. Osei-Akoto, and C. Udry. 2012. *Agricultural Decisions after Relaxing Credit and Risk Constraints.* No. w18463. Cambridge, MA: National Bureau of Economic Research.

Kenward, S., L. Cordier, and R. Islam. 2012. "Chars Livelihoods Programme: A Study to Assess the Performance of CLP Raised Plinths, Low Cost Latrines and Access to Clean Water during the July 2012 Flood." Chars Livelihoods Programme and Maxwell Stamp PLC, Dhaka, Bangladesh.

Kijewski-Correa, T., and A. A. Taflanidis. 2011. "The Haitian Housing Dilemma: Can Sustainability and Hazard-Resilience Be Achieved?" *Bulletin of Earthquake Engineering* 10: 765–71. doi:10.1007/s10518-011-9330-y.

Kinnan, C., and R. Townsend. 2012. "Kinship and Financial Networks, Formal Financial Access, and Risk Reduction." *American Economic Review* 102: 289–93.

Kunreuther, H., S. Pauly, and S. McMorrow. 2013. *Insurance and Behavioral Economics: Improving Decisions in the Most Misunderstood Industry.* New York: Cambridge University Press.

Macours, K., P. Premand, and R. Vakis. 2012. "Transfers, Diversification and Household Risk Strategies: Experimental Evidence with Lessons for Climate Change Adaptation." Policy Research Working Paper 6053, World Bank, Washington, DC.

Madajewicz, M., A. H. Tsegay, and M. Norton. 2013. *Managing Risks to Agricultural Livelihoods: Impact Evaluation of the Harita Program in Tigray, Ethiopia, 2009–2012.* London: Oxfam.

Mahul, O., and F. Ghesquiere. 2007. "Sovereign Natural Disaster Insurance for Developing Countries: A Paradigm Shift in Catastrophe Risk Financing." Policy Research Working Paper 6058, World Bank, Washington, DC.

Mannakkara, S., S. Wilkinson, and R. Potangaroa. 2014. "Build Back Better: Implementation in Victorian Bushfire Reconstruction." *Disasters* 38: 267–90. doi:10.1111/disa.12041.

Massiani, J., and G. Picco. 2013. "The Opportunity Cost of Public Funds: Concepts and Issues." SSRN Scholarly Paper No. ID 2321977, Social Science Research Network, Rochester, NY.

Mobarak, A. M., and M. R. Rosenzweig. 2013. "Informal Risk Sharing, Index Insurance, and Risk Taking in Developing Countries." *American Economic Review* 103 (3): 375–80.

Morduch, J. 1995. "Income Smoothing and Consumption Smoothing." *Journal of Economic Perspectives* 103–14.

Noy, I., and A. Nualsri. 2011. "Fiscal Storms: Public Spending and Revenues in the Aftermath of Natural Disasters." *Environment and Development Economics* 16: 113–28.

O'Donnell, O. 2007. "Access to Health Care in Developing Countries: Breaking Down Demand Side Barriers." *Cadernos Saúde Pública* 23: 2820–34.

Ouattara, B., and E. Strobl. 2013. "The Fiscal Implications of Hurricane Strikes in the Caribbean." *Ecological Economics* 85: 105–15.

Poontirakul, P., C. Brown, I. Noy, E. Seville, and J. Vargo. 2016. "The Role of Commercial Insurance in Post-Disaster Recovery: Quantitative Evidence from the 2011 Christchurch Earthquake." SEF Working Paper 01/2016, University of Wellington.

Ratha, Dilip, Soonhwa Yi, and Seyed Reza Yousefi. 2015. "Migration and Development." *Routledge Handbook of Immigration and Refugee Studies* 1 (3): 260.

Rogers, D. P., and V. V. Tsirkunov. 2013. *Weather and Climate Resilience: Effective Preparedness through National Meteorological and Hydrological Services.* Washington, DC: World Bank.

Sabates-Wheeler, R., and S. Devereux. 2010. "Cash Transfers and High Food Prices: Explaining Outcomes on Ethiopia's Productive Safety Net Programme." *Food Policy* 35: 274–85.

UNISDR (United Nations Office for Disaster Risk Reduction). 2014. *Financial Protection against Disasters: An Operational Framework for Disaster Risk Financing and Insurance.* Geneva: UNISDR.

White, E. J., and C. Porter. 2016. "Potential for Application of a Probabilistic Catastrophe Risk Modelling Framework to Poverty Outcomes: General Form Vulnerability Functions Relating Household Poverty Outcomes to Hazard Intensity in Ethiopia." Policy Research Working Paper 7717, World Bank, Washington, DC.

WHO (World Health Organization). 2013. *Universal Health Coverage: Report by the Secretariat.* Geneva: WHO.

World Bank. 2011. *Social Protection for a Changing India: Main Report.* Washington, DC: World Bank.

_____. 2013. *World Development Report 2014: Risk and Opportunity—Managing Risk for Development.* Washington, DC: World Bank.

_____. 2014. *Global Financial Development Report 2014: Financial Inclusion.* Washington, DC: World Bank.

_____. 2015a. "Another Nargis Strikes Everyday: Post-Nargis Social Impacts Monitoring Five Years On." Washington, DC.

_____. 2015b. *The State of Social Safety Nets.* Washington, DC: World Bank.

_____. 2016. "Humanitarian Cash and In-Kind Transfers across Sectors: Selection, Performance and Research Priorities." Background paper for the Inter-Agency Standing Committee (IASC), World Bank, Washington, DC.

TAILOR-MADE

**Policy priorities can be identified
at the country level.**

Chapters 5 and 6 investigated a variety of policies and provided estimates of their potential benefits on a global scale. They also identified countries in which these policies would be particularly promising. To develop a disaster risk management strategy in a given country, however, one needs an analysis of all available policies in that country.

Here, we propose using our analysis to identify promising options for action at the country level, and we illustrate this approach using a few countries with very different characteristics. The main finding of this chapter is that the potential of disaster risk management policies differs across countries, depending on their socioeconomic characteristics, their exposure to different hazards, and the actions they have already implemented to help people manage risks. In all countries, however, there are promising opportunities to reduce asset losses through risk mitigation and to increase resilience by enhancing the ability of people to cope with disaster losses.

Another important finding is that in many countries, especially low-income ones, very promising options to build people's resilience are also good poverty reduction and development policies—examples are financial inclusion or social protection. In these countries, it is very easy to align development priorities with disaster risk management and build on the synergies between these two objectives. We therefore largely confirm here the findings from chapters 2 and 3 that poverty reduction helps with risk mitigation and risk mitigation helps with poverty reduction.

Our estimates give insight into promising courses of action, but they do not indicate whether or what measures need to be implemented. As already pointed out, these estimates are based on global analyses and databases and would need to be refined using country-level data sources. But, most important, whereas we focus on potential benefits of actions, making actual decisions requires assessing the costs of various policies as well.

Such a cost assessment would, however, have to be performed at the country level, and we cannot provide a full cost–benefit analysis of the measures proposed here. Indeed, the cost of, say, reducing exposure to natural disasters by 5 percent depends on how this reduction is to be achieved. If it is carried out by building new dikes or pumping stations, the cost will include large up-front investment costs, as well as significant maintenance and operational costs over the lifetime of the protection system. If carried out through risk-sensitive land-use planning, there will be no large investment costs, but implementation and enforcement will require building strong institutions and a solid legal framework, and the indirect cost may be increased land scarcity. If carried out through ecosystem conservation, as suggested for Colombo in chapter 5, the costs will include investment costs (to restore and rehabilitate ecosystems if needed), opportunity costs from forgone development of land, and enforcement costs.

Obviously, our global analysis cannot reach this level of detail, but it can support a conversation on options to achieve various objectives. One way of engagement on this issue is to begin by assessing the benefits from a 5 percent reduction in exposure ($1.5 billion a year in Bangladesh, for example) and then explore the options to achieve such a reduction, looking in turn at those options that are regulation-based, infrastructure-based, or ecosystem-based, as itemized and discussed in chapter 5. Similarly, the benefits from the postdisaster support package as estimated here could be compared with the cost of various instruments able to ensure that affected people receive timely and appropriate help in postdisaster situations. Following the descriptions provided in chapter 6, it is possible to consider options such as developing insurance, making an existing social safety net scalable, or creating an entirely new program. Costs can then be estimated and compared with potential benefits.

Designing a disaster risk management strategy is challenging because it requires considering a very broad set of actions—from developing hard infrastructure to undertaking institutional measures such as devising land-use plans and social safety nets— that are usually designed and implemented by different agencies within a country (World

Bank 2013). This kind of endeavor creates difficult communication and coordination issues (Clarke and Dercon 2016). The assessment of multiple actions within a single framework, as proposed here, may provide a starting point for engaging multiple agencies and stakeholders in a constructive dialogue on what can and should be done.

Country-level disaster management profiles help identify promising policies

To identify promising policy options and help design consistent strategies, this report developed disaster management profiles for the 117 analyzed countries. The profile for Malawi shows the potential benefits of different actions on well-being and asset losses (figure 7.1). These profiles are available for all countries.

Figure 7.1: Many actions could reduce asset and well-being losses in Malawi

Effects of policy options on asset and well-being losses in Malawi

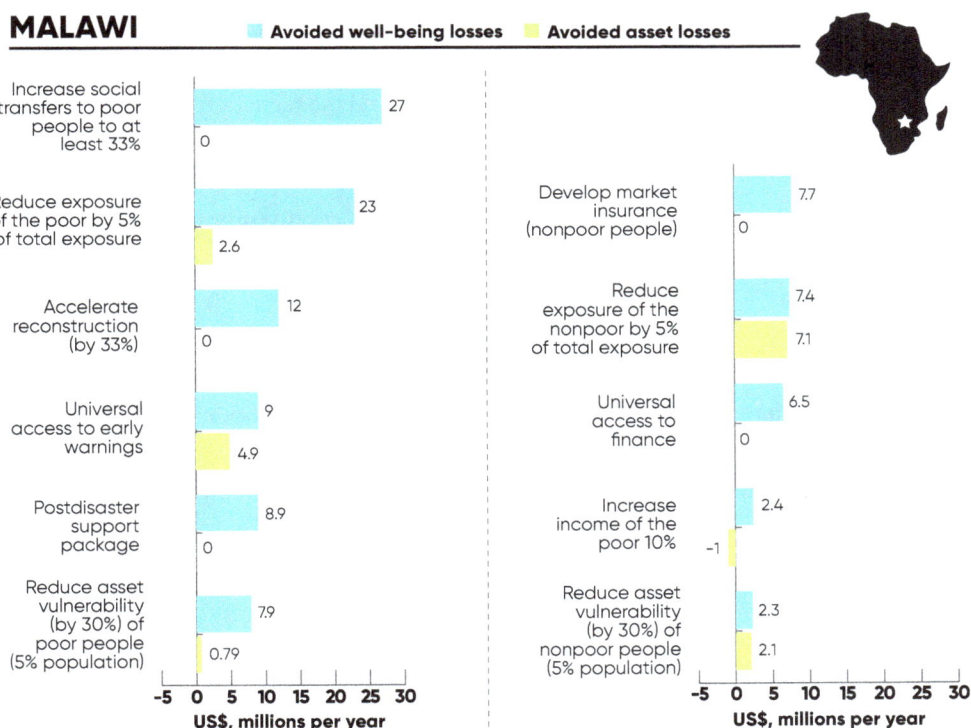

Source: World Bank estimates.

Note: U.S. dollars per year are based on a purchasing power parity exchange rate. This profile shows how different actions would reduce asset losses and the impact of disasters on well-being. It considers the same actions presented in table 6.2, as well as the effect of reducing poverty, but presents the benefits at the country level. Benefits are large when a country has a combination of two characteristics: (1) the measure has the potential to reduce losses, and (2) the country is lagging in the domain of the measure. For example, in countries in which early warning is already universally accessible, no more gain can be expected from this measure.

In Malawi, building up social protection systems so that poor people receive a larger share of their income from transfers would increase resilience and reduce the well-being effects of natural disasters, even if the income level of poor people remains unchanged. A well-being gain equivalent to a $27 million increase in consumption would be generated if the share of diversified income were to reach 33 percent. And this is only a fraction of the benefits that stronger safety nets can produce.

Making the safety net system responsive to disasters (by combining a financial instrument with delivery mechanisms) to enhance the government's ability to provide postdisaster support should generate well-being gains amounting to almost $8.9 million a year.

And reducing poverty – by increasing poor people's income by 10 percent – would lead to larger asset losses from disasters because richer people have more to lose. But, overall, the increase in resilience would more than compensate for such losses, and the well-being losses from disasters would be reduced by $2.4 million a year. The well-being losses from a disaster would be reduced further if the increased income was translated into more robust buildings or more savings in financial form. And the reduction in disaster impacts is in addition to the (much larger) direct well-being gains of being less poor.

Accelerating reconstruction and providing universal access to early warning would generate $12 and $9 million a year, respectively. These benefits from early warning do not include the lives that can be saved, but they are already likely to be higher than what would need to be invested to create and maintain such a capacity in Malawi.

As for exposure to natural disasters, reducing the exposure of poor people so that total exposure is lessened by 5 percent would prevent asset losses of $2.6 million a year and would generate well-being gains equivalent to $23 million a year. By contrast, reducing the exposure of the nonpoor would generate much higher gains in terms of avoided asset losses ($7.1 million a year), but much lower well-being benefits (only $7.4 million a year).

For floods only, reducing exposure by 5 percent, targeting poor people, would reduce asset losses by $2.2 million a year, which would generate well-being gains equivalent to $19 million a year. This corresponds to reducing exposure by about 80,000 people. The avoided well-being losses are thus equivalent to $230 a year per protected person, suggesting that the government of Malawi would have to be ready to pay up to $3,800 per person either protected by a dike or resettled in a safe area (with a 6 percent discount rate).

It now becomes possible to explore the various options available to Malawi to undertake such actions, including infrastructure, land-use plans, relocation programs, or ecosystem-based solutions. The investment and operational costs of these different solutions can be estimated and compared with the benefits per person protected estimated here.

Comparing countries can be helpful as well. In Bangladesh (figure 7.2), reducing the exposure of poor people so that total exposure is reduced by 5 percent would prevent asset losses of $360 million a year, but would generate well-being gains equivalent to $1.5 billion a year. For floods only, this corresponds to reducing exposure by about 1.5 million people—not an easy task—with a benefit to well-being amounting to $1.1 billion, or about $800 per person per year. The government could thus pay almost $13,000 per capita for protection or resettlement. Such a high value—more than three times higher than in Malawi—would mean that options that may not be economically viable in Malawi could make sense in Bangladesh. This result should affect the list of potential solutions that are explored and assessed by the government of Bangladesh.

Figure 7.2: Although reducing exposure is a priority in Bangladesh, resilience building could also result in large reductions in well-being losses

Effects of policy options on asset and well-being losses in Bangladesh

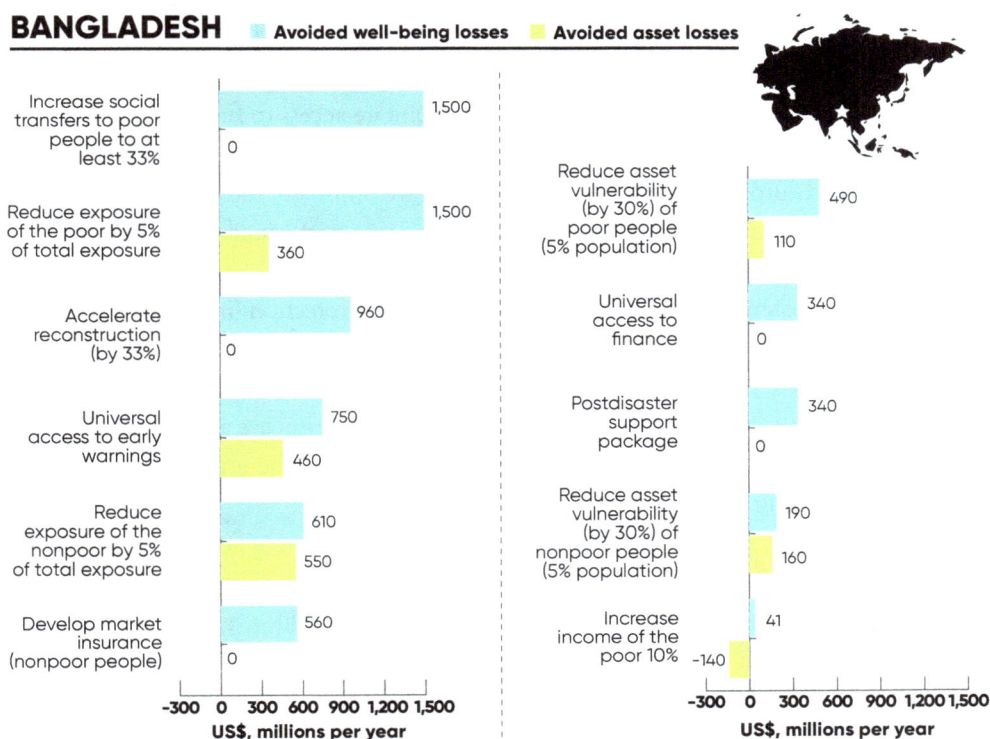

Source: World Bank estimates.
Note: U.S. dollars per year are based on a purchasing power parity exchange rate.

Implementing a package in Bangladesh to enhance the ability to provide postdisaster support (combining contingent finance with scalable social protection) would lead to well-being gains of $340 million a year. Adding insurance, even if only for the nonpoor, would add benefits amounting to $560 million. And if this postdisaster support can facilitate and accelerate the reconstruction phase, it would generate an additional $960 million a year in well-being gains.

For Angola, the results are different (see figure 7.3). The country has very low socioeconomic resilience—only 31 percent—because of large inequalities (the bottom 20 percent of wage earners account for only 5 percent of total income), a very weak social system (it is not very pro-poor), and liquidity constraints. In such a context, huge benefits can result from building socioeconomic resilience. Developing the toolbox to provide postdisaster support (combining liquidity instruments with scalable social protection) has significant potential, possibly delivering $180 million a year in well-being gains. Interestingly, the various components of such a toolbox, taken independently, are largely inefficient.

Making social protection more scalable does not deliver much benefit if a country remains liquidity-constrained after a shock, and improving access to liquidity in the aftermath of a disaster is not very useful in the absence of delivery mechanisms to transfer resources to affected people. This finding shows once more the complementarity between interventions that facilitate access to financial resources in the aftermath of disasters and interventions that improve preparedness (such as registries and automatic scaling-up mechanisms). Combined, these interventions produce much larger benefits than the sum of the two performed independently.

Increasing transfers, with more remittances and social protection (in particular, cash transfers for the poor), would also increase resilience and deliver gains in well-being, as would poverty reduction in general. This example shows that in low-resilience countries such as Angola, development and poverty reduction are already good resilience-building options. The alignment between development priorities and resilience building is strong.

As for early warning systems, they have large potential in a country in which they are largely nonexistent. They would deliver about $160 million a year in well-being benefits for a net present value of $2.7 billion. This amount is probably orders of magnitude larger than the cost of creating a functioning hydrometeorological organization with the capacity to deliver warnings.

Figure 7.3: In a low-resilience country such as Angola, resilience building should be a priority

Effects of policy options on asset and well-being losses in Angola

ANGOLA ■ Avoided well-being losses ■ Avoided asset losses

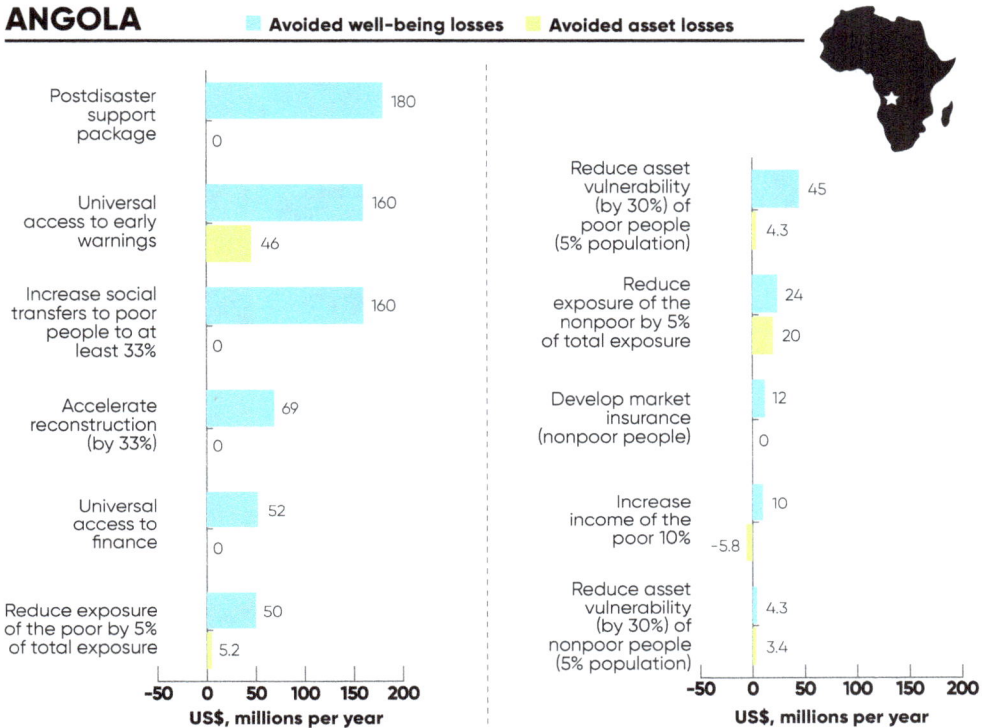

	Avoided well-being losses	Avoided asset losses
Postdisaster support package	180	0
Universal access to early warnings	160	46
Increase social transfers to poor people to at least 33%	160	0
Accelerate reconstruction (by 33%)	69	0
Universal access to finance	52	0
Reduce exposure of the poor by 5% of total exposure	50	5.2
Reduce asset vulnerability (by 30%) of poor people (5% population)	45	4.3
Reduce exposure of the nonpoor by 5% of total exposure	24	20
Develop market insurance (nonpoor people)	12	0
Increase income of the poor 10%	10	-5.8
Reduce asset vulnerability (by 30%) of nonpoor people (5% population)	4.3	3.4

US$, millions per year

Source: World Bank estimates.
Note: U.S. dollars per year are based on a purchasing power parity exchange rate.

In Colombia (figure 7.4), resilience is relatively low (45 percent) because of the large overexposure of poor people and their large asset vulnerability, as well as the small size of transfers, rendering people's income weakly diversified. As a result, the benefits in terms of well-being of reducing asset losses for the poor are quite large, and action targeting the nonpoor appears much less desirable. Also, increasing the strength of social protection for the poor—even without scalability—would yield large benefits in terms of gains in resilience and well-being, valued at about $2.7 billion a year.

In Germany (figure 7.5), resilience is very high (76 percent), and most of the socioeconomic options to increase resilience and enable people to better able to cope with shocks have already been implemented—not many low-hanging fruits are left. Thus the benefits of better access to finance, social transfers, postdisaster support, or contingent finance instruments are small. Also, because of the large resilience level, there is less difference between reducing risk for the poor or for the nonpoor than in most other countries.

Figure 7.4: Traditional and scalable social protection would increase resilience in Colombia and improve well-being

Effects of policy options on asset and well-being losses in Colombia

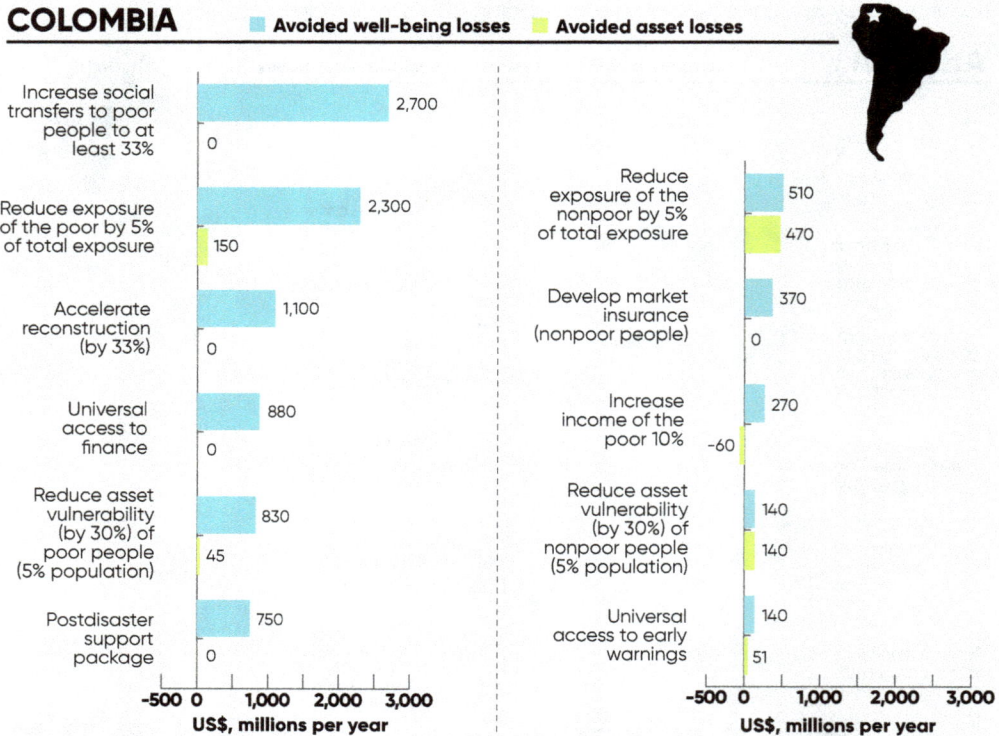

COLOMBIA   ■ Avoided well-being losses   ■ Avoided asset losses

Policy option	Value
Increase social transfers to poor people to at least 33%	2,700 / 0
Reduce exposure of the poor by 5% of total exposure	2,300 / 150
Accelerate reconstruction (by 33%)	1,100 / 0
Universal access to finance	880 / 0
Reduce asset vulnerability (by 30%) of poor people (5% population)	830 / 45
Postdisaster support package	750 / 0
Reduce exposure of the nonpoor by 5% of total exposure	510 / 470
Develop market insurance (nonpoor people)	370 / 0
Increase income of the poor 10%	270 / −60
Reduce asset vulnerability (by 30%) of nonpoor people (5% population)	140 / 140
Universal access to early warnings	140 / 51

US$, millions per year

Source: World Bank estimates.
Note: U.S. dollars per year are based on a purchasing power parity exchange rate.

The best options in Germany seem to be to further reduce the exposure of the population (poor and nonpoor alike) to natural disasters and the vulnerability of assets. Another interesting action would be to ensure more rapid recovery and reconstruction after disasters. Doing so could generate up to $240 million a year in well-being.

In Germany, increasing the income of the bottom 20 percent leads to an increase in asset and well-being losses from disasters. However, such an increase is not necessarily a bad thing for well-being: the nondisaster-related benefits from higher income and wealth for the poorest would largely dominate the increase in well-being impacts from disasters (here $18 million a year for the whole country).

The results of applying our model are thus country-specific, which supports the choice of using a model instead of a weighted average of subindicators in which the weights are global and are not adjusted to local circumstances like the other vulnerability or resilience indicators (see box 4.3). Indeed, the model allows identification of specific situations. For

Figure 7.5: In Germany and most other rich countries, resilience is already in place

Effects of policy options on asset and well-being losses in Germany

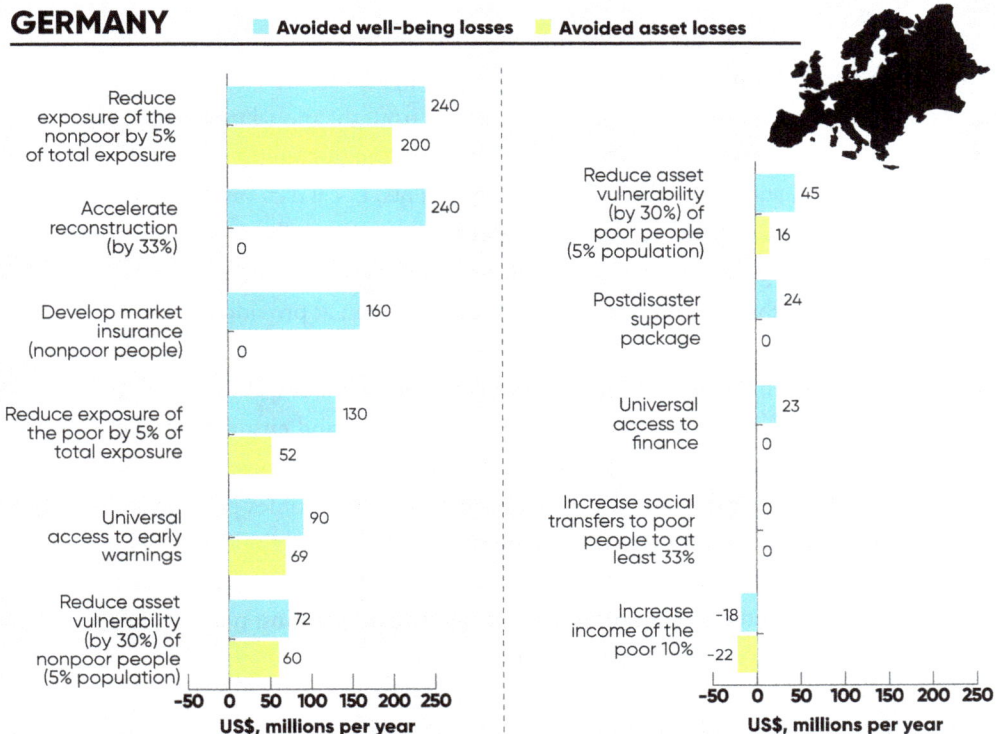

Source: World Bank estimates.

Note: U.S. dollars per year are based on a purchasing power parity exchange rate.

example, in countries in which poor people have assets that are much more vulnerable than those of the rest of the population (such as Costa Rica) or where the poor are particularly exposed (such as Zambia for floods), it is particularly important to protect the poor with social protection instruments. In Zambia, the package to improve postdisaster support (with financial instruments and scalable social protection) would deliver $21 million a year in well-being benefits, with a benefit-cost ratio of almost five.

As in the Mumbai case study, we ensure the robustness of these findings to uncertain parameters such as exposure and vulnerability to floods, the link between asset losses and income losses, income diversification, and the distribution of damages across affected households. These uncertainties matter for assessment of the level of risk, but not so much for assessment of policies. We find that the impacts of policies and their ranking are robust to these uncertainties. However, normative choices matter: changes in the elasticity of the marginal utility of consumption affect the implicit weight given to the poor and nonpoor and thus the relative merits of poverty and poverty bias reduction.

Summing up

This analysis should be understood as a first-round estimate using globally open data. It is a starting point for policy design and should be supplemented by local studies. At the local or national level, for example, the flood risks from the global model could be replaced with results from local analyses at higher resolution, including those of flash floods, small basins, and smaller but more frequent events. Local data on flood protection and better exposure data could be mobilized, and socioeconomic characteristics could be refined, accounting, for example, for the institutional capacity to scale up social protection beyond what a global database can reasonably aim at providing.

And yet the disaster management profiles can contribute to a discussion on a broad set of options to reduce natural risks and increase resilience and ensure that all options are discussed, from preventive actions such as flood zoning to ex post options such as insurance, contingent finance, and social protection. The profiles provide an integrated framework to discuss and compare these options, and they could even help break the silos in governments and local authorities, where ministries or departments in charge of social protection, building norms, and urban planning may not work well together or not even consider natural risks in their decisions.

It is hoped that this type of analysis will foster cross-sector dialogues at the country level, bringing together disaster risk agencies and experts with the rest of the government and agencies to ensure that development, poverty reduction, and disaster risk management are integrated into a resilient and sustainable development strategy that benefit the poorest.

REFERENCES

Clarke, D. J., and S. Dercon . 2016. *Dull Disasters? How Planning Ahead Will Make a Difference.* Oxford: Oxford University Press.

World Bank. 2013. *World Development Report 2014: Risk and Opportunity—Managing Risk for Development.* Washington, DC: World Bank.

APPENDIX

>> **Study results for 117 countries**

Country	GDP per capita (US$, PPP-adjusted)	Population (millions)	TODAY			WITH RESILIENCE PACKAGE (AND EARLY WARNING)			Annual well-being gains from resilience package (US$, millions, PPP-adjusted)
			Risk to assets (%of GDP)	Resilience (%)	Risk to well-being (% of GDP)	Risk to assets (%of GDP)	Resilience (%)	Risk to well-being (% of GDP)	
Albania	$9,961	3	0.99	69	1.43	0.91	84	1.08	92
Angola	7,488	21	0.15	31	0.48	0.12	60	0.20	441
Argentina	18,087	41	0.44	57	0.78	0.43	73	0.59	1,283
Armenia	7,527	3	0.73	71	1.03	0.70	81	0.86	34
Australia	42,834	23	0.20	72	0.28	0.20	82	0.25	272
Austria	44,056	8	0.24	73	0.32	0.24	82	0.29	113
Azerbaijan	16,593	9	0.26	61	0.43	0.26	73	0.36	106
Bangladesh	2,853	157	2.27	66	3.45	2.17	84	2.58	3,604
Belarus	17,055	9	0.36	64	0.57	0.35	76	0.46	164
Belgium	40,609	11	0.07	77	0.09	0.06	87	0.07	63
Benin	1,733	10	0.26	50	0.53	0.23	76	0.30	39
Bolivia	5,934	11	0.50	49	1.01	0.48	61	0.79	132
Bosnia and Herzegovina	9,387	4	0.62	63	0.98	0.52	79	0.67	109
Botswana	15,247	2	0.29	58	0.49	0.28	72	0.39	29
Brazil	14,555	200	0.19	62	0.30	0.16	76	0.21	2,721
Bulgaria	15,695	7	0.23	69	0.34	0.23	79	0.29	51
Burkina Faso	1,630	17	0.23	70	0.33	0.21	81	0.26	18
Burundi	747	10	0.38	59	0.64	0.36	76	0.48	12
Cambodia	2,944	15	1.90	53	3.61	1.52	74	2.05	678
Cameroon	2,739	22	0.27	47	0.57	0.26	66	0.39	108
Canada	41,899	35	0.10	70	0.14	0.09	80	0.12	291
Central African Republic	584	5	0.55	52	1.06	0.45	75	0.60	12
Chad	2,022	13	0.24	48	0.51	0.19	65	0.30	54

Continued

Country	GDP per capita (US$, PPP-adjusted)	Population (millions)	TODAY			WITH RESILIENCE PACKAGE (AND EARLY WARNING)			Annual well-being gains from resilience package (US$, millions, PPP-adjusted)
			Risk to assets (%of GDP)	Resilience (%)	Risk to well-being (% of GDP)	Risk to assets (%of GDP)	Resilience (%)	Risk to well-being (% of GDP)	
Chile	21,714	18	0.97	54	1.79	0.96	63	1.52	973
China	11,525	1,357	0.32	67	0.48	0.31	77	0.40	10,707
Colombia	12,025	48	1.37	45	3.04	1.36	63	2.16	4,959
Congo, Dem. Rep.	783	68	0.86	51	1.69	0.76	78	0.97	368
Congo, Rep.	5,680	4	0.59	51	1.18	0.48	69	0.69	120
Costa Rica	13,431	5	0.39	51	0.76	0.39	61	0.64	77
Croatia	20,049	4	0.58	74	0.78	0.57	85	0.67	86
Czech Republic	28,124	11	0.17	75	0.23	0.17	85	0.20	67
Denmark	42,483	6	0.01	81	0.01	0.00	90	0.01	2
Djibouti	2,903	1	0.25	59	0.42	0.25	73	0.34	2
Dominican Republic	11,795	10	1.18	64	1.85	1.15	77	1.49	411
Ecuador	10,541	16	1.94	66	2.93	1.92	79	2.43	729
Egypt, Arab Rep.	10,733	82	0.09	58	0.15	0.08	76	0.11	318
El Salvador	7,515	6	2.70	65	4.15	2.69	83	3.23	393
Estonia	25,254	1	0.23	60	0.39	0.19	72	0.26	42
France	37,217	66	0.18	72	0.25	0.18	81	0.22	580
Gabon	18,646	2	0.66	42	1.55	0.55	62	0.89	204
Georgia	6,930	4	0.95	68	1.40	0.94	77	1.21	53
Germany	42,884	81	0.10	78	0.13	0.10	86	0.11	458
Ghana	3,864	26	0.18	61	0.29	0.17	75	0.23	62
Greece	24,305	11	1.88	61	3.10	1.88	72	2.62	1,176
Guatemala	7,063	15	0.66	25	2.69	0.65	38	1.74	1,026
Guinea	1,213	12	0.44	63	0.70	0.40	82	0.49	28
Honduras	4,445	8	2.79	46	6.00	2.73	60	4.56	496
Hungary	22,707	10	0.93	80	1.16	0.93	89	1.04	222
India	5,244	1,252	0.28	63	0.44	0.26	77	0.34	5,852
Indonesia	9,254	250	0.33	69	0.49	0.32	81	0.40	1,850
Iran, Islamic Rep.	15,090	77	0.70	55	1.26	0.69	69	1.00	2,900
Iraq	14,471	33	0.52	56	0.92	0.49	73	0.67	1,123
Ireland	44,647	5	0.07	74	0.10	0.06	84	0.07	55
Israel	30,927	8	0.13	62	0.20	0.12	73	0.17	72
Italy	33,924	60	0.58	67	0.86	0.58	77	0.75	2,019
Jamaica	8,607	3	1.46	57	2.58	1.39	69	2.01	125
Japan	35,614	127	0.65	78	0.84	0.64	86	0.75	3,834
Jordan	11,405	6	0.22	73	0.30	0.22	89	0.25	33
Kazakhstan	22,470	17	0.27	62	0.43	0.26	74	0.35	257
Kenya	2,705	44	0.22	46	0.47	0.19	68	0.29	217
Kyrgyz Republic	3,110	6	0.83	55	1.51	0.82	68	1.20	51
Lao PDR	4,667	7	3.53	73	4.80	3.21	88	3.63	344
Latvia	21,833	2	0.64	65	0.99	0.52	76	0.68	133
Lesotho	2,494	2	0.96	60	1.60	0.90	79	1.13	22
Liberia	850	4	0.31	60	0.52	0.25	77	0.33	7
Lithuania	24,470	3	0.28	70	0.40	0.22	81	0.28	85
Macedonia, FYR	11,609	2	0.34	62	0.55	0.33	73	0.46	20
Madagascar	1,369	23	3.54	62	5.69	3.08	81	3.80	567
Malawi	755	16	1.01	60	1.69	0.97	80	1.21	56

Country	GDP per capita (US$, PPP-adjusted)	Population (millions)	TODAY			WITH RESILIENCE PACKAGE (AND EARLY WARNING)			Annual well-being gains from resilience package (US$, millions, PPP-adjusted)
			Risk to assets (%of GDP)	Resilience (%)	Risk to well-being (% of GDP)	Risk to assets (%of GDP)	Resilience (%)	Risk to well-being (% of GDP)	
Malaysia	22,589	30	0.31	59	0.53	0.31	74	0.42	692
Mali	1,589	15	0.26	40	0.64	0.23	62	0.38	62
Mauritania	2,945	4	0.55	36	1.54	0.50	60	0.83	80
Mexico	16,291	122	0.14	58	0.25	0.14	69	0.20	811
Moldova	4,521	4	0.90	75	1.21	0.82	85	0.97	36
Mongolia	9,132	3	0.40	57	0.69	0.37	69	0.54	39
Montenegro	14,152	1	0.23	66	0.35	0.22	79	0.27	6
Morocco	6,967	33	0.30	52	0.57	0.29	65	0.44	281
Nepal	2,173	28	1.04	63	1.64	0.93	81	1.15	282
Netherlands	45,021	17	0.09	78	0.12	0.09	87	0.10	74
Niger	887	18	0.57	54	1.07	0.52	77	0.67	61
Nigeria	5,423	174	0.12	48	0.24	0.11	63	0.18	592
Pakistan	4,454	182	0.60	65	0.92	0.56	82	0.68	1,828
Panama	18,793	4	0.22	49	0.44	0.22	66	0.33	79
Paraguay	7,833	7	0.19	51	0.38	0.18	65	0.28	50
Peru	11,396	30	2.10	40	5.24	2.09	57	3.65	5,366
Philippines	6,326	98	4.52	69	6.53	4.15	82	5.05	8,709
Poland	22,835	39	0.09	61	0.14	0.09	72	0.12	181
Romania	18,184	20	0.41	71	0.58	0.40	83	0.49	305
Russian Federation	23,564	143	0.19	52	0.36	0.15	65	0.23	4,073
Rwanda	1,426	12	0.36	60	0.60	0.35	71	0.49	17
Senegal	2,170	14	0.17	76	0.22	0.16	90	0.17	14
Serbia	12,892	7	1.39	72	1.94	1.24	84	1.48	389
Sierra Leone	1,495	6	0.53	65	0.82	0.51	81	0.63	16
Slovak Republic	25,759	5	0.33	73	0.45	0.32	83	0.38	87
Slovenia	27,368	2	0.57	77	0.74	0.57	87	0.65	40
South Africa	12,454	53	0.24	55	0.43	0.23	64	0.35	493
Spain	31,683	47	0.06	79	0.08	0.06	87	0.07	129
Sri Lanka	9,426	20	0.18	71	0.26	0.17	85	0.21	92
Sudan	3,265	38	0.17	50	0.33	0.15	64	0.24	112
Swaziland	6,471	1	0.54	56	0.96	0.52	74	0.70	20
Sweden	43,540	10	0.01	73	0.01	0.01	83	0.01	8
Syrian Arab Republic	4,959	23	0.41	66	0.62	0.40	85	0.47	161
Tajikistan	2,432	8	1.23	56	2.18	1.19	68	1.75	82
Tanzania	2,365	49	0.28	60	0.47	0.27	78	0.35	131
Thailand	13,932	67	0.65	51	1.28	0.62	64	0.98	2,701
Togo	1,346	7	0.32	59	0.54	0.27	77	0.35	17
Turkey	18,567	75	0.29	48	0.61	0.29	60	0.49	1,642
Uganda	1,621	38	0.17	49	0.36	0.17	61	0.27	49
Ukraine	8,508	45	0.60	73	0.82	0.48	86	0.56	962
United Kingdom	36,931	64	0.06	73	0.08	0.06	82	0.07	182
United States	51,340	316	0.24	66	0.37	0.24	75	0.31	7,989
Uruguay	18,966	3	0.06	58	0.10	0.05	73	0.07	18
Uzbekistan	5,002	30	0.25	44	0.57	0.24	56	0.42	207
Venezuela, RB	17,615	30	0.62	61	1.00	0.61	78	0.78	1,111
Vietnam	5,125	90	1.50	73	2.07	1.43	84	1.70	1,558
Yemen, Rep.	3,832	24	0.52	77	0.68	0.48	91	0.53	130
Zambia	3,800	15	0.20	40	0.50	0.19	59	0.33	94

Note: The countries that are not included in this table are those for which data were not available.

www.ingramcontent.com/pod-product-compliance
Lightning Source LLC
Chambersburg PA
CBHW080422270326
41929CB00018B/3125